Indians and Criminal Justice

Caught between the social and economic demands of the dominant American society and the expectations of their own traditional cultures, many Native Americans today find themselves unable to adapt to either world. Crime, alcoholism, violence, and anomie are increasingly commonplace among this group, who live on the margins of society. The authors of this book, several of whom are themselves Native Americans, examine the Indian system of justice—its history, philosophical-religious bases, and approaches to law enforcement—and assess the complex challenges the system faces in preserving both the social integrity and cultural identity of the community. Of interest to educators, students, and professionals in law, corrections, social work, and the social sciences.

Indians and Criminal Justice

edited by

Laurence French

ALLANHELD, OSMUN Publishers

ALLANHELD, OSMUN & CO. PUBLISHERS, INC.

Published in the United States of America in 1982
by Allanheld, Osmun & Co. Publishers, Inc.
(A Division of Littlefield, Adams & Company)
81 Adams Drive, Totowa, New Jersey 07512

Library of Congress Cataloging in Publication Data
Main entry under title:

Indians and criminal justice.

1. Indians of North America—Courts—Addresses, essays, lectures. 2. Indians of North America—Crime—Addresses, essays, lectures. 3. Criminal justice, Administration of—United States—Addresses, essays, lectures. I. French, Laurence, 1941-
KF8224.C6I528 345.73'05'08997 81-67871
ISBN 0-86598-063-2 347.30550897 AACR2

82 83 84/10 9 8 7 6 5 4 3 2 1

Printed in the United States of America

Contents

INTRODUCTION 1

PART I INDIAN SOCIOLEGAL ISSUES

1 CRITICAL LEGAL AND SOCIAL RESPONSIBILITIES FACING NATIVE AMERICANS 21
Teresa LaFromboise and Richard LaFromboise

2 THE PLURALISTIC BASIS OF AMERICAN INDIAN LAW 39
Elmer R. Rusco

3 THE ECONOMICS OF INDIAN CRIME 53
John Cross

4 NATIVE AMERICAN NEO-COLONIALISM 65
Laurence French

PART II INDIAN CRIME AND JUSTICE

5 BASIC DOCTRINES OF AMERICAN INDIAN LAW 75
Charles F. Wilkinson

6 NATIVE AMERICAN CRIME IN THE UNITED STATES 93
Sidney Harring

7 INDIAN LAW ENFORCEMENT 109
David Wachtel

8 ANOMIE AND VIOLENCE AMONG NATIVE AMERICANS 121
Laurence French

9 INDIAN VIOLENCE: The Cherokee Example 131
Laurence French and Jim Hornbuckle

10 AMERICAN INDIAN TRIBAL COURTS 147
Samuel J. Brakel

PART III INDIAN TREATMENT ISSUES

11 INDIAN ALCOHOLISM 165
Laurence French and Jim Hornbuckle

12 CONTEMPORARY INDIAN JUSTICE AND CORRECTIONAL TREATMENT 179
Laurence French

13 NATIVE AMERICAN PRISON SURVIVAL SCHOOLS 187
Laurence French

14 COUNSELING NATIVE AMERICANS 197
Laurence French

POSTSCRIPT 209

ABOUT THE AUTHORS 213

Acknowledgments

I wish to acknowledge permission to use material contained in this volume as follows:

1. Samuel J. Brakel's "American Indian Tribal Courts" is reprinted by permission of Richard H. Maas, Director of Dissemination for the American Bar Foundation.
2. Laurence French's "Anomie and Violence among Native Americans" is reprinted by permission of Dae H. Chang, Editor of the International Journal of Comparative and Applied Criminal Justice.
3. Laurence French's "Native American Prison Survival Schools" is reprinted by permission of Arlene R. Epstein, Director of Publications for the Adult Education Association of the United States of America.
4. Laurence French's and Jim Hornbuckle's "Alcoholism among Native Americans" is reprinted by permission of David Garrity for the National Association of Social Workers.
5. Laurence French's "An Analysis of Contemporary Indian Justice and Correctional Treatment" is reprinted by permission of Donald L. Chamlee, Editor, Federal Probation.
6. Laurence French's and Jim Hornbuckle's "An Analysis of Indian Violence" is reprinted by permission of the Society for American Indian Studies and Research.
7. Charles F. Wilkinson's "Basic Doctrines of American Indian Law" is reprinted by permission of the author.

I would also like to express my gratitude to the Native American scholars who made original contributions to this work.

Introduction: An Historical Analysis of Indian Justice

American Indians represent a social paradox in that they are one of the most misunderstood cultural groups in North America while at the same time being so closely linked to its historical development. The history of white/Indian contact was firmly established during the early 16th century when DeSoto explored what is now northern Mexico and the southern United States. Within the next century Indian aboriginal cultures began a long decline which transformed them forever, catapulting them from a stone age existence into the technological advanced world of Western societies.

White contact, competition and conflict with native groups led to a long history of discriminatory social policy including slavery, physical genocide, forced removal, allotment, reorganization, termination, relocation and self-determination. These policies in turn have had a tremendous impact upon the nature of Indian justice influencing both the nature of Indian crime and the administration of Indian justice. Indeed, the special legal status assigned American Indians over the years has placed them outside the customary boundaries of traditional North American jurisprudence, a phenomenon still common today. Special federal status, past treaty obligations and the issue of international sovereignty all contribute to the dilemma of Indian justice.

Historical Analysis of Indian Justice

Indian justice has an interesting historical development in North America in general and in the United States in particular. Clearly, the Cherokee, Apache and Sioux played significant roles in the transformation and adaptation from traditional legal customs to the contemporary accommodative situation.

Paradoxically the true nature of aboriginal customs, judicial concerns included, are lost to history since most native groups in America subscribed to a non-literate, oral tradition. Even then sufficient aboriginal attributes have survived, albeit modified over time, to the present.

Common to these aboriginal groups was the 'harmony ethos' with its world view of intra-group cooperation and interpersonal avoidance. This holistic view extended to the universe providing a metaphysical explanation of time and space, essence and being. From this perspective emerged the aboriginal sense of justice. These judicial ideas were rooted within the spiritual realm of 'Father Sky' where 'good' and 'evil' are viewed as relative terms determined by the definition of the situation and not by any moral prescript or natural law.

These relative situations in turn involve real world encounters - those directly affecting 'Mother Earth'. Culpability and responsibility for offenses, within this perspective, are determined according to the particular interpretation of the interaction between Father Sky and Mother Earth. Clearly this represents a marked departure from the tenets of the 'protestant ethic' where individual culpability is seen as an important norm.

The difference between the aboriginal harmony ethos and the Western, protestant ethic lie in how each metaphysical orientation views man's relationship to his natural environment. Western tradition views man as being god-like and therefore separate from other natural phenomena (Freud, 1931). Christian existentialism articulates this argument with its contention that man's destiny is linked to other-worldly forces--forces which do not necessarily have any relevance to nature per se. Indeed, a common theme of the Judaic/Christian/Muslim tradition is the presumption of innate rationality and individual culpability (Weber, 1956).

According to the harmony ethos, man is born powerless acquiring individual strengths and perhaps wisdom through a lifelong process of cooperative reciprocity with other living things. Within this perspective the power of other worldly sources, those associated with Father Sky, manifest themselves in the form of other living entities - most notably in animals. Vision quests, purification rituals (sweats, peyote, the black drink...), sacred communions with the spirits (peace pipe) and special rituals and dances honoring the hunted - all serve to illustrate the significance associated with the traditional view of Indian phenomenology and the acquisition of natural, albeit borrowed, power. Clearly, within this perspective man's responsibilities are shared with others as is his glory.

Consequently while responsibility is individualized within the Western perspective, resulting in a situation of personal culpability and internalized guilt, this same social attribute is shared within the traditional Indian perspective resulting instead in the distribution of guilt - a process known as shame.

Ostensibly, these contravening world views resulted in different social control mechanisms as well. Aboriginal controls mainly involved situational, consensual justice administered either by the clan (kin system) or through special councils. Clan leaders usually adjudicated domestic altercations, receiving complaints, investigating these complaints, and in many instances, enforcing customary sanctions against the wrongdoers. General tribal law and inter-tribal policy, on the other hand, fell within the jurisdiction of tribal leaders (Reid, 1970).

The aboriginal Cherokee legal structure most clearly illustrates the distinction made between domestic and external tribal issues. Domestic matters, including murder and infanticide, were adjudicated before the White chief (civil judge) with clan leaders (Painted Women) representing both the plaintiff (wronged clan) and the defendant (offending clan). Here the nature and extent of restitution, including capital punishment (blood vengeance), was determined by a jury comprised of all village adults - both males and females. Raiding and war policy was determined, administered and enforced by the Red Chief (War Chief) with the assistance of his war council, a body comprised of male and female advisors (Mooney, 1972).

Unlike the Cherokee, the Apaches and Plains Sioux were nomadic people, a factor which also effected their judicial system. Even then, marked differences distinguished the Apaches and the Plains Sioux. Clearly, the Apaches maintained one of the simplest aboriginal systems. Within this system the band was the basic social unit while a loose confederation of family networks linked these bands to the larger tribal unit. Clan and tribal leaders were absent among the Apache. Instead, leadership and justice was administered at the band level.

Significant Apache customs and rituals were initiated and enforced by family patriarchs. The council of patriarchs not only selected their respective band leaders, they also comprised the group's criminal justice apparatus, enforcing tribal customs as well as determining band hunting and raiding policy. Band leaders emerged from within the council of patriarchs and patriarchs were free to change their band affiliation in order to serve under a more charismatic leader.

In this sense, the early Apaches practiced a basic form of Rousseauan democracy where generally-held tribal customs and rituals provided the universal cultural boundaries of the group. And within these general normative boundaries Apache families had considerable liberty to join the band of their choice. Violations, the administration of customary justice, and the imposition of tribal sanctions were all handled at the band level with the council of patriarchs serving as jurors and the band leader acting as judge (Opler, 1969).

The Sioux were a patriarchal, mobile hunting and raiding society much like the Apaches. Yet their judicial system was quite different. Tribal customs and rituals were also maintained at the family (tiyospe) level but with much less personal discretion. Indeed, the Plains Sioux (Lacota) were unique in that they had their own domestic tribal police - the Akicitas. Moreover, the Plains Sioux (7 Lacota-speaking Tribes) maintained a Great Plains inter-tribal council (Wicasa Yatapikas). This Supreme Sioux Executive Council determined tribal laws which were then carried to the respective tribes by their council representatives (Naca elders).

Tribal justice was administered through a well structured criminal justice system. Tribal customs (verbally promulgated laws) were determined by the tribal council (Naca Ominica). This legislative body then assigned its own judicial committee (Wicasa Itacans) which served as an oversight committee, notably the supervision of the administration of tribal customs. The tribal police, on the other hand, enforced these laws. Justice among the Plains Sioux was swift and sure. Violations were often publically whipped inflicting both physical and social embarrassment (shame). This system of justice served the Sioux well adding a high degree of stability to a highly mobile and war-like society (Hassrick, 1967).

Cherokee Adaptations

White contact led to Indian adaptations along with pressure to model these changes after the Western criminal justice system. Formal controls soon replaced the aboriginal customary legal system among the Cherokee. As early as 1979, a tribal police force was created as a reaction to horse theft. This police force was known as the Regulating Companies and eventually led to the more permanent and better organized law enforcement agency (1808), the Light Horse Guard.

1808 also marked the Cherokee transition from a village and clan community structure into that of a nation/state, one with its own legislative body, written laws (Cherokee syllabary), and a separate, formal criminal justice system (police and courts). By 1816 the Cherokee Nation had a bicameral legislature consisting of the Standing Committee (upper house) and the National Council (lower house). Accordingly, the Nation was divided into eight (8) voting districts each with its own judge and marshall. These districts were further divided into four Circuits, each with its own judge and company of the Light Horse Guard.

In 1823, the Cherokee Nation established its own Supreme Court which had as its primary mandate the supervision of the circuit and district courts and law enforcement agencies. It also served as the ultimate court of appeals for Cherokee citizens. Following Removal to Indian Territory (Oklahoma) in 1838, the Cherokee were credited with establishing the first Indian run jails (circa 1840's). And in 1874 the Cherokee National Penitentiary was established. This prison still stands today in Tahlequah, Oklahoma in what was then the center of the new

Cherokee Nation.

Aboriginal ways still survived, however, resulting in the formation of secret police societies, such as the Kee-Too-Wah (pins). This particular secret society favored a return to the traditional customs and ways. These secret societies often took the law into their own hands in an effort to revitalize the old "law of blood" - that which existed prior to the formation of the Cherokee Nation. Obviously, these actions served to obstruct the development of a formal criminal justice system. During the Civil War competing Cherokee secret societies, notably the Kee-Too-Wah and the Knights of the Golden Circle, fought each other with the former advocating a return to the aboriginal ways and the latter supportive of the new Nation.

The transitional era ended for the Cherokee and most other tribes residing in Indian Territory with the Dawes Act (1887) which, among other things, abolished tribal ownership of Indian land. Later, the Curtis Act (1898) abolished tribal courts and laws forcing the Cherokee to now abide by the laws of the white-dominated, territorial government. These actions forced the Cherokee, as well as most of the other Indian groups in Oklahoma, into a state of lawlessness from 1898 until 1924, the year that American Indians were finally officially recognized as United States citizens (Mooney, 1972; Adair, 1930; Malone, 1956; Gearing, 1962; Collier, 1973).

Apache Adaptations

The transitional era for the Apache and other Indians of the Southwest did not actually begin until 1848 when the United States and Mexico signed the Treaty of Guadalupe Hidalgo. Nevertheless the Apache were at war with both American settlers and the Mexican government for 51 years beginning in 1835 and continuing until Geronimo's capture in 1886.

The 'Apache War', as it was known, was initiated by the Governor of Sonaro (Mexico) when he declared his "proyecto de guerre" plan in 1835. This genocidal concept declared open season on the Apache and was backed with a scalp bounty; 100 pesos for adult males, 50 pesos for female scalps and 25 pesos for Indian children. Obviously, scalps were taken from dead Indians.

America inherited this conflict from the Mexican government as part of the Treaty of Guadalupe Hidalgo and the situation worsened as more settlers entered the Southwest. The Americans soon established a network of 44 forts and military camps across the Southwest (Arizona, New Mexico and Texas) in an attempt to encourage permanent settlement of these territories. Moreover, a degree of success was made during this time (1851-1886) with periods of peace existing, albeit briefly, with the Chiricahua Apache chiefs: Mangas, Cochise, Victorio and, even Geronimo.

One of the more significant treaties was the 1873 compact, made with Cochise, which allowed the Chiricahua band to remain in their traditional homeland located in the Dragoon and Hauchuca mountains. A condition of this treaty was that these Apaches would be allowed to police themselves according to their aboriginal customs and that no outside soldiers or police would interfere in their internal affairs.

Hostilities continued at this time involving other Apache bands. Indeed at the Camp Grant Massacre Tucson vigilantes slaughtered over 100 Apache men, women and children, all who were from the peaceful Aravaipa band. And when President Grant's own personal intervention failed to bring these men to justice, Victorio, Geronimo, Mangas, Washez, Chichuahua, Chato and Nana, the most noted warrior leader of that time, took the law into their own hands engaging the United States in a fierce fight, one which lasted for fifteen years.

During this time an innovative individual became Indian Agent (1874-77). A civilian, John Clum, took charge of the San Carlos (Arizona) reservation at the young age of twenty-five, replacing General Crook who was sent north to engage the Sioux and Cheyenne Indians. San Carlos soon became a megareservation, the size of Rhode Island. It was the central collection point for Apache Indians incarcerating nearly 5,000 Apaches including the Chiricahua and Ojo Caliente Apaches as well as their leaders - Geronimo and Victorio.

Clum was credited with establishing the first reservation police force. This Apache police was so effective that the Army selected its Indian scouts from its officers. Indeed, during his tenure at San Carlos, Clum made remarkable progress with the Apaches, even offering them a chance to participate in reservation government. In addition to allowing local autonomy and establishing a reservation police, he also created a reservation trial court where the police prosecuted their own cases and where band leaders served as judges. Clum acted as the ultimate appellate judge reviewing all appeals.

Nevertheless, Clum's innovations were viewed as being premature and met with considerable resistance and resentment from both the white settlers and the U.S. Army and he was finally forced to leave his post in August, 1877. These innovative concepts of self-determination did, however, provide the model for the "Wheeler/Howard," Reorganization Act (1934). Clum went on to become the first mayor of Tombstone, Arizona and became founder and editor of the "Tombstone Epitaph".

Geronimo continued to raid settlements in the Southwest in spite of being pursued by a 5,000 man force under the direction of General Miles. Tom Horn, a civilian scout, finally convinced Geronimo and his small band to surrender in 1886. Given his reputation, the United States government felt compelled to punish all Chiricahua Apaches and consequently some four hundred Indians were imprisoned first in Florida, then Alabama and eventually in Oklahoma.

Even those who served as scouts for Generals Crook and Miles, including some who were personally decorated by the President of the United States, were arrested and interned along with the rest of the band. Indeed, the Chiricuhua Apaches remained interned in military prisons until 1914, six years after Geronimo's death and ten years prior to Indian citizenship. During this twenty-eight year period, all Indian children born in captivity were automatically ascribed prisoners' status (Opler, 1969; Stout, 1974; Terrell, 1972; Davis, 1929; Clum, 1936; Collier, 1977).

Sioux Adaptations

The aboriginal Siouan system of justice continued until the late 1800's when these Indians were finally forced off of the plains and onto reservations. It was within the reservation environment that their nomadic social structure, along with its police and warrior societies (Akicitas), proved ineffective and adaptations to a Western-style formal criminal justice system emerged. The reservation era for the Plains Sioux began, for all intent and purpose, with the Fort Laramie Treaty of 1868. Here, the United States provided Red Cloud (Oglala Sioux) with the Great Sioux Reservation, a land mass that extended from the Missouri River to the 103rd meridian on to the Black Hills. This 35,000 square mile track of land was designated to be the home for some 20,000 Sioux. The Great Sioux Reservation differed from San Carlos in that there was little outside interference and traditional customs, rituals and folkways still continued to dominate the Sioux people.

The 1868 treaty lasted six years until gold was discovered in the Black Hills (1874). Moreover, tribal reactions to illegal hostilities at the hands of the United States Army, notably the 7th Calvary, caused a split within the Sioux ranks with Red Cloud (Oglala) and Spotted-Tail (Brule) seeking peaceful accommodations with the whites while Sitting Bull, Crazy Horse, Gall and Hump advocated war. Blatant violations of the much heralded Fort Laramie Treaty, especially the desecration of the sacred Black Hills and continued harassment by the U.S. Army, culminated in the June 25, 1876 battle at the Little Big Horn, better known as "Custer's Last Stand". This was to be the Lacotas (Plains Sioux) last great victory over the white intruders. It also spelled the end to the Plains lifestyle and the beginning of forced reservation accommodation.

The United States was shocked at Custer's death and the defeat of the 7th Calvary and demanded that the Sioux and their Cheyenne allies be severely punished. The army pursued the militant Sioux and Cheyennes forcing Sitting Bull and Gall to hide in Canada while Crazy Horse and Hump continued to fight Generals Crook and Miles - the same generals who were also engaged in the Apache campaign. Things worsened for the militant

Sioux in the Fall of 1876 when the reservation faction signed away the Black Hills and all the land west of them, what is now Wyoming and Montana.

Crazy Horse eventually surrendered in the Spring of 1877 and was subsequently killed that Fall while in the stockade at Fort Robinson (Nebraska). However, things did not improve with the death of Crazy Horse and the Sioux continued to be moved onto more restrictive reservations. The 'warrior' and 'chief' societies were dismantled and sacred rituals, including the Sun Dance, were outlawed by the Indian Agent on the reservations. With little transition, reservation adjustment became extremely difficult for the Sioux. They did not adjust to either the confinement of these more restrictive reservations or to the white-imposed agrarian lifestyle which was substituted for the traditional buffalo hunts. Moreover, the Siouxs' attempt at self-rule suffered a serious setback when the Rosebud police chief, Crow Dog, killed the Brule Chief, Spotted Tail, in 1881.

This incident led to the Ex Parte Crow Dog decision of 1883 whereby the U.S. Supreme Court ruled in favor of Crow Dog. In this case, the white court took upon itself the task of adjudicating Crow Dog in the First Judicial District Court of Dakota (Deadwood, South Dakota) even though the Spotted Tail matter was already resolved according to traditional Sioux custom. Crow Dog was subsequently found guilty by a white jury and sentenced to be hanged. He appealed the verdict to the U.S. Supreme Court which ruled that state or territorial courts did not have jurisdiction over crimes committed by Indians on their own reservation. The Supreme Court further stipulated that Crow Dog had already settled the matter according to traditional Sioux custom, doing so by paying an agreed upon sum (blood money) to Spotted Tail's survivors. To convict him again for the same crime would constitute "double jeopardy" - a violation of the United States Bill of Rights.

The "superchief" concept also died with Spotted Tail and even more repressive controls were enacted on the Sioux reservations. Allotment and the Treaty of 1889 effectively terminated the conditions of the Laramie Treaty of 1868. Indeed, these conditions were enforced in spite of the fact that three-fourths of the adult Sioux males refused to recognize them. Corruption within the Indian Agency itself was widespread resulting in much of the reservation food supplies being misappropriated by white agents and sold elsewhere. Even the food that did reach the reservation was often sold to the Indians even though treaty conditions stipulated that these supplies were to be freely distributed, as partial compensation for their land.

These events generated a situation of despair and alienation for many of the traditionalists who now had to watch their people beg and starve. Indeed, these despairing Sioux were susceptible to an escape mechanism much like that provided by the Ghost Dance. The Sioux learned about the Ghost Dance directly from the Paiute prophet, Wovoka, in New Mexico and the movement gained momentum as the Sioux eagerly anticipated the "return of the buffalo" and their traditional ways. Furthermore, the Ghost Dance message advocated an end to the whiteman as well as the return of Sioux warriors killed in past battles with these intruders. All the great Sioux leaders supported the Ghost Dance movement including Red Cloud, Sitting Bull, Black Elk and Big Foot.

Unfortunately, the Sioux did not anticipate the white backlash and consequently, both Big Foot and Sitting Bull became victims of the Ghost Dance Movement. Sitting Bull was killed on December 15, 1890 when Indian police attempted to arrest him at Fort Yates (Standing Rock Reservation, North Dakota). After his death, many of Sitting Bull's followers joined Chief Big Foot at the Cheyenne River (Swift Bird, South Dakota) Reservation. Fearing a similar fate, Big Foot led his people off of the reservation for the protections of the Black Hills and the Bad Lands. His party of 370 was intercepted on December 28, 1890 at Wounded Knee Creek on the Pine Ridge Reservation southwest of Cheyenne River. Surrounded, and the Indians in the process of being disarmed, a shot was fired and the army panicked. Opening fire on the Indians with rifles and machine guns (Hotchkiss) 84 men and boys, 44 women and children were killed and another 33 wounded - many who later died. For all intent and purpose, the Wounded Knee massacre spelled the end of the Ghose Dance Movement and, along with it, the Sioux's hope for a return of their traditional ways (American Horse, 1970; Holder, 1970; Standing Bear, 1928).

At last the Sioux realized that they were now destined to reside on the reservations as wards of the federal government. Their dreams were dead. Black Elk captured the sentiment of his people at this time when he stated: "And so it was all over...A people's dream died there (Wounded Knee). It was a beautiful dream. (Now) the nation's hoop is broken and scattered, there is no center any longer, and the sacred tree is dead (Neihardt, 1932:230)." A decade later Hassrick made a similar assessment of the Lacota Sioux and reservation life: "Despair and resignation mark their countenance. They seem to carry on in a kind of insensitive, feelingless apathy, listless in their discouragement. For them there is no chance of victory and they have suffered their defeat. They have been characterized aptly as 'warriors without weapons', for they are men without a vision (Hassrick, 1964:342)."

Reservation Accommodation: The Legal Effects of Federal Paternalism

A number of significant events influenced the reservation criminal justice system, most notably: (1) 1883 Courts of Indian Offenses; (2) 1883 Ex Parte Crow Dog case; (3) 1885 Major Crimes Act; (4) 1887 General Allotment Act; (5) 1892 Rules for Indian

Courts; (6) 1898 Curtis Act; (7) 1924 Indian Citizenship Act; (8) 1934 Wheeler-Howard Act; (9) 1946 Indian Claims Commission Act; (10) 1953 Public Law 280; (11) 1954 Relocation; (12) 1968 Indian Civil Rights Act; and (13) the 1975 Indian Law Enforcement Improvement Act.

Reservation Accommodation: Law Enforcement

John Clums effective use of an Indian police force on the San Carlos Reservation did not go unnoticed in that Indian Commissioner Ezra A. Hayt made an official request for the general adoption of Indian police on reservations in his annual report to Congress in 1877. Congress responded by authorizing monies for 480 Indian police officers in 1878 and nearly doubling the appropriations the following year providing funds for some 900 Indian law enforcement officers (Hayt, 1877).

The effectiveness of the reservation police between 1878 and Reorganization (1934), is open to debate since traditionalists often viewed the Indian police with contempt. They felt that the Indian police actually represented the white-run Indian Agency and not tribal customs. Nonetheless, reservation law enforcement did play a significant role in maintaining order during the critical transition period when tribes were initially removed from their traditional homelands and forced to adjust to the new, and often alien, reservation environment.

Indian police usually worked with white Indian Agency administrators who, in turn, ruled on probable cause and sometimes even passed judgement and determined punishment for Indian violators. Later, with passage of the Courts of Indian Offenses (1883), Indian police and judges administered reservation justice. Problems still plagued reservation justice since most of these judges, like the police, were appointed by the Indian Agency or by Tribal leaders who themselves were appointed by the Agency. This system often led to exploitation, abuse of authority and selective justice. The Crow Dog case illustrates this dilemma well.

Standing Bear (1928: 157-160) recounted the events that led to the murder of the Rosebud Chief, Spotted Tail, in 1881. Spotted Tail apparently was favored by the Indian Commissioner, the local Indian Agents and Army detachment and subsequently was given the title of "Head Chief" of all the Sioux. This was a title conferred upon him by the whites and many of the Sioux, including his own people - the Brule Sioux - did not recognize Spotted Tail as deserving this honor, especially when it was Red Cloud, the Oglala Chief of the neighboring Pine Ridge reservation, who was most responsible for bringing peace to the area through the Laramie Treaty of 1868.

At any rate, Spotted Tail acquired considerable wealth and power in his new position, a situation that angered many Sioux. This resentment was further exacerbated when Spotted Tail relinquished the buffalo plains of northern Nebraska to white ranchers. And when he then stole another man's wife Sioux tradition warrented his death as just punishment. Crow Dog fulfilled this public mandate while at the same time avenging his own dispute with Spotted Tail who had him removed from his position as Rosebud Chief of Police.

Justice, according to tribal custom, required that Crow Dog pay blood money to Spotted Tail's survivors and he complied with this verdict. And in most instances, tribal justice would have sufficed. However, this particular incident was viewed as representing a major affront to white policy on Indian reservations. Consequently, Crow Dog was tried in Territorial Court before a white judge and jury, convicted of murder and sentenced to be hanged. The U.S. Supreme Court then responded favorably to Crow Dog's habeas corpus writ allowing tribal justice to prevail. Indeed, the white outcry now was even greater than before leading to the enactment of the Major Crimes Act of 1885.

The Major Crimes Act brought federal law enforcement officers onto the reservation while at the same time compelling Indian police to bound over Indian offenders who violated the Major Crimes (murder, manslaughter, rape, aggravated and murderous assault, arson, burglary, larceny...) to federal courts and not to process these cases before tribal courts. This served to compound reservation justice making reservations virtual hunting grounds for Indian, state, county (sheriffs) and federal police. Indeed, ever since 1885 Indian reservations have been 'overpoliced', a problem which continued to plague reservations even today.

Indians are usually ascribed the lowest status within the reservation police hierarchy with the federal agents having the greatest authority followed by the State Police, sheriffs, town police and, lastly, the Indian police. Conflicting Indian policy over the years, notably Allotment, Reorganization and Termination, only contributed to the confusion and ambiguity over reservation police jurisdiction. This situation lasted some 90 years from the initiation of the 1885 Major Crimes Act until passage of the Indian Law Enforcement Improvement Act of 1975.

Specifically, the bill (S.2010) provides for the improvement of law enforcement and the determination of civil and criminal jurisdiction and law in Indian country. Title I of the bill recognized the lack of a consistent congressional Indian policy in the past and the fact that this has resulted in unclear jurisdictional status within Indian country: "jurisdictional problems of increasing severity and magnitude in Indian country have demonstrated that subjecting Indians and Indian country to state or federal civil and criminal jurisdiction and law without regard to the unique cultural, political, geographic and social factors of each Indian tribe and reservation is unjust and unworkable... (Abourezk, 1975)."

Reservation Accommodation: The Courts

Traditional Indian justice has survived in spite of four hundred years of outside attempts to convert Native Americans to the Western model of formal justice. Early treaties (Six Nations Treaty of 1784 and the Hopewell Treaty of 1785) and Supreme Court decisions (Worcester v. Georgia of 1832 and Ex Parte Crow Dog of 1883) recognized Indian sovereignty, tribal rights and other aspects of customary justice.

The Civil War and massive westward expansionism as well as continued conflict with Indians over their land led to increased demands from the general public for greater regulation of Native American populations. Hence, not only were reservations subjected to more extensive surveillance by the U.S. Army and the Bureau of Indian Affairs (BIA) more internal controls designed to restrict their tribal authority was instituted as well. These actions followed the 1871 congressional decision to abolish further treaty negotiations with aboriginals, an action which many viewed as a de facto attempt to create legal policy. Under this plan past treaties would no longer have to be honored.

Actually, the establishment of the 'Courts of Indian Offenses' was itself an ethnocentric attempt to legislate morality and to impose white ways upon Native Americans. The Secretary of Interior, Henry M. Teller, articulated his reasons for establishing these courts in his annual report to Congress:

"... many of the agencies are without law of any kind, and the necessity for some rule of government on the reservation grows more and more apparent each day. If it is the purpose of the Government to civilize the Indians, they must be compelled to desist from the savage and barbarous practices that are calculated to continue them in savagery, no matter what exterior influences are brought to bear on them. Very many of the progressive Indians have become fully alive to the pernicious influences of these heathenish practices indulged in by their people, and have sought to abolish them; in such efforts they have been aided by their missionaries, teachers, and agents, but this has been found impossible even with the aid thus given...Yet a few non-progressive, degraded Indians are allowed to exhibit before the young and susceptible children all the debauchery, diabolism, and savagery of the worst state of the Indian race. Every man familiar with Indian life will bear witness to the pernicious influence of these savage rites and heathenish customs. In accordance with the suggestions of this letter, the Commissioner of Indian Affairs established a tribunal at all agencies, except among the civilized Indians, consisting of three Indians, to be known as the court of Indian offenses. The members of this tribunal consist of the first three officers in rank of the police force, if such selection is approved by the agent; otherwise, the agent may select from among the members of the tribe three suitable persons to constitute such tribunal (Teller, 1883: x-xiii)."

The Crow Dog case led to the passage of the Major Crimes Act of 1885 which restricted the authority of the Courts of Indian Justice as well as further curtailing traditional consensual justice. Congress passed the Major Crimes Act as an attempt to better regulate 'serious offenses' on the reservations. It was promptly tested before the U.S. Supreme Court in "United States v. Kagama" in 1886 in a case involving Indian murders on the Hoopa Valley Indian reservation in California. The Supreme Court upheld the constitutionality of the Major Crimes Act and the number of crimes increased over the years from the initial seven to thirteen today: murder; manslaughter; rape; carnal knowledge of any female other than wife; assault with intent to kill; assault with a dangerous weapon; assault resulting in serious bodily injury; arson; burglary; robbery; and larceny (Brakel, 1978).

Inconsistency in federal Indian policies often served to obviate both tribal and federal justice on the reservations. The General Allotment Act (Dawes Act) of 1887, the Curtis Act of 1898, Public Law 280 of 1953 (Termination) and the Civil Rights Act of 1968 all restricted tribal authority and justice in some fashion or other. Pressure from non-Indian settlers led to passage of the General Allotment Act. The Act stipulated that tribal collectivities would be broken up and that the land held in tribal trust would now be distributed to individual Indians as deeded land. All 'surplus' land would then be opened to non-Indian settlers (Washburn, 1975). The Curtis Act went a step further dissolving tribal government and Indian authority including the abolition of tribal courts. Indians would also now be required to register with the United States government and these registrations would be known as 'tribal rolls' (Curtis, 1898).

The Wheeler-Howard (Indian Reorganization) Act of 1934 was the result of the energies of the progressive Indian Commissioner during the Roosevelt Administration - John Collier. This Act reversed the policies of Allotment and the Curtis Act. Reservations were again given back to the tribes and tribal autonomy was encouraged as well as a rebirth of the traditional culture and customs. Indian lands could once again be held in tribal collectivity but now under federal trust. Tribal customs, including law enforcement and criminal and civil adjudications, were revitalized during this time (Philip, 1977). This experiment at tribal self-determination was short-lived however and in 1953 the Eisenhower Administration supported a new policy determined to destroy the reservation system. This was the combined polices of 'Termination' and 'Relocation'. Indeed, one of the first casualties of Public Law 280 was tribal justice. The Act conferred:

> "...jurisdiction on the states of California, Minne-

sota, Nebraska, Oregon, and Wisconsin, with respect to criminal offenses and civil cases of action committed or arising on Indian reservations within such states, and for other purposes (Prucha, 1975:234)."

Even with these curtailments, the American Bar Foundation noted that:

> "In theory, the tribal courts are left with jurisdiction over all civil and criminal matters that occur within reservation boundaries with the exception of the 13 federal crimes as long as 'due process' is observed in criminal cases (Brakel, 1978:8)."

Few tribes, however, have the resources to exercise their legal authority, especially under these conditions, and therefore most tribes must continue to rely upon outside, usually county or state, courts for reservation offenses.

Reservation Accommodation: Corrections

Traditionally, Indians rarely found the need to detain offenders in jails or similar devices. Most aboriginal justice was immediate involving either blood vengeance (death) or parity restitution (blood money). Even under a sentence of death condemned persons were usually released to the custody of their family or clan. Among the southeastern tribes it was customary to assign a personal executor to each condemned Indian with the former moving into the same household as the latter. It has even been suggested that it was not unusual for the executor and offender to become friends during the interim period.

One southeastern tribe, the Cherokee, often resolved blood vengeances during their seasonal stick ball games. Here it was understood that the condemned man would be beaten to death by the avenging clan players. This was seen as being a most honorable death one which not only resolved the personal vengeance but restored honor to the offender's entire clan. Reluctant offenders, on the other hand, could either attempt to run to a 'neutral' village, where he or she would have to remain until after the New Years Spiritual Rebirth ceremony, or they could be executed in a dishonorable fashion such as being tied and thrown over a cliff with their remains left for the buzzards.

During the early reservation era, that time when tribal autonomy prevailed, flogging was a common form of corporal punishment. The reservation police usually carried out these sentences on-the-spot usually without benefit of judicial processing or review. This form of swift justice was administered for public drunkenness, child and wife battery and other related offenses. Indeed, the 'whip bearers' were important members of all Plains societies, including the Sioux police societies.

As mentioned earlier, it was the Cherokee who built the

first tribal-run correctional institution. Stockades provided a similar function on the plains reservations. They differed from the Cherokee Penitentiary in that they were run by the U.S. Army or the civilian Indian Agency. Indian police were also utilized in the stockades and as the army left these stockades came under civilian control usually for the incarceration of any offender - white, black, or Indian. Actually, Indian correctional facilities decreased greatly over the years where today few reservations have even holding jails. This may change in the future as Indian focus is fixed upon the innovative correctional philosophy instituted on the Cheyenne River reservation.

The Swift Bird Indian Correctional facility is located on the Cheyenne River reservation in South Dakota and housed in an abandoned Job Corps Center overlooking the Missouri River. The facility is a voluntary pre-release institution designed to serve Native American clients who have been convicted and sentenced for crimes in South Dakota, North Dakota, Nebraska, Minnesota, and Montana.

The Swift Bird mandate is to provide individualized, cultural resocialization for short-termed Indians convicted of non-violent felonies or misdemeanors in either federal or state courts. The staff is entirely Native American and the project is sponsored and endorsed by both the Native American Rights Fund (NARF) and the National Institute of Justice (NIJ). The major drawback to the program is that the parent correctional facility retains original jurisdiction over the Indian clients while they are at Swift Bird. These Indian clients are in effect placed on parole to the Swift Bird correctional program.

The cultural program utilized at Swift Bird is similar to those used by Indian 'survival schools'. They first stress the positive attributes of 'Indianism' - the process of learning about your heritage and being proud about being Indian. This initial stage is then followed with counseling and training techniques which are designed to better prepare the Indian ex-offender to cope within the larger United States society.

Many Indian leaders envision Swift Bird as a prototype for a system of Indian-run correctional facilities across the nation. It is anticipated that in the future each major Indian linguistic group (Algonkian, Iroquois, Athapaskan, Siouan, Pueble...) will have its own correctional facility. And if this philosophy is carried over to the other criminal justice components, law enforcement and the judiciary, then perhaps we will be finally embarking on a viable 'PanIndian' solution to the 'Indian problem' (French, 1979).

REFERENCES

Abourezk, J. Indian Law Enforcement Act of 1975 (S.2010). Washington: U.S. Government Printing Office (Parts 1 & 2), 1975.
Adair, J. Adair's History of the American Indian (S. Williams, ed.). Johnson City: East Tennessee State University Press, 1930.
American Horse, L. & Joseph Cress Lacota Stories. Pine Ridge: Red Cloud Indian School, Inc., 1970.
Brakel, S. American Indian Tribal Courts. Chicago: American Bar Foundation, 1978.
Collier, J. American Indian Ceremonial Dances. New York: Bounty Press, 1977.
Collier, P. When Shall They Rest. New York: Holt, Rinehart & Winston, 1973.
Clum, W. Apache Agent. Lincoln: University of Nebraska Press, 1936.
Curtis Curtis Act. Washington: U.S. Statutes at Large, (30:497-98) 1898: 502,504,505.
Davis, B. Truth About Geronimo. New Haven: Yale University Press, 1929.
Freud, S. Civilization and its Discontents (J. Strachey, ed.). New York: W.W. Norton, 1931.
French, L. "Corrections and the Native American Client," Prison Journal, Vol LIX, No. 1 (Spring-Summer), 1979.
Gearing, F. Priests and Warriors. Mesasha, Wisconsin: American Anthropological Association, 1962.
Hassrick, R. The Sioux. Norman: University of Oklahoma Press, 1967.
Hayt, E. Annual Report of the Commission of Indian Affairs. Washington: House Executive Document No. 1, 4th Congress, 2nd Session, Serial 1800 (November): 1877: 358-399.
Malone, H. Cherokees of the Old South. Athens: University of Georgia Press, 1956.
Mooney, J. Myths of the Cherokee and Sacred Formulas of the Cherokee. Nashville: Charles Elder Publisher, 1972.
Neihardt, J. Black Elk Speaks. New York: William Morrow, 1932.
Opler, M. Apache Odyssey. New York: Holt, Rinehart & Winston, 1969.
Philip, K. John Collier's Crusade for Indian Reform 1920-1954. Tucson: University of Arizona Press, 1977.
Prucha, F. Documents of United States Indian Policy. Lincoln: University of Nebraska Press, 1975.
Reid, J. A Law of Blood. New York: New York University Press, 1970.
Standing Bear, L. My People the Sioux. New York: Houghton Mifflin, 1928.
Stout, Jr., J. Apache Lightning. New York: Oxford University Press, 1974.
Teller, H. "Courts of Indian Offenses," Annual Report of the

Secretary of the Interior. Washington: House Executive Document No. 1, 48th Congress, Serial 2190, 1883: x-xiii.

Terrell, J. *Apache Chronicle*. New York: World Publishing, 1972.

Sioux Trails. New York: McGraw Hill, 1975.

Washburn, W. *The Assault on Indian Tribalism*. Philadelphia: J. B. Lippincott, 1975.

Weber, M. *The Protestant Ethic and the Spirit of Capitalism* (T. Parsons, ed.). New York: Charles Scribner's Sons, 1956.

Part 1

Indian Sociolegal Issues

Chapter 1
Critical Legal and Social Responsibilities Facing Native Americans

TERESA LA FROMBOISE and
RICHARD LA FROMBOISE

Indian people are very skeptical of basic human rights since they have experienced numerous instances in which their rights have been denied due to the oppressive policies of the United States government (such as removal, allotment, termination).

"For oppressors, there exists only one right, their right to live in peace, over and above the right, not always recognized but simply conceded, of the oppressed to survival (Freire, 1968)"

The Indian's survival as 'poorest of the poor' is not only a material poverty but a poverty of reasonable choices, a lack of freedoms, and a poverty of spirit (Warrior, 1970). Indians will be more likely to stand up for themselves against criticism once they've developed a positive belief system which can justify assertive actions. They will understand better how to act in a situation once they know what their individual and special rights are. They will find it easier to stand up for themselves when they realize that they are also asserting the rights of Indian people in general. Before they can experience these effects, they must become aware of existing techniques which have sabotaged Indian efforts to stand up for their rights.

1. Making an Indian feel as if he or she is a non-person by referring to them as 'pagan', 'savages', and 'drunkards' or by legally distinguishing between Indians and whites on the basis of the dehumanizing criteria of blood quantum. Human rights are for people.

2. Stealing human rights by obtaining thanks from the victims. Indians are often made to feel indebted and that they should be appreciative for the numerous sacrifices and hard work vested in solving the 'Indian problem'.

3. Instilling fear in Indians that their attempts to regain their rights they already have. Indians are often told that things could be worse and they should be grateful for the human rights they have rather than complain about their loss of human rights.

4. Setting up the oppressors as the protectors of the Indians' human rights so that the protectors can selectively act in ways which further their own interests while ostensibly acting on behalf of the Indians.

5. Pretending that the reason for the loss of human rights is for some other reason than that a person is Indian (such as drinking, being late, nonconformity).

6. Pointing to the common good of all people. Indians are presented as being selfish if they represent their wishes when there are competing interests. For instance, Indians can't only think of their rights, they must also think of the other hunters or the sporting goods industry.

7. Removing rights so gradually that Indians don't realize what has happened until it is too late. Another hunting rights example would be to first restrict the geographical area where hunting is permitted, then cut the season to certain times of the year, then insist on licensing, and then Indians will be on the same grounds as non-Indian sportsmen.

8. Holding conferences on HUMAN RIGHTS to allow Indians to blow off steam and go home feeling that things are well in hand (Waubageshig, 1970, p. 197-8).

These examples illustrate the kinds of experiences Indian people have regularly encountered and which indicate that the majority society usually acts with total disregard for the rights of Indian people. The responsibilities of Indian people and the responsibilities of the Federal government in carrying out these Indian rights in a mutually respectful way will be discussed throughout in hopes that eventually rights will no longer be used as weapons. To Indian people, freedom and responsibility come from the right to decide what is best for themselves and to run their own affairs.

Few people realize that American Indians comprise the only minority group which possess a special legal status within the United States (Washburn, 1976). Although they are citizens like everybody else, they are also, by virtue of their tribal affiliations, possessed of special rights which eminate from the special legal status of 'internal sovereignty'. This concept has often puzzled and irritated white Americans. This status was attained by treaty negotiations between Indians and whites which established that the Indian land Americans now enjoy would be held in trust by the United States government if Indians could live autonomously, free from external control, and maintain their own authority within the limits of their own reservation lands. The special rights of Indians were established by executive orders and judicial doctrines created in response between them and the United States (Zionitz, 1975). Non-Indian

Americans enjoy their rights directly from the supreme law of the land called a constitution. The secondary law of the land eminates from statutes passed by the legislature and from treaties both of which are equal (Holland V. Missouri). Although most Indian tribes have their own constitutions, their rights flow not from the local concern but from the national concern. Indians believe that they have fulfilled their obligations to the treaty (land release) and expect the same from their counterparts.

Unfortunately, as individual Indians entered into a variety of associations with whites, these relationships became characterized by inequality and political separation (Washburn, 1976). It became evident that laws would need to be enacted to protect the Indian's individual rights. Consequently, legislation was passed: the Dawes Act of 1887 attempted to reconcile Indian status; Indians were declared U.S. citizens in 1924; the Indian Reorganization Act was created to give legal recognition to tribal governments distinct from federal, state and local governments in 1934; the Indian Claims Commission was created in 1946 to hear disputes between Indians and the U.S. government. Most recently, the Indian Civil Rights Act of 1968 emphasized rights of Indians as U.S. citizens, so that the individual rights in the U.S. Constitution would be upheld in Indian communities over and above local constitutions (25 U.S.C. S.S. 1301-41 (1970)). Many Indians question the desirability of this act since it weakens Indian self-government in the name of protecting individual Indian rights from arbitrary and unjust actions of tribal governments. (S. Rep. No. 841, 90th Cong., 1 Sess. at 6 (1967)). By attempting to protect Indians from their own people, the Indian Civil Rights Act threatens their special status as sovereign entities because now Indian self-government is subject to the same limitations and restraints imposed on federal, state, and local government by the Constitution of the United States (Senate Committee on the Judiciary, Protecting the Rights of the American Indian, S. Rep. No. 92-294, 91st Cong., 1st Sess. 2 (1969)). These restraints however have been interpreted by the Supreme Court quite favorably toward Collective Indian rights rather than individual Indian rights (Santa Clara V. Martinez, 1978).

As Indian associations with whites continue, Indians continue to ask that their special history, status, and circumstances be allowed to be worked out within the framework of their own rights and beliefs and in collaboration and harmony with those around them (*American Indian Journal*, 1978).

The relationship between an Indian and his tribe is very different than the relationship between non-Indian citizens and their city and state government (Zionitz, 1975; Lindstrom, 1978). Indian tribes are considered to be governmental bodies of dependent nations within the borders of the United States, occupying territory over which they have the power of self-government. The principles underlying the sovereign status of Indian tribes is classically stated by Cohen as follows:

"The whole course of judicial decision on the nature of Indian tribal powers is marked by adherence to three fundamental principals: (1) An Indian tribe possesses, in the first instance, all the powers of any sovereign state, (2) Conquest renders the tribe subject to the legislative powers of the United States and, in substance, terminates the external powers of sovereignty of the tribe, e.g., its power to enter into itself affect the internal sovereignty of the tribe, i.e., its powers of local self-government, (3) These powers are subject to qualification by treaties and by expressed legislation of Congress, but, same as thus expressly qualified full powers of internal sovereignty are vested in the Indian tribes and in their duly constituted organs of government (Cohen, 1942, p. 123).

To fully safeguard guidelines for federal courts in dealing with Indian sovereignty questions, Indians must stand up for their sovereign rights to:

1. Function as governments with sovereign powers over their territory and people.
2. Maintain their own values and concepts of fairness and justice to the fullest extent.
3. Maintain respect for tribal self-government by demanding that courts recognize the tribes own institutions of government, their constitutions, ordinances, and regulations.
4. Maintain a tribal society which is closed or limited to outsiders, if it chooses, and reject cultural pluralism in order to protect its community character.
5. Maintain the tribe's inherent right to determine its own membership.
6. Impress upon the courts the importance of avoiding action which would undermine the authority of tribal courts over reservation affairs and, in turn infringe on the rights of Indians to govern themselves (William V. Lee, 358 U.S. 217 (1959)).

The following pages contain a detailed discussion of the rights commonly discussed in the Indian Bill of Rights Exercise (see Assertion Training with Indian Adults chapter). Since almost all interpersonal interactions or communications imply certain personal rights, it is important that Indian people recognize what their rights are in order to know how to stand up for them, how to act on them, and how not to deny them. For these reasons they are presented in detail as a guide to Indian behavior.

Treaty Rights

Historically, the treaties entered into by English colonists for the direct purchase of land were done so in a very solemn and formal manner (Morison, 1952). Unfortunately this form of negotiating differences between Indians and whites was frequently the object of ridicule and shame by laymen and historians. The classic example cited by them is the purchase of Manhattan Island by the Dutch for twenty-four dollars from the local Indians. This agreement illustrates the different values and interests and differences of power since Indians placed greater value on trade items (i.e., guns and beads) than on marginally used lands (Washburn, 1976).

The making of treaties with the U.S. first took the form of verbal discussion between the Commissioners and Indians. The written texts, with their legalistic construction were later prepared by government lawyers. Even though the formal written treaties are often insufficient reports of the verbal promises exchanged by Indians and whites, Indian people still visualize treaties as the basis of all their rights and status (Waubageshig, 1970). Indians have believed that the content and spirit of the treaties must be their guide, not the precise letter of the foreign language in which they are written.

Under mounting pressure, Indian people surrendered their remaining lands for the rights of services relating to education, welfare, health and economic development.

a. The guarantee to hold certain lands called 'reserves' for the sole use and benefit of the Indian people forever, and assistance in the social, economic and cultural development of the reserves.

b. The provision of health services to the Indian people on the reserve or off the reserve at the expense of the Federal government.

c. The provision of education of all types and levels to all Indian people at the expense of the Federal government.

d. The right of the Indian people to hunt, trap and fish for their livelihood free of government interference and regulation and subject only to the provision that the exercise of this right must not interfere with the use and enjoyment of private property (Waubageshig, 1970, p. 11).

Therefore, these benefits are not handouts because Indian people have paid dearly for them.

Right to Self-Government

One of the main aspects of tribal sovereignty is the Indian's right to govern themselves (Martone, 1976). Sovereignty includes authority of tribal courts over reservation affairs which are not to be undermined by federal courts (William V. Lee, 358 U.S. 217 (1959)). The right to self-government is not new. Laws dealing with Indians have been passed with the promise that the government would eventually step aside and let Indians run their own affairs and assume transference of the power of the Department of the Interior (Josephy, 1971).

Indian self-government is a form of government in which

decisions are made by people who are most directly affected by the decisions (Cohen, 1942).

"There are two primary justifications for self-government by Indian tribal groups found in the documents on Indian sovereignty: (1) the extent to which a particular Indian group is entitled to exercise power to define the rules of behavior for its membership; and (2) the extent to which it is easier, wiser, more civilizing and necessary to allow Indian groups to engage in self-rules (Price, 1973).

This concept was consciously used by Franklin and Jefferson and incorporated in the philosophy of the U.S. Constitution. Self-government by Indians today has run into some amount of opposition seemingly related to the fact that most officials in favor of self-government are so egocentrically involved that they appear to be actually opposed to self-government in the area over which they are expert and have jurisdiction. If Indians continue to yield to each expert division in the matters in which it is concerned, there will be no Indian self-government. For example, the Bureau of Indian Affairs has interfered for more than 100 years and justified its powers on the grounds that their help was only needed for a brief, temporary period until authority could be conveyed to Indians themselves (Cohen, 1942). It also follows that this same Bureau is the primary mediator when the confrontation formerly described becomes reality.

Right to Jurisdiction

Another controversial Indian right provided for under tribal sovereignty is the right to jurisdiction, or the tribal jurisdiction, or the tribal right to exercise effective governmental authority over the entire reservation and all Indian and non-Indian persons within its boundaries. Some tribes have asserted this right through an 'implied consent' ordinance to obtain jurisdiction over those who enter reservation lands. Other tribes have asserted this right through their inherent tribal authority since it has never been withdrawn by congressional acts (Zionitz, 1975).

The supreme court has mandated in its latest decision of Oliphant V. Suquamish Indian tribe (1978) that Indian tribes do not have inherent criminal jurisdiction over non-Indians, stipulating there may be jurisdiction if bargained for, in a treaty, or given to the tribe by congressional act. The inherent authority relating to civil jurisdiction over non-Indians has yet to be tried. Thus, logically using the meaning of jurisdiction as power to regulate, Indian tribes are put to the task of having the supreme court decide what the non-Indians have agreed to. However, in the event that there are ambiguous or unclear meanings to the treaties, they are to be interpreted in favor of the Indian (Choate V. Trapp, 224 U.S. 665, 675 (1912)). Therefore, Indians have the right to full jurisdiction over Indians within the reservation to the same extent that the state has jurisdiction over Indians outside the boundaries of the reservation.

Right to Exclusion

Many Indian people believe that they have the right to exclude anyone from the tribe who is a troublemaker or who upsets the serenity of the community. This applies to Indians as well as non-Indians. The rare case of exclusion or banishment of Indians from the tribe was used as a means of controlling unacceptable social behavior. In serious cases, non-Indian outsiders were excluded for: preaching a political or religious doctrine offensive to the tribe, its members or its government; and meddling or interfering in internal tribal affairs because they threatened Indian cultural preservation. This exclusionary power was the only means with which a tribe could deal with non-Indian offensive behavior, since it has no jurisdiction over non-Indians in tribal courts (Zionitz, 1975).

This right was well-established prior to the Civil Rights Act of 1968. Now after the decision of Dodge V. Nakai, which overruled tribal exclusion on a number of grounds, the validity of this right is open to judicial question. Nevertheless, current Indian thinking supports the tribal right to exclude outsiders under appropriate ordinances such as those in the Navajo Tribal Code which enumerate specific grounds for exclusion and which bear a reasonable relationship to the preservation of peace and harmony of the community (Zionitz, 1975).

Right to Leadership

Another Indian right that is often sabotaged is a right to leadership among their tribes. People often ask where the leaders like Sitting Bull, Tecumseh, and Chief Joseph, who lead Indians to help their own, are today. Unfortunately, current political leaders have to encounter techniques common within the bureaucratic structures today which impede leadership and keep Indian people superficially involved by:

1. Keeping the tribal group split by dealing with groups outside the recognized tribal government and perpetuating the myth that 'Indians never agree, even if there are only two of them'.

2. Asking advice of Indians and advisors from different or dissident groups.

3. Permitting only the Indians who agree with the administration to be heard.

4. Keeping policy-making decisions uniform at a regional or national level rather than addressing the highly specific needs of reservation programs.

5. Giving Indians a superficial voice by forming advisory committees rather than decision-making committees.

Indian people are becoming aware of this situation and understand the power of unity. They are choosing to follow tribal leaders who give the appearance of agreeing with a white viewpoint while reserving what Indian view possible, and using both to the tribe's benefit.

Another reason for the lack of Indian leadership concerns the Bureau of Indian Affairs involvement in the election of tribal chiefs. The right to tribal self-government and selection of its officials, like all rights under tribal sovereignty, is subject to Congressional change. Until PL 91-495 was enacted by Congress in 1970, the right was removed from some tribes and the power of appointment was placed in the hands of the President and the Secretary of the Interior (Cohen, 1942).

Many Indian people, especially those who adhere to the American Indian Movement have expressed their wish to return to traditional forms of leadership selections. This entails the discontinuance of the election procedure outlined by the Indian Reorganization Act (Deloria, 1974). Whether the price to be paid in the form of disorganization uncertainty, and (at least) temporary vulnerability would be worth the gain, is a topic of controversy at the present time.

Right to Indian Preference

According to Congressional mandate:

> "An Indian has preference by law on initial appointment (in the Bureau of Indian Affairs, Indian Health Service, and programs directly effecting Indian Reservations) provided that the candidate has established proof that he is one-fourth or more Indian and meets the minimum qualifications for the positions to be filled (Morton V. Mancari, 417 U.S. 535 (1974))."

The precedent for giving preferential treatment to Indians in employment relating to Indian affairs was established by Congress as early as 1834 (Act of June 30, 1834, 4 Stat. 737). The purpose of Indian preference is to make Indian people the principle agents in their own economic and cultural survival. In recent years the Secretary of the Interior has liberalized the right to Indian preference to extend beyond initial appointment and also include preference in promotions, reappointments, training, and reductions-in-force (Indian Civil Rights Issues in Oklahoma, 1974).

In order to maintain this right, Indian people must speak up against administrative techniques designed to interfere with

Indian preference such as:

1. Seeking negative information about each Indian applicant, thus justifying hiring a non-Indian.
2. Relocating talented Indians in areas far from their tribal group (i.e., Washington, D.C.).
3. Overhiring or deliberately hiring unqualified Indians to have them on the payroll, thus perpetuating the stereotype that Indians are ignorant and incompetent, then hiring a white person to do the unqualified Indian's job.
4. Underhiring or hiring a skilled Indian at a lower pay level than a non-Indian with equal skills would be paid.
5. Training Indians in various career development programs that lead to no useful placement for numerous years, rather than encourage intellectual development (Waubageshig, 1970).

Right to Determine Membership

The ability of a tribe to define its own membership has long been determined an Indian right due to its sovereign nature, (Court of Appeals of New York in Patterson V. Council of Seneca Nation; 245 NY. 433, 157 N.E. 734, 736 (1927)). A tribe has the complete authority to determine all questions of its own membership by regulating the abandonment of membership, the adoption of non-members into the tribe, and the types of membership it may choose to recognize (Cohen, 1971). Indians believe that this right is necessary for the self-preservation and integrity of the tribe. The right to self-determination has been seen as paramount in decisions affecting tribal membership.

Many tribes show a flexible view with regard to blood quantum requirements, while others are more rigid in its standard for interpretation of tribal membership status. For example, the Santa Clara Pueblo V. Martinez case (98 S. Ct. 1670, (1978)) tested the validity of the Santa Clara Pueblo's membership ordinance which precludes membership for children of female members of the Pueblo who married nonmembers, but grants membership to children of male members of the Pueblo who had married nonmembers. The court held in favor of the Pueblo and supported the ordinance which was adopted to deter the sudden increase in mixed marriages which threatened the self-preservation of the Pueblos.

Even though most tribes use blood quantum requirements to define themselves for membership purposes, many Indian people feel that they themselves have a right to determine who is Indian regardless of the degree of Indian blood one possesses. They feel that an Indian is considered Indian by the way one thinks and acts, not by the amount of Red blood running through his or her veins.

They reserve judgment about Indianness until the person has proven him/herself worthy of the title. Besides many native people prefer to be labeled by their tribal name (Sioux, Shoshone, etc.) rather than answer to a name bestowed upon them by Columbus when he mistakenly arrived in this hemisphere. This adherence to tribal identity and membership policies is a mechanism of social, psychological, and cultural self-definition.

Right to Self-Determination

In 1973 Congress officially adopted the policy of self-determination in its relations with Indian people (P.L. 93-638, 88 Stat. 2203). This policy gives Indians the right to decide programs and policies for themselves, to manage their own affairs, to govern themselves, and to control their land and its resources (Josephy, 1971). In short, the primary goal of Indian people is to be free of non-Indian paternalism and to survive as tribal people in modern-day society (Josephy, 1971). All the right to self-determination requires is that Indians will be allowed to be responsible for the results of their own actions, a privilege long standing for fellow Americans.

Self-determination is not acknowledged by Indians to be a substitute for the original treaty obligations and trust agreements. It is rather a right accepted as a supplement to help implement the original rights of health, education and welfare agreed upon in treaty negotiations. However, in 1974 the National Advisory Council on Indian Education reported that "the national policy of self-determination for Native Americans is for the most part being ignored by the Federal Officials responsible for the implementation of this policy." They further asked Congress to determine the reasons for this gross oversight and asked them to create corrective actions to terminate the blatant defiance of congressional directions.

Recently, the Policy Review Commissions (1977) in making tentative recommendations, cited the responsibility of the Department of the Interior to manage natural resources. Thus, at least two functions have been identified to be out of the department's scope of expertise, Indians and their territory, since they relate to people-orientated matters. This criticism transcends the actual program implementation of the Bureau of Indian Affairs.

Right to Hunt, Fish and Trap

Many of the disputes concerning an Indian's right to hunt, fish, or trap on reservations concerns whether or not their treaty agreement specifically stated these rights or merely implied the rights in such phrases as "this treaty sets apart certain lands for the use of the tribe," leaving the term 'use' to legal interpretation. Historically, one of the traditional uses of the land by numerous tribes was for hunting and fishing (McDonald, 1978). States have generally not attempted to regulate reservations and allotted lands in terms of conservation. The states' few attempts at regulation have been unsuccessful (State V. Cooney, 77 Minn., 518, 80 N.W. 696 (1899); Pioneer Packing Co., V. Winslow, 159 Wash. 655, 294 P. 557 (1930); State V. Cloud, 179 Minn., 180, 228 N.W. 611 (1930)). Nevertheless, in cases where the treaty for formal agreement in which immunity is claimed but not authorized by Congress, it has been determined that the state does have regulatory powers over reservations and allotted lands (Organized Village of Kake, etc. V. Egan, etc., 369 U.S. 60, 82 S. Ct. 562, 7 L Ed. 2d 573 (1962)).

In most cases, the court has generally implied the continued existence of hunting and fishing rights even when treaties and federal legislation have appeared to avoid those rights (Menominee Tribe of Indians V. United States, 91 U.S. 404 (1968). States do not have jurisdiction to control the activities of non-Indians or nonmember Indians in hunting and fishing on Indian reservations for purposes of controlling the exploitation of the tribes fundamental rights (Ray V. Martin, 326 U.S. 496, 501 (1946)). Also, the state can pursue its conservation goals off the reservation but cannot force the tribe to conserve on the reservation (Puyallup Tribe V. Department of Game, 391 U.S. 392, 88 S. Ct. 1725, 20 L. Ed. 2d 689 (1968)).

Before Indian people can determine whether or not they and their tribe enjoy the right to hunt, fish, or trap, they must take the responsibility to investigate the following:

1. Is this right specifically stated in their treaties?
2. What was the traditional use of land, waters, and bordering territory?
3. If granted, what was the proper outcome of the hunting or fishing, sustenance of life or economic gain?

They must also responsibly accept the fact that matters which are vague and unspecified must be decided by the courts as witnessed above.

Water Rights

Indian water rights are a subject of life-and-death importance to most Western tribes because "water is to the land what blood is to the body." Without the protection of Indian water resources, Indian survival, by way of natural resources, is at stake. The Indian's right to use water especially in arid and semiarid regions is a necessary catalyst to the economic development of western reservations. Without water these reservations are uninhabitable, the minerals remain in place, and poverty prevails (Josephy, 1971).

The Indian's right to water in the streams and lakes which arise upon, border, traverse or underlie their reservations are accord by the Supreme Court in the case of Winters V. United States (207 U.S. 564, 574, 28 S. Ct. 207, 52 L. Ed. 340 (1908)).

In 1939 the Court confirmed its earlier position. However, a more recent decision of the Supreme Court in United States V. District Court (Eagle County), 401 U.S. 520 (1971) opened up the possibility that Indian water rights may be decided in state courts. The question in these cases often "becomes not who owns the water but how best can it be used: for the reservations and their relatively few inhabitants or for the industrial metropolises of the southwest?" (Price, 1973, p. 310).

The responsibility to uphold Indian water rights and administer these rights solely for the benefit of Indians lies with the administrators, engineers, and scientists within the Department of the Interior. However, they are also charged with the administration of land and rights to the use of water claimed in connection with reclamation projects, administration of grazing districts, and other land uses requiring the exercise of rights to the use of water, fish and wildlife projects, recreational areas, and other activities regarding rights to the streams. The responsibility to defend, protect and preserve title to the land of Indians and their rights to the use of the water lies with the lawyers of the Justice Department. They are also to act as adversaries against the Indian claims for seizure of their lands and rights to use of the water. Both the Department of the Interior and the Department of Justice hold conflicting responsibilities which prevent them from fulfilling the trust obligation to Indians regarding their natural resources.

It is the Indians responsibility to demand that Congress enact legislation that would create an agency, independent of the Department of the Interior or the Department of Justice, with full responsibility for the protection, preservation, administration, development and control of the lands and rights of the Indian reservations. Indians also have the responsibility to take an inventory of Indian rights to waters arising on, bordering on, traversing, or underlying their lands in order to determine: how to best use them in light of the increasing population and water demands of the western United States (Veeder, 1971); and how to most responsibly assert their right to the use of water found on their lands.

Right to Health Care

Most Indian people who are of one-fourth or more Indian blood are entitled to free comprehensive medical care through the Federal government on the basis of treaty or congressional mandate (25 U.S.C.:13; 42 U.S.C.: 2001). The government's responsibility for Indian medical care by directly providing the service by reimbursement originated in the Indians concern for medical supplies due to the ravages of scarlet fever, measles, and smallpox incurred by Indians in the 1870's.

Despite these well-intentioned laws and treaties, there is

a major problem concerning Indian entitlement to health services. Of the 790,000 Indian citizens of the U.S. 1970 census, approximately 460,000 reside on or adjacent to Federal Indian reservations and in identifiable Indian communities in Oklahoma and Alaska. The remaining 300,000 Indians live on state reservations or in towns and cities throughout the nation. Even though they are one-fourth or more degree of Indian blood, they must maintain a special relationship with the Federal government or be denied the right to free medical care (Department of Health, Education and Welfare, 1972).

Right to be Different

Indian people often like to dress or maintain an appearance which uniquely identifies them as Indian and, in effect, different from other Americans. This may appear in numerous ways that pay respect to ancestral mannerisms and ways of dress: wearing beaded ties, necklaces, belts and headbands; wearing ribbon shirts; sporting long hair; and speaking Indian. They dress differently to establish their right to decide personal appearances for themselves and reaffirm the difference between themselves and non-Indians. Indians, like other minorities, have found that they cannot denounce their differences without denouncing themselves in the process. For many years the melting pot theory was an unwritten national goal and, unfortunately, it is still the implicit assumption of many 'culturally encapsulated' citizens. Yet this country's national motto E. Pluribus Unum reaffirms that American's source of strength is not in its sameness, but in its plurality (Breslin & Pedersen, 1976).

School officials and employers frequently denounce Indian people for the nonconforming behavior of wearing long hair in Indian cultural fashion. This right to be different has been tested in both public and BIA boarding schools. Francis Wise, Chairwoman of the Native American Rights Movement, describes her experience with this right when she tried to enroll her children in the Lawton, Oklahoma public school system:

> "Before I signed the necessary enrollment cards, I spoke to the principal...and I explained to him that my children were Indian and that my sons had long hair and I would like to know if this was going to be a problem. He said, "let's finish our business, and then we will discuss it." Then I proceeded to finish the enrollment cards, and I paid their activity fees. He then informed me that my sons could not attend school because their hair was too long. I then, of course, explained to him that we are Native Americans and it is our traditional cultural and religious right to wear our hair long and flowing or rather in braids. It is up to the Indians to decide because we are Indians. He told me that he could not make the decision

himself since it was school policy (Indian Civil Rights Issue in Oklahoma, 1974, p. 15).

In another public school system, 25-30 Indian students were expelled because they refused to have their long hair sheared or take a paddling (Leitka, 1971). It may well be that conformity provides assurance to many people. Perhaps because of this, situations continue to occur in which the right of Indian people to appear different than the current style is abused.

Right to Worship

The Indian's right to worship as he or she pleases is one of the most important of all Indian rights since Indian ways of life are based predominantly on traditional religious beliefs. This right is supported in a joint Resolution relating to American Indian Religious Freedom, introduced by Senator Abourezh from South Dakota, and unanimously passed by the Senate in April, 1978. This eventual act recognizes the American tradition of freedom for individuals to express and exercise their traditional religions but points out that this freedom has not been enjoyed by traditional American Indians, in many cases because of a lack of clear, comprehensive and consistent federal policy on this matter. The act hopes to clarify federal policy on the Indian right to freedom of worship (American Indian Religious Freedom Act, P.L. 95-341 (1978)).

The religious practices of Indians are an integral part of their culture, tradition, and heritage and often form the basis of Indian identity and value systems. This resolution intends to remedy past restraints to Indian religious freedom, originating in the early efforts of Christian churches to bring an end to Indian religious beliefs and practices in order to civilize and encourage them to give up their nomadic way of life for more secure permanent settlements (Waubageshig, 1970). It is doubtful that any other group of people in the United States has had their religious beliefs and practices as systematically suppressed and denied as the Native American.

Right to an Education

Indian people are becoming aware of their right to have a voice in the education of their children. The right to an education was well established in treaties which imparted a strong moral duty to educate Indians held in guardianship or in a trust relationship with the federal government. Many of the treaty agreements are said to be invalid (Rosenfelt, 1974) since the educational provisions are vague. Some agreed to provide teachers and other educational services for a limited number of years, long since past, or for the duration of time determined by the President, or for no period of specified time. Most of these treaties do not even specify how the government will discharge its obligations (Rosenfelt, 1974).

Consequently, Indian people face an educational situation which infrequently responds to the needs of Indian children which is marked by a dismal record of high drop-out rates and negative self-image which discriminates against Indian children attending State public schools in terms of curriculum, treatment by school officials, and in exercise of their cultural values and which frequently misuses federal funds designated to meet the special needs of Indian children that are different from those of the middle-class American students (Indian Civil Rights Issues in Oklahoma, 1974).

The federal government takes the position that the legal responsibility for Indian education rests with the states. The supreme court has ruled emphatically that the opportunity for public education is a right which must be made available to all citizens on equal terms (Brown V. Board of Education, 347 U.S. 483, 493 (1954)). Indian children, as citizens of the state in which they reside, are entitled to a free public education to the same extent as other citizens. Even Indian children who reside on remote reservations not now served by public schools have a constitutional right to education from the state (Rosenfelt, 1974).

A look at the results of an Indian educational system historically lacking in local control or parental input does not reveal schools as very good places for Indians to be. In order to improve this situation, the federal government subsidizes Indian education to compensate for the burden placed on local school districts and to provide basic support. During the last half decade, the Indian Education Act, the Indian Self-Determination and Education Assistance Act, the revised Johnson-O'Malley regulations, and the improved administration of Title I have provided an administrative framework that makes it possible for Indian communities to shape educational programs in a more flexible, relevant and responsive manner (Rosenfelt, 1976). This federal assistance must be coupled with an insistence that the states discharge their responsibility to provide an adequate, non-discriminatory, basic education.

Indian people realize that the responsibility for a well-rounded education system which fosters independence and turns out a reservoir of trained and progressional Indian people must fall on themselves. They must make a concerted effort to change the current situation since government agencies have tried to provide this to date. Navajos have found that change can be best implemented through local control and cultural identification (Roessel, 1968). However, Indians may be hesitant to become involved in Indian education because they often encounter people of expertise who make decisions for them.

Until recently, Indians have not recognized their right to

be wrong. "The right to be wrong and the right to be right are essential American perogatives--privileges of democracy" (Roessel, 1968, p.3). The right to be wrong was officially granted to Indians through the War on Poverty when the Office of Economic Opportunity established Indian Community Action Programs. The freedom to try new ideas make mistakes and learn from them showed Indians that they have the ability, skills, and the programs which benefit their own people. Indian people are now beginning to realize that they do not have to be passive observers and allow education to slip through their hands into the hands of experts and professionals. If the American dream is the dream of the right to be wrong and the involvement of all people, then however humble the role is, Indians have a choice to be involved. Indian parents can have local control by taking the responsibility to provide input concerning what they want the finished product of education to be, what they want out of education, what they want their children to learn, and how they think the school should teach these things (Indian Education Act, P.L. 92-318 (1972)).

The current goal in Indian education is to take the best of the dominant culture and the best of the Indian culture and put these together in the classroom so the child grows up with a positive sense of well-being, a positive self-image, and with pride in his or her heritage. This is done by including recommendations that selected biographies and history texts be used and tribal language be taught in the classroom so that Indian children can learn about Indians of today--their problems and opportunities. The responsible involvement of Indians in Indian education will produce Indian students proud of being Indian as well as proud of being Americans.

Summary

Indian people have come to realize that freedom inherent in their individual and special rights will be acquired only by constantly and responsibly pursuing recognition of these rights. The literature warns of a possible danger of trainees becoming agressive due to becoming overly rights conscious (Lange & Jakubowski, 1976). Another predicted danger of 'rights consciousness' is the possibility of dead-end conflicts arising in which both parties adamantly stick to their positions, each adhering to their own rights (Lange & Jakubowski, 1976). The author questions whether this impasse is any different than past Indian-white relations. To improve on this stalemate, mutual responsibility and compromise are emphasized. Much of responsible assertiveness relies on an awareness of the consequences of assertive action and the willingness and ability to reach mutually acceptable compromises. It is hoped that Indian people will have the freedom to choose to be assertive or non-assertive while standing up for their rights based upon their determination of how important the right is to them, how they are likely to feel if they do not assert their rights, and how much it will cost them to assert their rights in a particular situation (Lange & Jakubowski, 1976). It is also hoped that Indians will reassess the very nature of their values, ways of living, and beliefs about mankind as they continually challenge America to keep her promise that Indian property, rights, and liberty no longer be abused.

REFERENCES

Alberti, R., and M. L. Emmons. Your Perfect Right. San Luis Obispo, Ca.: Impact Press, 1970.

Breslin, R. W., and P. Pedersen. Cross-cultural Orientation Programs. New York: Gardner Press, 1976.

Cohen, F. Handbook of Federal Indian Law. Washington: U. S. Government Printing Office, 1942.

Cohen, F. S. "Indian Self-government," Red Power (Josephy, A.M. ed.). New York: McGraw-Hill, 1971.

DHEW. Indian Health Programs (No. 72-502). Washington: U. S. Government Printing Office, 1972.

Freier, P. Pedagogy of the Oppressed. New York: Seabury, 1970.

Josephy, A. M. Red Power. New York: Seabury, 1971.

Kennedy, E. M. Congressional Record, 124, 1978: 1.

Lange, A. J., and P. Jakubowski. Responsible Assertive Behavior. Champaign, Ill.: Research Press, 1976.

Lindstrom, V. "Constitutional Law," American Indian Law Review, 6, 1978: 205-216.

McDonald, D. R. "Native American Fishing/Hunting Rights," Indian Historian, 11, 197-: 57-62.

Martone, F. J. "American Indian Tribal Self-Government in the Federal System," Notre Dame Lawyer, 51, 1976: 600-635.

Morey, S. M., and O. L. Gilliam. Respect for Life. New York: Waldorf Press, 1972.

Morison, S. E. "Mourts' Relation," Of Plymouth Plantation. New York: Knopf, 1952.

Oklahoma State Advisory Committee to the U. S. Commission on Civil Rights. Indian Civil Rights in Oklahoma. Washington: U. S. Commission on Civil Rights, 1974.

Price, M. E. Law and the American Indian. Indianapolis: Bobbs-Merrill, 1973.

Rimm, D. C.,and J. C. Masters. Behavior Therapy. New York: Academic Press, 1974.

Roessel, R. A. "The Right to be Wrong and the Right to be Right," Journal of American Indian Education, 7, 1968: 4-8.

Rosenfelt, D. M. "Legal Obligations to Provide Educational Services for Indians," Journal of American Indian Education, 13, 1974: 4-8.

Rowe, W., J. Eoyang, and T. LaFromboise. "Native American self-determination through Self-control," American Personnel and Guidance Association monograph. Dallas, 1977.

Warrior, C. "We are not Free," Red Power (Jospehy, A. M., ed.). New York: McGraw-Hill, 1971.

Washburn, W. E. "The Historical Context of American Indians Legal Problems," Law and Contemporary Problems (Rosen, L., ed.), 40, 1976: 12-24.

Waubageshig, T. The Only Good Indian. Toronto: New Press, 1970.

Zionitz, A. J. "In Defense of Tribal Sovereignity," South Dakota Law Review, 20, 1975: 1-58.

Chapter 2
The Pluralistic Basis of American Indian Law

ELMER R. RUSCO

Native Americans, hereafter also called Indians in this chapter, have a legal position which is different from that of any other group in this country (Cohen, 1942; Deloria, 1971; Getches, 1979; Price, 1973). Federal law recognizes the existence of Indian societies with rights of self-government which are not limited by the United States Constitution. For example, only some of the Bill of Rights apply to tribal councils, and such councils may act in ways which would be forbidden to other governments in the United States.

In effect, the federal courts have recognized the validity of cultural pluralism in the case of Indians, though not in the case of any other ethnic group. It is the argument of this chapter that this recognition is fundamentally on extraconstitutinal grounds, though the usual explanation for the recognition does not stress this, and that the United States Supreme Court has given intimations that the doctrine is supported by the constitutional protection of religious freedom.

While upholding Indian separatism, the courts have refused to uphold or recognize cultural pluralism with respect to any other groups. Even when, from 1896 to 1954, the Supreme Court was justifying gross inequalities in the governmental treatment of Black and White Americans, under the guise of 'separate but equal', it was not in fact recognizing cultural pluralism; the constitutional doctrine continued to be that Black Americans were persons entitled to equal protection of the laws and due process in the same manner as other Americans. Specifically, there was never any intimation that Black Americans had their own organs of government and cultures separate from that of White Americans which they had a right to uphold (Kluger, 1976). Likewise, the position of Spanish-speaking Americans has never been recognized as one which acknowledges cultural pluralism. It is true that former citizens of Mexico theoretically had their property and other rights under Mexican law recognized by the United States, and that these rights were protected by treaty. However, the rights involved were individual rights, not group rights, and they were theoretically on no different basis than the rights of other Americans (Steiner, 1969; Meier, 1972). The Chinese in this country had rights guaranteed by treaty until national law was changed in the 1940s to allow Chinese to become naturalized citizens, and this to a degree parallels Indian treaty rights. However, the treaties were not with the Chinese in America, but with the government of China, and they recognized neither rights which were in theory different for the Chinese than for other Americans, nor rights of self-government (Konvitz, 1946).

Indians, in contrast, have a legally-protected 'right to be different' which does not depend solely on the Constitution. For example, perhaps the best known statement of the status of Indian tribes, by Felix Cohen, is that

> "those powers which are lawfully vested in an Indian tribe are not, in general, delegated powers granted by express acts of Congress, but rather inherent powers of a limited sovereignty which has never been extinguished....The statutes of Congress....must be examined to determine the limitations of tribal sovereignty rather than to determine its sources or its positive content (Cohen, 1942:122)."

Thus, Indian tribes in fact represent a third level of government, separate from either the states or the federal government (see Native American Church V. Navajo Tribal Council, 1959). A standard corollary of this view has been that, while the limited sovereignty of tribes remains, it can be and has been in the past reduced by action of Congress and, by extension, could be eliminated altogether by Congress (Abourezk, 1977). If this is the case, in an ultimate sense the federal government is supreme over Native American societies, although nothing in the Constitution says this. More important, the survival of the limited sovereignty of tribes is dependent on Congress alone and is not protected by the Constitution of the United States.

The 'plenary power' of Congress over Native American societies, as it has usually been called, has been accepted as a fact which cannot be altered without constitutional amendment. This understanding leads Dario F. Robertson, for example, in a recent article which parallels the arguments of this chapter, to inconsistent conclusions. He begins by asserting that he

> "will argue that the tribal sovereignty doctrine has gradually been incorporated into the conceptual fabric of modern federalism to such an extent as to allow courts to declare the doctrine explicitly constitutionalized. This would have the effect of conferring upon the tribes a degree of constitutionally inviolate sovereignty (Robertson, 1978:374)."

However, after making an excellent case for this position, he concludes that acceptance of his doctrine of 'constitutionalization' would leave "the authority of Congress over the tribes ...largely unimpaired. Constitutionalization, however, would probably extinguish the congressional power of tribal termination (Robertson, 1978:393)." Likewise, Russel Lawrence Barsh and James Youngblood Henderson, after an extended criticism of the incompatibility of much of Indian law with American principles of 'political liberty', conclude that tribal sovereignty should have constitutional status but that this can be achieved only by formal constitutional amendment (Barsh, 1980). It will be the argument of this chapter, however, that the United States Supreme Court could interpret the history of actual Indian/White relations and of the development of doctrines of tribal sovereignty to grant to the tribes constitutional protection for their limited sovereignty. The basic argument will be that tribes once possessed full sovereignty and that neither the Constitution nor any actions by the tribes themselves has fully extinguished this sovereignty. In short, tribal sovereignty is extra-constitutional, and has in fact been recognized largely by the courts, not Congress; therefore, Congress cannot unilaterally end it.

The extra-constitutional basis of Indian legal status is apparent from reading a number of Supreme Court opinions involving Indians with actual historical conditions in mind. For example, there is the case of <u>United States v. Kagama</u> (118 US 375, 1886). In that case, the Supreme Court was asked to determine the constitutionality of a statute of Congress, which has become the Major Crimes Act, which applied part of the United States criminal law to Indians living on reservations, without the consent of the Indians. The statute in question had been passed to overturn a previous decision, <u>Ex Parte Crow Dog</u>, in which the Supreme Court had invalidated a criminal conviction of an Indian living on a reservation by pointing out that the statutes of the United States had been held not to apply to Indians in his situation. Even though their territories had been greatly reduced and their control over external relations transferred to the government of the United States, the tribes had not lost their sovereignty. Congress reacted to this decision by passing a statute which, without expressing a constitutional doctrine, specifically asserted that certain acts committed by Indians against Indians on reservations constituted federal crimes. The Supreme Court upheld the constitutionality of this act in the <u>Kagama</u> case. It is important to realize, however, that it did so by resorting to extra-constitutional arguments.

The Supreme Court began its review of the constitutionality of the statute in the customary way, by asking what constitutional provisions had been adduced to justify it. There were (and are) only two constitutional provisions specifically mentioning Indians. One omitted 'Indians not taxed' from the census, which is used to determine the number of seats in the House of Representatives to which each state is entitled; this obviously had no bearing on the point at issue. The second provision authorized Congress to regulate interstate commerce and commerce with 'foreign nations' and 'Indian tribes'. The court concluded that

> "it would be a very strained construction of this clause that a system of criminal laws for Indians living peaceably in their reservations...was authorized by the grant of power to regulate commerce with the Indian tribes."

The opinion also discussed the treaty clause because, although it does not mention Indians specifically, most relations with Indian societies were by means of treaties until Congress halted the practice by statute in 1871. The treaty clause, however, provided no basis for upholding a general criminal statute, because the tribes had not by treaties transferred authority for such statutes from their governments to the government of the United States.

At this point, if the normal practice in constitutional cases had been followed, the court should have invalidated the statute; if there is no constitutional basis for an assertion of authority by the federal government, the assertion is unconstitutional. Instead, the Court upheld the statute, by referring uncritically to extra-constitutional doctrines enunciated by Chief Justice Marshall. First, it asserted as constitutional dogma that there are only two levels of government in this country - the nation and the states. In fact, this was not the case at the time; Native governments existed which were held by themselves and recognized by the executive branch of the national government to possess authority not derived from either the federal government or the states (Barsh, 1980). Neither does the federal Constitution state any such conclusion; instead, it assumes the existence of states, with a range of authority not granted by the Constitution and only partly limited by that document, and then authorizes the creation of a federal government. In fact, the existence of Native governments was also assumed by that document, in the sense that its framers knew that such governments then existed and took no steps to eliminate them.

Next, the Court asserted that "These Indian tribes are the wards of the nation. They are communities dependent on the United States, -- dependent largely for their daily food; dependent for their political rights." After noting that the states were often the worst enemies of the Indians (which was irrelevant since no state action was in question) the opinion concluded that

> "From their very weakness and helplessness, so largely due to the course of dealing of the federal government with

them, and the treaties in which it has been promised, there arises the duty of protection, and with it the power. This has always been recognized by the executive, and by Congress, and by this court, whenever the question has arisen."

No link between the doctrine of 'protection' and the penalties imposed by a criminal statute was specified. Presumably, the Court believed that tribal governments on the reservations were no longer in existence and that therefore no prohibitions of the offenses specified in the statute would exist in the absence of federal law. Such an assumption could not have been supported by the facts at that time, however, at least for more than a few reservations.

Kagama is a less than competent treatment of the extra-constitutional realities which have resulted in establishing the Indian legal status, particularly if it is read as granting Congress plenary authority over tribes. But it does illustrate the nature of key legal doctrines regarding Native Americans. They do not derive from the Constitution itself, but from a judicially-constructed version of the course of Indian-White relations.

If one examines the principal cases which established the Indian legal status, one finds the same extra-constitutional reasoning, but one also finds no basis for asserting that only Congress can determine what Indian rights are. In fact, the courts have largely created the structure of Indian law, and there is no good reason why they need to abdicate their right to continue to recognize the extra-constitutional factors, in spite of their adject failure to do so in the Kagama and other cases.

One of the most basic Indian cases is Johnson and Graham's Lessee v. McIntosh, decided in 1825. The case is important because it was the first full-scale attempt by the Supreme Court to describe the situation of the Indians within American constitutional life, because the prevailing opinion was written by Chief Justice Marshall (who went into the issue in more depth than in any other case of his career except the Aaron Burr treason case) and because it realistically described the basis of both Indian and non-Indian property rights in this country. The specific litigants and their contentions are of such little importance in basic terms that no mention will be made of them (Beveridge, 1916).

Marshall, in the McIntosh case, began by asserting that it is necessary

> "to examine,...those principles of abstract justice, which the Creator of all things has impressed on the mind of his creature man, and which are admitted to regulate, in a great degree, the rights of civilized nations..."

However, he also said that it was necessary to determine "those principles...which our own government has adopted in the particular case, and given us as the rule for our decision", and in fact he did not resort to abstract principles at all, apparently relegating them to the status of "private and speculative opinions of individuals...respecting the original justice of the claim which has been successfully asserted (Faulkner, 1968)." He also declined to discuss an important rationalization for European seizure of Indian lands which had been presented to the Court as the case was being argued. This was the notion that Europeans were agriculturists while Native Americans were not, and that the former have a natural right to 'use' land which hunters really do not 'use' (Deloria, 1971). Marshall said:

"We will not enter into the controversy, whether agriculturists, merchants and manufacturers, have a right, on abstract principles, to expel hunters from the territory they possess, or to contract their limits."

Instead, Marshall asserted that American land titles stem directly from the doctrine of 'discovery', which is simply the assertion by all European nations that the title to lands held by native peoples lay with whatever European nation was first on the scene. In fact, Marshall described the 'discovery' doctrine as primarily a means by which European countries minimized conflict with each other. He said that

"as they were all in pursuit of nearly the same object, it was necessary, in order to avoid conflicting settlements, and consequent war with each other, to establish a principle, which all should acknowledge as the law by which the right of acquisition, which they all asserted, should be regulated, as between themselves. This principle was, that discovery gave title to the government by whose subjects, or by whose authority, it was made, against all other European governments, which title might be consummated by possession."

However, while the Europeans gained fee title by mere discovery, the Indians still retained another kind of property right, which he described as a right of 'occupancy'. Marshall thus described European land claims as an 'impairment' of Native property rights, not an extinguishment of them. Specifically, he asserted that the Natives, in spite of the doctrine of discovery, remained "the rightful occupants of the soil, with a legal as well as just claim to retain possession of it, and to use it according to their own discretion." In practice, he held, the doctrine of discovery gave the European nations, and later the federal government, the sole right to extinguish Indian property rights, by agreement with them, purchase, or conquest in a just war.

Marshall's own skepticism about the moral validity of the

'discovery' doctrine and his belief that its principal justification was the simple fact that it had happened can be discovered from this statement:

> "However extravagant the pretension of converting the discovery of an inhabited country into conquest may appear; if the principle has been asserted in the first instance, and afterwards sustained; if a country has been acquired and held under it; if the property of the great mass of the community originates in it, it becomes the law of the land, and cannot be questioned."

The statement in the McIntosh opinion that "Conquest gives a title which the courts of the conqueror cannot deny..." has been read as an assertion that land titles in this country rest on conquest of Native peoples. However, the opinion taken as a whole clearly states that conquest is only one way by which Native Americans lost land, and it was not the universal fact. The original holdings of Native Americans have been drastically reduced by a number of means, not all of which were legal under American law, but there are many Native groups who were never conquered by the United States. Examples which readily come to mind are the Eastern and Western Pueblos, the tribes which inhabited what are now California and Washington, and the Native inhabitants of Alaska. Indian governments which have never legally lost their lands are today asserting that they still own these lands, and are finding judicial support for these assertions.

Marshall also gave another set of arguments in favor of the actual behavior of European countries, but in doing so made it clear that this defense is something less than satisfactory in terms of those 'abstract principles' to which he had referred. He said that

> "Although we do not mean to engage in the defense of those principles which Europeans have applied to Indian title, they may, we think, find some excuse, if not justification, in the character and habits of the people who rights have been wrested from them."

He then went on to argue that, while normally in international law the conqueror was restrained by "humanity...acting on public opinion" to incorporate the conquered people(s) into the conqueror's society so that eventually they would become 'one people', this was not possible in the case of the Indians. Asserting that they were "fierce savages, whose occupation was war, and whose subsistence was drawn chiefly from the forest", he claimed that "it was impossible to mix" with them and also that they "could not be governed as a distinct society (Beveridge, 1916)." Since this was the case, "The Europeans were under the necessity either of abandoning the country, and relinquishing their pompous claims to it, or of enforcing those claims by the sword." In other words,

> "That law which regulates, and ought to regulate in general, the relations between the conqueror and conquered, was incapable of application to a people under such circumstances."

Indeed, Marshall believed that Indian societies were not part of the United States, and therefore subject solely to its governments, and would not become part of the United States.

While Marshall's argument as a whole lacks complete consistency and can be read as a cynical argument justifying the doctrine that 'might makes right,' there is an alternative reading. Marshall was aware at the time of this decision that Native societies still existed as self-governing entities in full possession of varying amounts of the lands which had been theirs before Europeans arrived on this continent. He was aware also that the Constitution had not abolished these self-governing societies; indeed, by implication it recognized them, by listing them as entities with whom the federal government could regulate commerce. His opinion thus is based on an attempt to deal with the actualities of the situation in a way which was consistent with the Constitution. The result was a logically outrageous assertion that Europeans had acquired Native properties merely by observing them; but it was also a recognition that Indian societies were still self-governing entities and still possessed significant property rights which had to be acknowledged by federal and state governments.

In _Cherokee Nation v. Georgia_, Marshall returned to attempts to define the relationships of Indians with the United States (Prucha, 1975). In that case he refused to recognize Indian societies as foreign states, although he did recognize them as states with rights of self-government as he had done in the _McIntosh_ case (Cohen, 1942). The distinction was important because if they were foreign nations, the Cherokees and all other Indian nations could initiate cases in the Supreme Court, since the Constitution gave original jurisdiction to the Court in cases involving 'foreign states'. In trying to explain how a Native society could be a nation without being foreign, Marshall made some assertions about Indian societies which do not square with his treatment of them in the _Worcester_ case during the next term of the Court. Most important was the fact that he asserted that the relation between Indian governments and the government of the United States "resembles that of a ward to his guardian." No explanation of how this relationship came to be was offered, and this formulation has been used since then to justify numerous intrusions on the rights of Indians. The fact that his later opinion in the _Worcester_ case does not repeat this language has introduced some confusion into Indian law as in the _Kagama_ case.

The greatest single case spelling out the status of Indian societies is undoubtedly Worcester v. Georgia, in which Marshall and the Supreme Court vainly attempt to overturn actions by the state of Georgia which, as he had stated in Cherokee Nation, were intended to

> "annihilate the Cherokee as a political society, and to seize for the use of Georgia, the lands of the nation which have been assured to them by the United States, in solemn treaties repeatedly made and still in force (Prucha, 1975)."

After accepting jurisdiction of the case, which had been brought to them through a different route than the Cherokee Nation case, Marshall moved to the heart of the conflict before the Court. Revisiting the doctrine of 'discovery' which he had discussed in the McIntosh case, Marshall repeated that "power, war, conquest, give rights, which, after possession, are conceded by the world; and which can never be controverted by those on whom they descend." We must, he said, "proceed...to the actual state of things..."

This was, according to Marshall, that discovery had transferred title to the land to the European nations, subject to the still-existing right of occupancy of the native peoples. However,

> "The extravagant and absurd idea, that the feeble settlements made on the sea-coast, or the companies under whom they were made, acquired legitimate power by them to govern the people, or occupy the lands from sea to sea, did not enter the mind of any man."

What European nations claimed by discovery was merely "the exclusive right of purchasing such lands as the natives were willing to sell." The 'power of making war' defensively was also simply assumed by Europeans, and embodied in colonial charters, but this did not justify wars of 'conquest'. With the Revolution and the adoption of the Constitution, the United States became the inheritor of the rights established by discovery, and could not inherit more than these rights had given Great Britain.

In brief, the 'actual state of things' was that Great Britain and subsequent American governments had no more than a partial claim to ownership of land and a tradition of treaties under which various Indian groups had put themselves under the 'protection' of the United States. Contradicting himself in the Cherokee Nation case, Marshall argued that the relationship created by these protection agreements in no way limited the sovereignty of Indian societies, for "Protection does not imply the destruction of the protected."

In his summation of the status of Indian societies, Marshall said:

"The Indian nations had always been considered as distinct, independent, political communities, retaining their original natural rights, as the undisputed possessors of the soil, from time immemorial, with the single exception of that imposed by irresistible power, which excluded them from intercourse with any other European potentate than the first discoverer of the coast of the particular region claimed; and this was a restriction which those European potentates imposed on themselves, as well as on the Indians. The very term 'nation', so generally applied to them, means 'a people distinct from others'. The constitution, by declaring treaties already made, as well as those to be made, to be the supreme law of the land, has adopted and sanctioned the previous treaties with the Indian nations, and consequently, admits their rank among those powers who are capable of making treaties. The words 'treaty' and 'nation', are words of our own language, selected in our diplomatic and legislative proceedings, by ourselves, having each a definite and well-understood meaning. We have applied them to Indians, as we have applied them to the other nations of the earth; they are applied to all in the same sense.

Again, the point of this line of argument is that the position of Indians in the American governmental system is a matter of the 'actual state of things', not explicit constitutional doctrine. But this actual state is one in which the sovereignty of native societies was never completely abolished and in which the consent of those societies was necessary to limit their sovereignty, except in the case of just wars and, partially, with respect to European land claims.

While the rest of this chapter must be brief, I believe that an excellent case can be made that the situation outlined by Marshall, expecially in the Worcester case, has not changed fundamentally. The legal status of Indians today is still determined to a substantial extent by the 'actual state of things,' specifically the fact that previously sovereign nations have never completely given up their sovereignty. Congress put an end in 1871 to the negotiation of new treaties with Indian nations, although there have been many 'agreements' with such societies since then. However, this 1871 law specifically stated that existing treaties were still valid, and most treaties are valid today (Cohen 1942). While some treaties have been abrogated, neither Congress nor the Supreme Court has ever declared that Indian sovereignty as represented in the treaties has been abolished.

Two particularly important examples of the continuing force of the 'actual state of things' in this century are two Supreme Court opinions, dealing with Indian rights to resources, which remain important elements of Indian law. United States v. Winans, in 1904, decided that a treaty protected the right of the Yakima Nation to fish at off-reservation locations (Cohen,

1942). The treaty, however, was not regarded as the source of this right; rather, the source was the preexisting Indian right which had not been abrogated by the treaty. The Court stated that

> "The right to resort to the fishing places in controversy was a part of larger rights possessed by the Indians, upon the exercise of which there was not a shadow of impediment..."

Further, while the treaty was a 'limitation' of these rights, it was not a 'taking away' of them, for "the treaty was not a grant of rights to the Indians, but a grant of rights from them --a reservation of those not granted." In 1979, the United States Supreme Court upheld sweeping fishing rights for a number of the Washington tribes.

Winters v. United States, the case which established Indian water rights which are stronger than water rights under state appropriation laws, likewise relied on the idea that the Indians, by an agreement (not a treaty), had reserved water rights (Cohen, 1942). The Court noted that, at the time the Indians in question had agreed to move to a reservation (in 1888) they

> "had command of the lands and the waters -- command of all their beneficial use...Did they give up all this? Did they reduce the area of their occupation and give up the waters which made it valuable or adequate?"

Somewhat clumsily but decisively, the Court answered no to these questions.

> "If it were possible to believe affirmative answers, we might also believe that the Indians were awed by the power of the government or deceived by its negotiators. Neither view is possible. The government is asserting the rights of the Indians."

While this opinion has been interpreted as only asserting a judgment about the will of Congress, in fact Congress has never explicitly legislated to any significant degree on Indian water rights, but instead has accepted judicial interpretations of these rights (Clyde, 1967; National Water Commission, 1973). And while subsequent opinions on Indian water rights have talked chiefly about federal reservation of water rights for Indians, no opinion has specifically overruled the underlying logic of the Winters case.

Finally, the United States Supreme Court has come to a similar conclusion on the rights of a religious minority in a manner which strongly suggests that their opinions on Indian cases have been based implicitly on an acceptance of cultural pluralism where the evidence for the existence of extensive cultural differences is substantial and related to religion.

That the Supreme Court has long held the rights of religious communities in high esteem can be argued from several grounds. A particularly striking evidence of this is the fact that the Supreme Court, in 1925, struck down an action by a state which restricted religious freedom before they had decided explicitly that the First Amendment applied to states because of the incorporation of some of the Bill of Rights into the Fourteenth Amendment (Butts, 1950).

In 1972, in the Yoder case, the United States Supreme Court upheld the right of an Amish community in Wisconsin to refuse to send their children to 'formal (non-Amish) high school' until the age of 16. The Court forbade Wisconsin to compel Amish parents and children to abide by this law on the basis of the First Amendment's protection of religious freedom, applied to the state by the Fourteenth Amendment. In doing so, however, it indicated that it was also protecting the right of the Amish community to be different. The rationale was that religious beliefs were so closely tied up with every aspect of Amish life that it was not possible to separate the two. Denying that a similar claim could be made on 'purely secular' grounds, the Court's opinion asserted that

> "the record in this case abundantly supports the claim that the traditional way of life of the Amish is not merely a matter of personal preference, but one of deep religious conviction, shared by an organized group, and intimately related to daily living."

Throughout the opinion there are references to 'the way of life' of "the separated agrarian community that is the keystone of the Amish faith" and to the notion that what was at stake was "the continued survival of Amish communities as they exist in the United States today."

The Supreme Court suggested that its conclusions would 'probably' apply to 'few other religious groups or sects' because such other groups probably could not demonstrate such a powerful connection between religion and other aspects of the existence of the group. However, it seems clear to me that many traditional Indian communities could make such claims with at least as much justice as the Amish communities. If this is so, the freedom of religion provides another constitutional protection for Indian societies (Deloria, 1973).

In summary, Indians are different, and their unique legal status has roots which are extra-constitutional. It is important to recognize this fact, for there are small numbers of Indians today in relation to the wider society, and Indians still own substantial resources which the general society values highly. The survival of Indians as Indians is questionable unless the wider society sees validity in the ways of life of Native Americans and is willing to grant their right to exist as separate societies with self-governing capacities.

REFERENCES

Abourezk, James American Indian Policy Review Commission: Final Report. Washington: U.S. Government Printing Office, 1977.

Barsh, Russel Lawrence, and James Youngblood Henderson The Road: Indian Tribes and Political Liberty. Berkeley: University of California Press, 1980.

Beveridge, Albert J. The Life of John Marshall. (four volumes) Boston: Houghton Mifflin Co., 1916-1919.

Butts, F. Freeman The American Tradition in Religion and Education. Boston: Beacon, 1950.

Clyde, Edward W. " Indian Water Rights," pp. 373-399 in Robert Emmet Clark, ed., 2 Waters and Water Rights. Indianapolis: Allen Smith Company, 1967.

Cohen, Felix S. "Powers of Indian Tribes," 55 Decisions of the Department of the Interior, 14-67, 1934.

--- Handbook of Federal Indian Law. Washington: U.S. Government Printing Office, 1942.

Deloria, Vine, Jr., ed. Of Utmost Good Faith. San Francisco: Straight Arrow Books, 1971.

--- God is Red. New York: Grosset and Dunlap, 1973.

Faulkner, Robert Kenneth The Jurisprudence of John Marshall. Princeton: Princeton University Press, 1968.

Getches, David H., with Daniel M. Rosenfelt and Charles F. Wilkinson Cases and Materials on Federal Indian Law. St. Paul, Minnesota: West Publishing Co., 1979.

Keim, Albert N., ed. Compulsory Education and the Amish: The Right Not to be Modern. Boston: Beacon Press, 1975.

Kluger, Richard Simple Justice: The History of Brown v. Board of Education and Black America's Struggle for Equality. New York: Alfred A. Knopf, 1976.

Konvitz, Milton R. The Alien and the Asiatic in American Law. Ithaca: Cornell University Press, 1946.

Meier, Matt S., and Feliciano Rivera The Chicanos: A History of Mexican Americans. New York: Hill and Wang, 1972.

National Water Commission Water Policies for the Future: Final Report... Washington: U.S. Government Printing Office, 1973.

Price, Monroe E. Law and the American Indian. Indianapolis: Bobbs-Merrill, 1973.

Prucha, Francis. Documents of United States Indian Policy. Lincoln: University of Nebraska Press, 1975.

Robertson, Dario F. "A New Constitutional Approach to the Doctrine of Tribal Sovereignty," VI American Indian Law Review 2: 1978, 371-394.

Rusco, Elmer R. The MX Missile and Western Shoshone Land Claims. Ms. in possession of author.

Satz, Ronald N. *American Indian Policy in the Jacksonian Era*. Lincoln: University of Nebraska Press, 1975.

Schusky, E. *The Right to be Indian.* San Francisco: American Indian Historian Press, 1970.

Steiner, Stan *La Raza: The Mexican Americans*. New York: Harper and Row, 1969.

Veeder, William H. "Indian Prior and Paramount Rights to the Use of Water," 16 *Rocky Mountain Mineral Law Institute* 631, 1971.

Chapter 3

The Economics of Indian Crime

JOHN CROSS

The political, economic and social problems facing American Indians are varied and pervasive. On virtually every measure of social welfare, Indians rank well below the white population, as well as below other racial and minority groups (U.S.B.C., 1973). This ranking also holds true with respect to the criminal justice system. Various studies conducted throughout the last four decades have shown the crime rate for Indians to be consistantly higher than the crime rates for whites and other non-white groups (U.S.D.L., 1971). Between 1920 and 1930 Hayner reported the crime rates on three reservations in the Northwest to be significantly higher than the national average (Hayner, 1942). During the next decade Von Hentig reported the Indian arrest rate (2,510 per 100,000) to be three times higher than the national rate for whites (836 per 100,000)(Hentig, 1945).

Approximately two decades followed these early studies of Indian criminality before other research was conducted. Stewart's analysis of the 1960 federal Bureau of Investigation crime reports showed that the overall arrest rate for Indians was eight times greater than that for whites and three times greater than arrest rates for blacks (Stewart, 1964). One of the more recent studies of Indian criminality surpassed the previous studies mentioned. In his analysis of Indian criminality over an 18-year period (1950-68), Charles Reasons (1972) substantiated these earlier studies. Reasons found that overall arrest rates of Indians are three times those of blacks and ten times those of whites (Reasons, 1972). Studies of specific criminal offenses such as homicide, suicide, and alcohol-related offenses have also shown Indian rates to be higher than the national average (Levy, 1969; Bynum, 1972).

The most recent revelations of Indian 'criminality' have come from reports of various state advisory committees to the United States Commission on Civil Rights (New Mexico, Arizona,

South Dakota). These reports have documented problems of prejudice and unequal treatment encountered by American Indians in the criminal justice system in various parts of the country. Attitudes of the dominant white community are shown to be antagonistic toward Indian people. Similiar attitudes are seen to exist among the various agents of the criminal justice system. The use of force and harrassment are common techniques practiced by law enforcement officials. Within the court system there exists a type of inherent discrimination occurring in jurisdiction, procedures, staffing, acquiring defense counseling and/or bail, jury make-up and attitudes, and sentencing.

Despite the foregoing studies and reports, there is an immense dearth of systematic information on crime and the American Indian. Contemporary literature dealing with race and crime is almost exclusively of a black/white nature. Of particular interest is that texts in criminology and criminal justice have given little attention to American Indians, even though analysis of data at national, state, city and reservation levels have verified the high incidence of crime among American Indians in relationship to other racial groups.

Theoretical (Scapegoat) Explanations of Crime

Within each historical period the outstanding characteristic in all criminology discussions has been the underlying assumption of a qualitative difference between the criminal and the non-criminal. This early contrast was sharpened by prepossession of social theorists with the conflict between absolute good and absolute evil which was personified by 'God', on the one hand, and the Devil, on the other. This underlying conflict has persisted in one form or another despite translations in terminology from a 'good/evil' distinction to a 'normal/abnormal' distinction.

During the Middle Ages evil (criminal) action was explained by the term 'possession.' Later, during the seventeenth and eighteenth centuries, evil doings were explained by such concepts as rationalism, reason, and notions of equality. Theological theories of causation were being rejected as explanations of evil. Evil doings were explained in terms of choice rather than in terms of possession or seduction by an evil one. All men were assumed to be reasonable and wise about their own interests and if one chose to do evil, it was because of the pleasure it would bring him. This view postulated a free moral agent, confronted with a choice between doing right and doing wrong, and choosing freely to do wrong.

The early development of psychology and anthropology, the growing practice of measurement, the use of statistics, and the development of the theory of evolution have aided this distinction. These new additions dealt primarily with how good persons were to be distinquished from evil persons. Generally, the physical constitutions or characteristics of criminals were offered as evidence of the criminality of a person. The later development of psychology and the annihilation attack on earlier morphological theories shifted the explanation of criminality once more from external to internal evidence. Again the terms changed, but they still served the old purpose. The new mode of identifying criminality was aided by statistical techniques as naive as earlier morphological techniques. The new rule was to measure intelligence despite the fact that a definition of intelligence was, or is now, no more easily formulated than one of 'possession.' This game continued until it was shown that no relationship existed between intelligence and the criminal or the non-criminal.

Under the influence of recent psychological thought, a new body of theories has developed which focus on the emotional def--iciency rather than the mental deficiency of the criminal. A new series of tests and devices have been brought into play to reveal that the criminal is not 'normal.' Even though these interpretations have a qualitative aspect, the impact of the idea of 'law', adopted from the physical sciences, and the use of statistical tables and mathematical formulas have led to the imputation of psychic abnormality. On the basis of crude scientific assumptions, conclusions about criminality have been drawn which imply definiteness and absolutism. The fact that the qualities or traits measured are intangible or irrelevant did not prevent this process from gaining widespread acceptance.

Other contemporary explanations have been offered for the understanding of crime and race. Predominant among these explanations have been sociological, economic and legal theories. Generally these theories have an inherent bias which view the individual as a pliable, malleable component of the criminal justice system who needs to be changed so that he may fit or become better adjusted to the system. This notion of pliability has within it a strong conviction that people are perfectable. This 'perfectability' is to be achieved through creation of perfect social systems which guide the interrelationships of individuals and influence their goals. Under the influence of good (rational) institutions, the perfectability of individuals, and thus their harmony with themselves and society, can be achieved. The issue of the limits of pliability or the conception of a deviant society are seldom raised under these theories. Underlying the pliability assumption is the presence of deviant individuals or subcultures - but never a deviant institution or society.

Neo-orthodox economic theories of crime usually structure their analysis by assuming that individuals try to maximize their objective function. This amounts to a kind of assumption about 'individual sovereignty.' The implication is that persons have a variety of choices and that their situations, ceteris paribus, can be viewed as optima freely choosen. Further, the implication is that persons have a nearly unlimited range of opportunities in the course of their lifetime. This inclination to view crime in terms of maximization and choice have two principal applications in the analysis of criminality. First, it leads to some inputation about rationality and irrationality. Second, in the analysis of (measured) returns to criminal behavior, economic theories of crime have tended to ascribe rationality to those who invested in criminal behavior with high rates of return (Becker, 1968).

Sociological theories of crime have been developed predominately around the concepts of anomie and differential association. This latter concept has dominated much of the writing about criminal behavior. Society provides the person with direct contacts with both law-abiding and law-breaking patterns of behavior and attitude. The person's own behavior is determined by whichever persons and groups with whom he has the most contact - and subsequently the most influence over his/her own personality and behavior (Sutherland, 1980). The concept of anomie is also an important perspective on criminal behavior. According to this perspective, criminal behavior is most often a result of normlessness. This is a condition in which adequate norms to inform people how to act are lacking. There is either a confusing lack of norms or an awareness that appropriate ones are missing (Durkheim, 1951).

On the assumption that crime is aggressive behavior, psychological theory has developed the concept - 'frustration/aggression.' According to this theory, aggression is produced by frustration and everyone can tolerate frustration only up to a certain point (Merton, 1938; Palmer, 1960; Merrill, 1947). Early social/psychologists have also used a similar approach to set the pattern for later researchers to adopt eclectic approaches and multi-factor techniques (Glueck, 1934). This kind of research rejects the idea that any single factor will produce criminal behavior and emphasizes the idea that a combined effect of a number of handicaps will do so. A person may resist one or two unfavorable factors, but everyone has a 'resistance limit' beyond which they cannot go. Various other theories have offered an explanation of criminal behavior. One such explanation is containment theory. The attempt here is to identify why certain persons become offenders through a general effort to isolate conditions under which social controls prevent crime. In this approach the concept of the social role is used to analyze those control processes that prevent criminal conduct (Reckless, 1961).

The foregoing indicates the pattern of criminological discussions which mold the general dominant policies and laws within the criminal justice system. The fact that this accumulation of knowledge has been based upon naive theories and assumptions is beside the point. The point is that remnants of these ideas still inform many scholars seriously dedicated to the study of criminality. Whether the explanation for 'unsocial' behavior of the individual has been through terms such as possession, free will, physical stigma, intellectual inferiority or emotional instability, each has left unchallenged society's institutional set-up, both theoretical and practical.

The problem with the above perspectives is that they rely primarily on the idea of individual sovereignty. They concentrate on the results of free choice among a given group of behaviors, but rarely focus on the way institutions tend to define or limit the behavior available for choices. In their attempt to move away from one-factor to multi-factor determinism, these approaches have also produced a kind of tautological reasoning. If there is no other measure of a resistance limit or breaking point other than criminal behavior, then this is an exercise in circular reasoning. Such problems have not helped greatly in the explanation of crime.

Race And Law: The Subordination of Racial Groups

The fate of American Indians has been to fall victim to these conventional criminal definitions and techniques. The result has been to find that Indian criminality has been caused by sudden increases in income, poverty, anomic conditions, culture conflict, and excessive use of alcohol. There is an increasing need to develop a better general framework for understanding crime. Renewed interest has been expressed in localizing the cause of crime within institutional networks rather than assuming crime to be an individual pathology.

Since people are social beings and operate in social setting, the 'criminal' must also be an adjusted, social being as opposed to a person who is unadjusted and exhibits unsocial behavior. The difference between criminal and non-criminal social beings is the conflict which arises out of conflict between a racial group and the dominant society. The question is how does a group grow up into a conflict group and how does an individual become adjusted to that group rather than to some other group in society? (Minnis, 1963; Johnson, 1969; Jessor, 1968; Riffenburg, 1964; Sellin, 1938; Carr, 1958; Dozier, 1966).

The shape and character of the legal system in a complex society (one which is stratified economically and politically) is derived from conflicts inherent in the structure of these societies. Usually the legal system in its normative strictures and organizational operations exhibit those norms and practices that maintain and enhance the position of entrenched power holders. The broad principles underlying the legal order are ramified in and attenuated by the organizational aims of complex societies. The law then will differentially reflect the perspectives, values, definitions of reality, and morality of the middle- and upper-classes while being in opposition to the morality and values of the poor and lower-classes. Given this character of the legal system it would not be surprising that the poor should be criminal more often than the non-poor.

This systematic induced bias in society against the poor goes considerably further than having values incorporated within the legal system which are antithetical to the poor's life conditions. In complex societies, the decision to enforce laws against certain persons and not against others will be determined primarily by criteria derived from the bureaucratic nature of law enforcement agencies. The empirical data make it clear that poor people do not recieve the same treatment at the hands of law enforcement agents as do the well-to-do. This differential treatment is systamatic and complete through practices where police, prosecuting attorneys, and the like, choose to look for and impose punishments for offenses that are characteristically committed by the poor while ignoring those offenses committed by the more affluent members of the community. Where offenses (e.g., gambling) are equally likely to be committed by persons from different social classes, the police will look for these crimes in under-class neighborhoods.

That such selective enforcement is not a function of what is most pressingly needed by the society is clearly indicated by enforcement of laws prohibiting the use of 'dangerous drugs.' For example, laws prohibiting marihuana smoking are enforced vigorously as long as it is concentrated among the poor. However, once the spread of marihuana reached into the middle- and upper-class youth, the potential 'criminal' population increased substantially. This brought into view the problem of selective inforcement which characterized the United States legal process. This increased visibility of selective police activity did bring about changes in policy and law. Studies in Nebraska and Utah found that when arrests of prominent people's children occurred the marihuana laws were promptly altered to reduce the penalties. It is unlikely, however, that these changes have substantially altered the tendency of the legal system to select for enforcement laws dealing with acts of the poor (Galliher, 1974).

A Dual System of Justice: The Network of the Economic and the Legal Institutions

The perspective adopted here pays more attention to institutions and their impact on producing crime. It is generally assumed that social institutions serve certain useful purposes and persist because of this function. However, very little is explained by saying that a social institution exists because it serves certain social needs. It is inconveivable that any institution in a large, complex society would not serve some needs. It is equally inconceivable that any institution would serve the needs of every group or social class simultaneously. The question then is if an institution serves certain needs, whose needs are served? Or if an institution persists because it is functional, for whom is it functional?

The focus of this perspective is the economic institution and how it aids in producing criminal behavior as a primary behavior alternative for the underclass. The economic institution is comprised of several components, one of which is the labor market. A new paradigm has been developed which depicts separate work forces within the labor market rather than a homogeneous labor force. Various writers divide the labor market into multiple-segments, but there is general agreement about the sector in which the underclass is located. Piore describes this sector as one where:

> Jobs tend to be low-paying, with poorer working conditions, little chance of advancement, a highly personalized relationship between workers and supervisors which leaves wide latitude for favoritism and is conducive to harsh and capricious work discipline; and with considerable instability in jobs and a hign turnover among the labor force (Piore, 1975: 125).

For those persons relegated to this sector, the pattern of economic life is largely unconventional in its learning of opportunity structures. The occupational skills learned in this market place do not fit into the occupational categories of the primary labor market. Thus, economic mobility is severely limited for a significant segment of the working poor.

The experiences of the underclass with the occupational structure of the secondary market have a direct influence on their experience with the police. To most property-owning, middle- and upper-class United States citizens, strict law enforcement poses no threat to anyone except those who break the law. But to most non-propertied, non-white citizens, justice is a privilege of race and class. To them most laws are biased and justice is largely inaccessible. In short, the legal institution is a political instrument protecting the social position and cultural values of predominately one class and one race of citizens. Just as with the dual labor force, there is in fact a dual system of justice - one for mainstream society and one for the underclass - which creates a barrier to obtaining justice for the underclass. The important concern is how conditions created by their economic situation effect the experiences the underclass have with the police. To the hard-core unemployed, legal and occupational discrimination are reinforcing institutions. The greatest obstacle to employment is a police record and the greatest obstacle to low contact with the police is unemployment.

To the underclass, living in the ghetto is living in legal jeopardy. In law enforcement semantics these areas are referred to as high crime areas. It follows that the implication for this pejorative for police procedures is 'high crime area,' 'fringe aream' 'fringe tactics, ... Because a high crime area is a known location for nefarious activities and a collecting ground for 'shady' characters, people in these areas will see more police than people in the middle-class communites, In addition, there are a variety of legal and quasi-legal options policemen can use as tactics to flush out 'criminals' and 'prevent' crime. Thus, being poor and powerless members of a high crime population, these persons are frequently exposed to these tactics. One tactic is 'field investigation,' - the right to stop and question any person for whatever reason. On the surface this appears harmless enough, but for ghetto residents the results are often disasterous. The simple stopping of a vehicle of a ghetto resident may result in multiple charges. For example, when contact between a policeman and a ghetto resident (urban Indian) becomes emotional, multiple charges may develop including eluding the police, disturbing the peace, resisting arrest, and assulting a police officer.

Repeated arrests are annoying and when they occur frequently, they are oppressive, especially when wages are forteited from lost work and/or fines. Weekend arrests are also frustrating since the person is usually detained until the following Monday, almost always a work day. Because of their high exposure to traffic surveillance in a high crime area and their low economic standing, ghetto residents cannot afford accidents, expensive repairs, traffic fines, or attorney's fees. The response then is of a short-term strategy for evading the formal rules which often leads to bench warrants, suspended or revoked licenses, which in turn leads to such coping patterns as ignoring tickets, multilating out-of-state driver's licenses or forging new ones, or simply driving without a license ad finitim. This phenomenon is best illustrated by the 'reservation car' - an old, large vehicle which while accepted on the rural reservation certainly does not conform to off-reservation inspection and registration criteria. Yet, these are the vehicles which Native Americans rely on when commuting between reservation and urban ghetto.

The problem created by a perons's low position in the occupational structure have received considerable study. Having meaningful employment allows a person to impose some order and structure to his/her world, rather than being victimized by disorder and chaos. Holding employment which allows one to impose this order provides a sense of mastery of the world. The inability to make one's sense of order prevail follows from lack of meaningful work or employment. More recent studies have found similar results among persons who participate in marginal employment (Liebow, 1967; Hannery, 1969).

The existing theories of crime have failed to consider a person's position in the occupational structure as an important factor in determining his contact with law enforcement personnel and agencies. Tom Wicker has noted in an article in the New York Times:

> In 1974, as a declining economy progressively forced people out of work, the rate of crime rose by 17 per cent nationally, compared to a rise of only 0.75 per-

> cent in the more prosperous year 1973. The rate of violent crime doubled, the rate of property crime tripled, and...(a) link to rising unemployment was suggested (Wicker, 1975:33).

What suggested the link between crime and unemployment to Wicker at this time was three factors:

> 1. The cities which had the largest increases in unemployment also had the largest increases in crime.
> 2. Those months that had the largest increases in unemployment also had the largest increases in crime.
> 3, The type of crime that increased most was the type most likely to be committed by a poor, unemployed person, that is, street crime for small sums of money.

Thus, crime as well as other characteristics such as cynicism, hostility, frustration, anomie and finally family instability are manifestations of the economic institution as proxied by occupational positions, unemployment or marginal employment. These are the same factors which conventional theories have posited as 'causes' of crime. Research carried out by the National Institute for Mental Health (NIMH) has also shown that work problems of parents can contribute to delinquency of their children (Shore, 1964).

The disabilitative effects of the lack of meaningful work has been documented also among persons in rehabilitative institutions such as prisons (Bartlett, 1972). Other writers have shown high crime rates in ghetto areas to be a product of their economic condition. Organized crime often referred to as 'illegitimate business' has been shown to flourish in ghetto areas because residents usually have no other means by which to earn a living. The pervasiveness of lucrative 'illegal businesses' enhances many residents to turn to illegal activity as a way of earing a means of financial survival. According to Richard Quinney:

> ...there is sufficient observation to recognize the obvious fact that unemployment produces criminality. Crimes of economic gain increase whenever the jobless seek ways to maintain themselves and their families. Crimes of violence rise when the problems of life are further exacerbated by the loss of life-supporting activity.... Permanent unemployment - and acceptance of that condition - can result in a form of life where criminality is an appropriate and consistant response (Quinney, 1977: 58).

Quinney further notes that with contemporary data collected by various agencies it is difficult to get statistical evidence to show conclusively the relationship between crime and unemployment because such statistics are politically constructed in the beginning to obscure the failings of the economy. On a cognitive basis one can say there is a dual system of law and order - one for mainstream society and another for poor minorities, notably urban, ghetto dwellers. The empirical question is at what interstices do these two systems influence each other (Spradley, 1970).

Native Americans, especially young Indians, have long been encouraged to leave the reservation and join the mainstream, American society. Toward this end magnet cities, in the 1950's, were targeted for urban Indian migration. But without adequate job training and skills, suitable housing or education, these urban Indian communities quickly became 'Indian ghettoes.' Today, the situation has not improved much. Federally-funded urban Indian centers are primarily 'hang-outs' for marginal, unemployed (unemployable!) Indians, many who have drinking problems and criminal records.

REFERENCES

Allen, R. A. Black Awakening in Capitalists America. Garden City: Anchor, 1970.

Bartlett, L. "Production Participation," Occupational Mental Health, 1, 1972.

Becker, G. "Crime and Punishment," Journal of Political Economy, 3, 1968.

Bynum, J. "Suicide and the American Indian," Native Americans Today (Bahr, et. al. ed). New York: Harper and Row, 1972.

Carr, A. and S. M. Johanson. "Extent of Washington Criminal Jurisdiction over Indians," Washington Law Review, 33, 1958: 289-302.

Dozier, E. "Problem Drinking among American Indians," Quarterly Journal of Studies on Alcohol, 27, 1966: 72-87.

Durkheim, Emile. On the Social Division of Labor. Glencoe, Ill.: Free Press, 1951.

Galliher, J., L. McCartney and B. Baum. "Nebraska's Marihuana Law," Law and Soceity Review, 8, 1974: 441-455.

Glueck, Sheldon, and Eleanor Glueck. One Thousand Juvenile Delinquents. Cambridge: Harvard University Press, 1934.

Hannery, U. Soulside. New York: Columbia University Press, 1969.

Hayner, N. "Variability in the Criminal Behavior of American Indians," American Journal of Sociology, 47, 1942: 602-613.

Jessor, R., et. al. Society, Personality and Deviant Behavior. New York: Holt, Reinhart & Winston, 1968.

Johnson, H. W. Rural Indian Americans in Poverty. Agricultural Economic Report, 167, Washington: U. S. Department of Agriculture, 1969.

Levy, J. E., S. J. Kunitz, and M. Everett. "Navajo Criminal Homicide," Southwest Journal of Anthropology, 25, 1969: 124-

150.
Liebow, E. Tally's Corner. Boston: Littel, Brown, 1967.
Merton, Robert. "Social Structure and Anomie," American Sociological Review, 3, 1938: 672-682.
Merrill, M. A. Problems of Child Delinquency. Boston: Hough Mifflin, 1947.
Minnis, M. S. "The Relationship of the Social Structure of an Indian Community to Adult and Juvenilt Delinquency, Social Forces, 41, 1963: 395-403.
Padfield, H., and R. Williams. Stay Where You Were. New York: Lippincotte, 1973.
Palmer, Stuart. The Psychology of Murder. New York: Thomas Y. Crowell, 1960.
Piore, M. J. "Notes for a Theory of Labor Market Segmentation," Labor Market Seqmentation (Edwards, R. C, et. al. eds). Lexington: D. C. Heath, 1975.
Quinney, Richard. Class, State and Crime. New York: McKay, 1977.
Reckless, Walter. "A New Theory of Delinquency and Crime, " Federal Probation, 25, 1961.
Reasons, Charles. "Crime and the American Indian," Native Americans Today (Bahr, H., et. al. eds). Evanston, Ill.: Harper & Row, 1972.
Riffenburg, A. A. "Cultural Influences and Crime among Indian Americans of the Southwest," Federal Probation, 28, 1964: 38-46.
Sellin, Thurston. Culture, Conflict and Crime. New York: Soccial Science Research Council, 1938.
Shore, M. F., and J. L. Massimo. "Job-Focused Treatment for Anti-Social Youth," Children (July/August, 1964).
Spradley, James P. You Owe Yourself a Drunk. Boston: Little, Brown, 1970.
Stewart, O. "Questions Regarding American Indian Criminality," Human Organization, 23, 1964: 61-66.
Sutherland, Edwin, and Donald Cressey. Principles of Criminology Philadelphia: Lippincott, 1980.
United States Bureau of Census. U. S. Census of Population: 1970, Subject Report: Amerian Indians. Washington: U. S. Government Printing Office, 1973.
United States Department of Labor. Manpower Report of the President. Washington: U. S. Government Printing Office, 1971.
Von Hentig, H. "The Delinquency of American Indians," Journal of Criminal Law and Criminology, 36, 1945: 75-84.
Wicker, Tom. "Unemployment and Crime," New York Times (April 25, 1975): 33.

Chapter 4

Native American Neo-colonialism

LAURENCE FRENCH

All the abuses of colonialism exist within America's Indian reservation system including forced accommodation and cultural genocide. United States Indian policy reflects a history of contemptuous actions supportive of the maintenance of a rigid colonial caste system whereby Native Americans are treated as third-class citizens. This places Native Americans on the bottom rung of the social hierarchy, a notch below blacks, Hispanics, females and other 'second-class' citizens. In Marxist terminology, the American Indian is assigned the status of lumpenproletariate or that of a 'dangerous' group.

Theoretical Perspectives

Essentially, this selection looks at social policy and the effects this policy has upon the Native American target population. Hence, we are talking about majority/minority relationships and within this context we contend that Native Americans have been, and continue to be, subjugated by the larger white-dominated society. Furthermore, we are looking at a social process mandated by legal authority (dejure subjugation) and not one which merely emerged (defacto subjugation) accidently due to indirect consequences of societial development and majority biases. White/Indian relations have always involved varying degrees of confrontation which can be best illustrated by four interaction models:

1. The Annihilation Model.
2. The Assimilative Model.
3. The Forced Accommodation Model.
4. The Pan-Indian Model.

The Annihilation Model: Here, interaction involves serious conflict between the aggressing colonial power(s) and the native population with little effort made to preserve the indigenous aboriginal population by the colonial power(s). One of the most vivid historical examples of colonial annihilation was that which involved the Tasmanian aboriginals, while examples of contemporary annihilation are alleged to occur in Brazil and Columbia - with the aboriginals living along the Amazon River basin being the target population. Within a colonial perspective, the annihilation model stresses physical genocide. This process either involves the outright destruction of native populations through combative or biological warfare, or both, or it can entail a more subtle form of annihilation such as slavery. Either way, the motivating factor is usually the same - the removal of the indigenous population from the coverted land. Indian wars, Indian slavery and small pox infested blankets (biological warfare) are historical examples of white/Indian confrontations reflective of the annihilation model while the concept of 'cultural genocide' is indicative of contemporary United States Indian annihilation policy.

Assimilative Model: This model also has its roots in early white/Indian relations. Eastern intellectuals held that the 'nobel savage' should be formally educated and converted to Christianity. History indicates that many of these academic liberals fought strongly for the Native American cause as the well documented congressional battles over Removal attest. These same liberals provided the incentive for the Civilized Tribes (Cherokee, Choctaw, Chickasaw, Creek, and Seminole) to alter their social structures and to model them after that of the white European model. This resulted in the creation of highly successful societies (Indian Nations), especially among the Cherokee and Chickasaw tribes. Yet assimilation policies sometimes were as harsh as those associated with the genocide and forced accommodation models.

Early assimilative attempts combined religious conversion and education and due to this enculturation combination 'church schools' were the first major white institutions to appear among Indian groups. These were first established in the East prior to Removal and provided the incentive for certain of the Civilized Tribes to establish and maintain their own educational systems. But part of the punitive aspects of Reconstruction led to the destruction of the Indian-run boarding school system. These schools continue to operate in some areas evey today, notably the mid-West. Examples of past educational techniques employed to aid the Indian student in his or her resocialization (i.e., to abandon their traditional culture and adopt the 'superior' white/European model) included having one's mouth washed out with soap, whippings, humiliation, and the like, for such infractions as speaking in their native languages or subscribing to traditional rituals and customs.

This assimilative policy suffered many shortcomings. First, it assumed that all Native Americans were similar hence they herded them together indiscriminately. Secondly, they (control agencies of the dominant society) took young Indian children away from their families and cultural environments at the crucial formative years without substituting any viable alternatives to meet their primary needs. And, thirdly, the boarding schools relied heavily on the punitive end of the reward/punishment continuum effectively stripping the Indian of his or her cultural heritage and primary needs while clearly instilling animosity and bitterness toward the white dominant culture which supported and administered these programs.

This entire resocialization process did much to create the dependent, culturally-ambiguous reservation Indian. Indian names were Anglicized, native languages forbidden and earlier behavioral patterns reflective of their Indian encluturation were punished while little effort was made to fully prepare these Indian students to adequately compete or assimilate into the larger dominant culture. Instead, shame, guilt, derrogated self- and group-images and latent inferiority were the skills best taught at these boarding schools.

Vine Deloria, Jr., and other scholars of the American Indian and Amerian Indian scholars, contend that many so-called 'assimilation policies' were and continue to be thinly disquised attempts to accommodate or, more significantly, to eliminate the unique American Indian cultrual heritage. Nonetheless, contemporary academic liberals continue to foster the 'assimilative' argument as did their earlier counterparts decades ago. Today, however, many academic liberals interpret assimilation within the 'structural/functional' perspective, now calling this process 'structural assimilation.' Simpson (1977) sees structural assimilation as reflecting partial assimilation - a situation whereby majority integration and assimilation of Native Amerians is limited due to cultural differences. But many feel that this neo-liberal assimilation model wreaks of elitist ethnocentrism. Support for this position is found in the common liberal arguments offered for the 'failure' of Native Americans to become fully assimilated and integrated into the larger dominant society. Judging American Indians through the existentially-oriented, Protestant ethic, liberals commonly use culturally-biased biological, psychological, cultural and social/structural factors to explain what they feel to be "...the inherent inferiority of American Indians."

Forced Accommodation Model: Within this perspective lies the justification for much of the harsh treatment shown Native Americans: genocide, Removal, deceit and the reservation system. This view, like the others, gained momentum during the early years of the Republic (United States), especially during the white/Indian contact in the original Thirteen Colonies. The controversial Removal policy focused about the fierce struggle between the Eastern elite (assimilative model) and the Western frontiersmen. The former wanted to civilize the 'nobel savage' through education and religious conversion and eventually absorb them into the larger cultural mainstream while the latter wanted to exterminate them or drive them out of their traditional lands. The Frontiersmen won. And the American Indian has been losing more each year - ever since this process of physical and cultural genocide began. Those wanting to accommodate the Indian continued to wield considerable influence regarding federal policy toward this group. The extremist sought total elimination through genocide, a process illustrated by a long history of brutality, including scalpings, hangings and massacres at the hands of white vigilantees, federal troops and state and local agencies.

The less extreme accommodative view sees the Indian as an inherently inferior being, one that needs to be separated from the dominant society so that they will not contaminate the white members. By labeling the Indian as inferior, white leaders often felt little compunction when forcefully removing the Indians to 'worthless' lands and when reneging on promises and treaties. The reservation concept and its policy of federal paternalism also stems from this perspective. Indians are viewed as dependent wards who can not adequately care for themselves thereby compelling white agencies to regulate their lives. An ulterior motive, many contend, is to better control Native Americans. Following decades of reservation life and federal control, a self-fulfilling prophecy emerged whereby the once self-sufficient, fiercely proud American Indian became co-opted into playing the inferior, dependent role of the 'reservation' Indian.

The reservation environment is not a healthy one as the high incident of criminal and alcohol pathologies attest. Today, Native Americans have the highest crime rate of any racial group in the Nation, according to available data (Reasons, 1972). Child suicide is another phenomonen common to reservation life resulting from dire physiological and psychological conditions conducive to this environment. In essence, reservation life merely ratarded the genocide process so that at the time they were awarded citizenship in 1924 only a quarter million Native Americans survived out of millions at the time of white contact. Today this figure has risen to a half million recognizable Indians and another 300,000 people with Indian-affiliation (mixed-bloods). Yet, even today, alcoholism and violence are common-place on Indian reservations accounting for more Native American lives than any other factor (Wax, 1973).

Moreover, the accommodative perspective also has much to do with the vulgar Indian image so often conveyed in the movies, on television, in comics and novels. Here, the Indian's inferior status is portrayed through his savagery and intellectual primitiveness. It is often implied that the Indian kills indiscriminately and for the pure joy of the act. He is seen as being a semi-literate, unwashed barbarian who is easily duped with cheap trinkets or alcohol, or both. And associated with the latter is the popular myth of the 'drunken Indian.' All told, the vulgar Indian image presents the American Indian as a childlike creature vacillating between uncontrolled aggressiveness and impulsive indulgence. What is often overlooked is that Native Americans themselves are exposed to this negative stereotype with some accepting it as valid in lieu of any other viable models to adopt.

Pan-Indian Model: Unlike the other models, Pan-Indianism represents a Native American approach to the solution of Indian problems. It is seen as a renaissance in Indian acculturation since it represents the expression of a new, nation-wide identity. Pan-Indianism represents an attempt to create a universal American Indian ethnic image, one that transcends tribal, reservation, and urban Indian ghetto boundaries offering all Native Americans a positive, shared cultural identity. The current Pan-Plains variation of Pan-Indianism relies heavily on the Plains Indian stereotype much like the vulgar Indian image does - but for different reasons. English currently is the common Indian language while the visible traits and institutions of the Plains Indians have come to symbolize the new ethnic Indian.

Contemporary Pan-Indianism emerged as a reaction to the depersonalization and deculturalization associated with forced accommodation and its policy of cultural genocide. It is an attempt to create a positive cultural base for these otherwise marginal Indians while also allowing mobile and displaced Native Americans to better adjust to situations outside the reservation setting.

Historically, the Pan-Indian movement first appeared in the East with Handsome lake's 'Good Message' during the early 1800's. The Good Message was a blend of traditional Seneca religious prescriptions and those of the Quackers, an influential group among these people at this time (white assimilation model). Apparently this was the first attempt toward an organized universal Indian religion. Handsome Lale preached his message among the Iroquois for sixteen years and his influence is still evident among the Six Nation Iroquois Reservation (Reserve) in Canada (Wax, 1973).

The Western Ghost Dance movement of the late 1800's was yet another attempt toward a universal Indian belief system, again one reflecting inter-tribal cooperation and adaptation to the new 'white threat.' A common element of the Ghost Dance was the appearance of a prophet with a message concerning the disappearance of the white man and the return of the Indian dead and, most significant, a return to the old ways. This seemingly radical theology alarmed the whites as some felt that the Ghost Dance would stimulat Indian militancy such as the 1872 Modoc and 1877 Nez Prece wars. Later, the Ghost Dance movement proved to be the salavation for the Plains Indians - a group which had long suffered from economic, cultural and psychological poverty. The Ghost Dance instilled a fire within the younger Warriors and a promise of an end to the poverty, privations and drudgery of reservation life. This proved to be the needed catalysis for the expression of the Sioux's mass alienation. The Ghost Dance resulted in the Wounded Knee massacre in December, 1890. This led ot its demise but this spirit was rekindled in the late 1960's and 1970's resulting in Wounded Knee II in 1973.

Other religious movements gained prominence such as the Native American Church commonly associated with the peyote cult. This belief again combines Christian and traditional rituals much like the Good Message did. Many elements of the Protestant ethic are incorporated into this movement including self-reliance, brotherhood, and abstinence from alcohol. Yet, white Protestantism is reluctant to accept or recognize the Native American Church due to its use of peyote - a hallucinogen drug derived from certain cactus plants (buttons). This is unfortunate since the basic objective of the Native American Church seems to be to help Native Americans bridge the gap between Indian traditionalism and the demands of the dominant white society.

While these Indian religious movements contributed to contemporary Pan-Indianism none seem sufficient in themself to explain the current phenomenon. It took an incident like the Second World War to initiate a movement that truly transcends the various tribal and geographic barriers obstructing earlier cooperative efforts. These young Indian servicemen (some 25,000) returned, some national heroes (Ira Hayes...), with a different outlook on life and set about educating others in their communities. This interest led to the creation of the National Congress of American Indians (NCAI) in 1944. Although other white-sponsored Indian organizations preceded the NCAI, this was the first viable Native American-sponsored program. A major shortcoming of this organization is its attempt to work within the existing system. The result is that little is accomplished mainly because of inter-tribal competition for limited resources - a situation exacerbated by the neo-colonial nature of white/Indian relationships and policies.

A more radical, youth-oriented Native American group later surfaced in the 1960's (1961) primarily as a reaction to the perceived ineffectiveness of the National Congress of American Indians. The National Indian Youth Council (NIYC) served as the parent organization for the more radical group - the American Indian Movement (AIM) - much like the Students for a Democratic Soceity (SDS) fostered the more radical 'Weatherman' faction. NIYC not only was critical of the more conservative NCAI organization, they protested the fact that it (NCAI) allegedly spoke for the vast majority of Native Americans. These two Native American factions clearly represent what has always been evident to students of American Indian culture since the advent of white contact - the existence of a variance between conservative and radical Native Americans. The former seeks to maintain the status quo while the latter supports drastic change. Interestingly, the alliances of these two groups have changed overtime. In the past the conservatives represented the more traditional Indians while the radicals wanted to adapt to the white/European model. Today the opposite is true. The radical (NIYC) supports 'Indianism' while the conservatives (NCAI) want to work within the larger white system (neo-colonialism). And the battle continues as the conservatives and radical Indian elements vie for the support and conversion of the largest group of Native Americans - the 'marginal Indians.'

REFERENCES

Brown, D. Fighting Indians of the West. New York: Charles Scribner's Sons, 1975.

Collier, Peter. When Shall They Rest. New York: Holt, Rinehart & Winston, 1973.

Deloria, Jr., Vine. Custer Died for Your Sins. New York: Dell, 1969.

-We Talk, You Listen. New York: Dell, 1970.

-God is Red. New York: Dell, 1973.

-Behind the Trail of Broken Treaties. New York: Dell, 1974.

Fanon, F. The Wretched of the Earth. New York: Grove Press, 1968.

French, Laurence. "Emerging Social Problems among the Qualla Cherokee," Appalachian Notes, 3 (2), 1975.

-"Social Problems among the Cherokee Female," The American Journal of Psychoanalysis, XXXVI (2), 1976.

French, Laurence, and Jim Hornbuckle. "The Historical Influence of the Eastern Indians on Contemporary Pan-Indianism," The Indian Historian, 10 (2), 1977.

Hagen, W. American Indians. Chicago: University of Chicago Press, 1962.

Hertzberg, H. The Search for an American Indian Identity. Syracuse: Syracuse University Press, 1973.

Josephy, A. The Indian Heritage of America. New York: Alfred A. Knopf, 1968.

Lauber, A. Indian Slavery in Colonial Times. Williamstown, MA.: Corner House, 1970.

Nash, G. Red, White and Black, Englewood Cliffs, N. J.: Prentice-Hall. 1974.

Reasons, Charles. "Crime and the American Indian," Native Amercans Today (H. Bahr, et. al., ed.). New York: Harper & Row, 1972.

Simpson, G. 72 Annual Proceedings: Washington: American Sociological Association, 1977.

Washburn, W. The Assault on Indian Tribalism. Philadelphia: J. B. Lippincott, 1975.

Wax, M. Indian Americans. Englewood Cliffs, N. J.: Prentice-Hall, 1973.

Part 2

Indian Crime and Justice

Chapter 5
Basic Doctrines of American Indian Law

CHARLES F. WILKINSON

It is almost always a mistake to seek answers to Indian legal issues by making analogies to seemingly similar fields. General notions of civil rights law and public land law, for examples, simply fail to resolve many questions relating to American Indian tribes and individuals. This extraordinary body of law and policy holds its own answers, which are often wholly unexpected to those unfamiliar with it.

This article examines the root doctrines of the Federal-tribal relationship. Ultimately, these doctrines allocate legal and political power among three sets of governments - the tribes, the United States, and the States - on more than 50 million acres of Indian land. For better or worse, law plays an enormous role in the lives of American Indians - perhaps a greater role than is the case with any other group of American citizens. Because of that, the doctrines peculiar to Indian law will continued to play the same crucial role that they have played in the past; they will determine whether, and to what extent, American Indians will be able to control their own destinies.

Tribal Sovereignty: Indian Tribes as Government

Sovereignty means the authority to govern, to exercise those powers necessary to maintain an orderly society. The powers of sovereign governments are familiar: the power to enact laws; the power to establish court systems; the power to require people to abide by established laws; the power to tax; the power to grant marriages and divorces; the power to provide for the adoption of children; the power to zone property; the power to regulate hunting and fishing; and so on. 'Sovereignty,' therefore is a collection of all or some of those powers which governments (such as the United States, counties, and cities) have and exercise on on a regular basis (Cohen, 1971).

When we talk about tribal sovereignty, then we are saying a very simple but deeply fundamental thing: Indian tribes are governments.

The status of Indian tribes as sovereigns, or governments, has been uniformly recognized by Congress and the courts from prerevolutionary days through the present. This sovereign status is reflected in the early treaties, the early cases, the recent cases, and the recent legislation. Since tribal sovereignty is a doctrine which has evolved and has been clarified over more than 200 years, it is helpful to trace the development of the doctrine.

The single most important court decision, which is still relied upon by courts, is Worchester v. Georgia, 31 U. S. (6 Pet.) 515 (1832). This case resulted from the struggle between the State of Georgia and the Cherokee Nation, whose lands became surrounded by the State of Georgia. In the late 1820's Georgia passed a series of laws which effectively abolished the Cherokee government. One of the laws included a requirement that any non-Indian residing on Cherokee land must first obtain a permit from the Governor. The Georgia courts convicted the missionaries of violating the State law, but the United States Supreme Court overturned that conviction.

Chief Justice John Marshall's opinion in Worcester v. Geogia stuck down the Georgia State laws which purported to operate on Cherokee lands. Interpreting the treaties, the Constitution, and the Indian Trade and Intercourse Act, Chief Justice Marshall found that Indian tribes were "disctinct, independent, political communities having territorial boundaries, within which their authority (of self-government) is exclusive...." Thus, the State laws could have no effect on Cherokee lands because the Cherokee Tribe was a separate sovereign government.

While the opinion in Worcester v. Georgia holds that Indian tribes are not subject to State law, later cases make it clear that Indian tribal sovereignty, or self-government, is subject to the superior legislative authority of Congress. To put it another way, Georgia could not regulate affairs on the Cherokee reservation, but the United States could. The doctrine of tribal sovereignty, as first set forth in Worcester v. Georgia, has been explained in its most classic form by Felix Cohen, then Assistant Solicitor, Department of the Interior, a writer who is still considered by the courts to be the leading authority on Federal Indian law:

> The whole course of judicial decision on the nature of Indian tribal powers is marked by adherence to three fundamental prinicples: (1) An Indian tribe prossesses ... all the powers of any sovereign state. (2) Conquest renders the tribe subject to the legislative power of the Unites States and in substance, terminated the external powers of sovereignty of the tribes... but does

> not by itself affect the internal sovereignty of the tribe, i.e., its powers of local self-government. (3) These powers are subject to qualification by treaties and by express legislation of Congress, but, save as thus expressly qualified, full powers of internal sovereignty are vester in the Indian tribes and in their duly constituted organs of government (Cohen, 1971:123).

The doctrine of tribal sovereignty, or self-government remains the starting point for any current discussions concerning the powers of Indian tribes. An Indian tribe inherently possesses all powers held by a government. The tribe continues to hold these sovereign powers until they are expressly relinquished by the tribe, as in a treaty, or until they are expressly taken away by Congress.

Since Worcester v. Georgia in 1832, the Supreme Court has treated tribal sovereignty as an evolving doctrine. This evolution is not unnusual; many provisions of our Constitution itself, including the Commerce Clause and the Bill or Rights, have also undergone great change during the same period. In the late 19th and early 20th centuries, the Supreme Court emphasized the plenary authority of Congress in relation to tribal sovereignty as Congress began to exercise its broad power to deal with Indian affairs. In the latter part of the 19th century, the Court implicitly limited tribal sovereignty by finding that a crime committed by a non-Indian against a non-Indian on the reservation was wholly the concern of the States, not of the Federal Government.

With passage of the Curtis Act of 1898 (30 Stat. 495) and the abolishment of the Indian Territory, tribal government lapsed into a period of dormancy. The policy trend toward destruction of tribal government was reversed in 1934 with passage of the Indian Reorganization Act (25 U.S.C. sec. 461-479). In 1959, in Williams v. Lee, 358 U. S. 217 (1959), the Supreme Court gave recognition to the continued strength of the doctrine of tribal sovereignty.

In the early 1960's, the Supreme Court itself seemed to be caught up in the termination era. Most particularly, Organized Village of Kake v. Egan, 369 U.S. 60 (1962), set forth the previously unprecedented proposition that State laws would apply to Indians on the reservations, in spite of notions of tribal sovereignty, unless the State laws infringed upon tribal self-government or were prohibited by Federal law. This finding, which was not raised by the facts of the case and which has since been limited by the Supreme Court, was a clear departure from earlier cases finding that reservation Indians were beyond the reach of State authority.

But the Supreme Court decisions of the 1970's have reemphasized the importance of tribal sovereignty. McClanahan v. Arizona Tax Commission, 411 U.S. 164 (1973), found that "the Indian sovereignty doctrine is relevant, then, not because it provides a definitive resolution of the issues in this suit, but because it provides a backdrop against which the applicable treaties and Federal statutes must be read." Thus, Federal treaties and statutes must be "read with this tradition of sovereignty in mind." The Supreme Court then ruled that a reservation Indian is not subject to State income tax for income earned on the reservation. The Court restated most of the basic law of tribal sovereignty first established by Chief Justice Marshall in Worcester v. Georgia:

> (T)he policy of leaving Indians free from state jurisdiction and control is deeply rooted in the Nation's history... this policy was first articulated by this Court 141 years ago when Mr. Chief Justice Marshall held that Indian nations were "distinct political communities having territorial boundaries, within which their authority is exclusive, and having a right to all the land within those boundaries, which is not only acknowledged, but guaranteed by the United States."

An even more recent case is United States v. Mazurie, 419 U.S. 544 (1975), which dealt with the right of tribal governments to exercise regulatory authority over non-Indians. The Wind River Tribes, acting pursuant to Federal statutes and with the approval of the Secretary of the Interior, passed a law requiring that sellers of alcoholic beverages must obtain liquor licenses from the tribe. This pattern of regulation is, of course, similar to regulation by State governments. A non-Indian was denied a liquor permit from the tribe. The operators of the liquor store continued to operate without a license and a Federal prosecution followed. The Tenth Circuit Court of Appeals ruled that the tribe had no power to regulate a liquor license because it was not a government. According to the appellate court, the tribe was nothing more than a 'private, voluntary organization.' The Supreme Court rejected that reasoning and upheld the requirement of a tribal license. Justice Rehnquist, writing for a unanimous Court, relied upon notions of tribal sovereignty and found that Indian tribes are "a good deal more than 'private voluntary organizations'":

> Thus it is an important aspect of this case that Indian tribes are unique aggregations possessing attributes of sovereignty over both their members and their territories, Worcester v. Georgia, 6 Pet. 515, 557 (1882); they are "a separate people" possessing "the power of regulating their internal and social relations..."

Thus, today's Supreme Court has made it clear that tribal sovereignty remains a vigorous and far-reaching doctrine. The absolute view of complete sovereignty, first set forth in Worcester v. Georgia, has been slightly eroded. Nonetheless, Worcester is repeatedly cited by the courts and the results consistently affirm sovereign tribal rights. The present law fully and unequivocally supports the conclusion that Indian tribes initially possess all elements of internal sovereignty and that their sovereign attributes can be diminished only by Congress, not by the state. These sovereign attributes include such basic governmental powers as the following:

1. The power to establish legislatures, usually called tribal councils.
2. The power to establish tribal courts.
3. The power to tax.
4. The power to grant marriages and divorces.
5. The power to provide for adoptions and guardianships.
6. The power to regulate hunting and fishing.
7. The power to control economic development through zoning regulations and other land use planning devices.
8. The power to regulate non-Indian individuals in Indian country.

Other sovereign powers could be added to this list. The point, however, is not to enumerate all sovereign powers of Indian tribes, but simply to give examples for the purpose of showing that Indian tribes are in fact governments. Congress has the unquestioned power to limit those sovereign rights, but all inherent governmental powers remain intact until Congress expressly acts. The importance of strong tribal self-government has been manifested in all recent congressional legislation.

The Trust Relationship: The United States' Special and Unique Relationship with Indians

The trust relationship between the United States and American Indians was first set forth in Cherokee Nation v. Georgia, 30 U.S. (5 Pet.) 1 (1831). This opinion, which was written by Chief Justice John Marshall, stands with Worcester v. Georgia as one of the most significant opinions in Indian law. The two cases retain their vitality today and are repeatedly cited by modern courts.

Cherokee Nation v. Georgia was handed down one year before the Worcester decision and also involved the Cherokee Nation's resistance to Georgia's attempts to enforce State law on Cherokee lands. The Cherokee Nation filed an action in the United States Supreme Court, seeking to enjoin enforcement of the State statutes which effectively outlawed the Cherokee government and laws. The Supreme Court refused to accept the case because the tribe was not a 'foreign state' within the meaning of Article III of the Constitution. As a result, the Court did not have jurisdiction over the case.

Chief Justice Marshall, however, proceeded to discuss the legal status of Indian tribes and their relationship to the Federal Government. In doing so, he drew upon international law, colonial and United States treaties, Federal statutes, and the Constitution. The Chief Justice characterized the relationship between the two governments as "perhaps unlike that of any other two people in existence" and "marked by peculiar distinctions which exist nowhere else." Marshall agreed with the Cherokee Nation that it was a 'state' in that it was "a distinct political society...capable of managing its own affairs and governing itself." But he found that the Cherokee Nation was not 'foreign' because it was within the jurisdictional limits of the United States and because the treaties with the Cherokees acknowledged dependency upon the United States.

Marshall concluded that Indian tribes, rather than being foreign states, "may, more correctly, perhaps, be denominated domestic dependent nations...." He then invoked the trust relationship by concluding that the relationship of the tribes to the United States "resembles that of a ward to his guardian."

This duty has always been recognized by the courts and has been variaously characterized as a 'fiduciary' relationship, a 'trust' responsibility, and a 'guardian-ward' relationship. Marshall's analysis that our law has no direct parallel to this trust relationship has been often emphasized by the United States Supreme Court, which has described the relationship between Congress and Indians as 'solemn,' 'unique' or 'special,' and 'moral.' The Court, in utilizing such unusually forceful language, has relied in large part upon political principles which have emerged throughout the history of Indian Affairs. Although Cherokee Nation v. Georgia involved a treaty. later decisions have found that the trust relationship is created not only by treaty but also by other methods of Federal recognition such as statutes, agreements, and Executive orders.

The trust relationship, like the Bill of Rights in the Constitution, cannot be defined with precision in all respects. It is an evolving, dynamic doctrine which has been expanded over the years as changing times have brought changing issues. Nevertheless, the trust relationship is a mature doctrine about which several generalizations can fairly be made.

Indian trust title to land is one important manifestation of the trust relationship. Title to land in Indian country is held by the United States in trust for the tribe. Trust land is not subject to taxation, and individual Indians on trust land are free of State taxes. Trust lands, and their resources, must be managed for the sole benefit of the tribe so that they will be preserved. In some instances, land is held in trust by the United States for individual Indians. Some tribal funds are also held in trust and, in some cases, funds are held in trust for Individual Indians.

Land held in trust for Indian tribes or individuals must be carefully distinquished from the so-called 'public lands,' such as those administered by the National Park Service, the Bureau of Land Management, and the Forest Service. Public lands are administered for the public-at-large. Different rules often apply for Indian trust lands which are held, and administered solely for, the affected Indians (Cohen, 1971).

The scope of the trust responsibility extends beyond specific real or personal property which is held in trust. The United States has the obligation to provide related services, and to take other appropriate actions necessary to protect tribal self-government. The doctrine may also include a duty to provide adequate social services to Indians. These conclusions flow from the basic notion that the trust responsibility is a general obligation which is not limited to specific provisions in treaties, Executive orders, or statutes; once the trust relationship has been acknowledged, administrative action is governed by the same high duty which is imposed on a private trustee.

The tribes have recourse in the courts if the trust responsibility is breached. For compensable claims arising before 1946, tribes are permitted to sue for money damages in the Indian Claims Commission. For claims arising after that date, the proper court is the U. S. Court of Claims. Many successful suits have been brought for loss of land and for mismanagement of timber, water, and mineral resources.

In addition, although the trust responsibility cannot be enforced in court against Congress itself, executive officials are subject to suits for injunctive and declaratory relief for breach of the trust duty. A leading example is Pyramid Lake Paiute Tribe v. Morton, 354 F. Supp. 252 (D.D.C., 1972), where a Federal district court enjoined the Department of Interior from diverting water to a Federal project which reduced the water quality of Pyramid Lake in Nevada. Pyramid Lake is located on a downstream Indian reservation. The court held that the Government's trust responsibility to the tribe was violated by the upstream diversion, even though the diversion was not on the reservation.

These principles clarify the crucial distinction between Congress and executive agencies in the administration of the trust responsibility. Although Congress is not subject to suit for violation of the trust responsibility, administrative officials are directly accountable to the tribes through court actions. Administrative agencies operate only pursuant to delegations of authority from Congress. Basic administrative law principles dictate that administrative officials are subject to judicial review for most situations in which they exceed their delegated authority. Accordingly, Indian tribes and individuals will often have recourse against the Department of the Interior, or any other agency which violates the trust responsibility.

Many basic aspects of the trust obligation extend to an individual Indian wherever he or she may be. The duty to protect his tribal government, the duty to protect this trust resources, and the duty to acknowledge his tribal identity continue undiminished even though the individual Indian may have left the reservation.

The research of this Commission shows that the Bureau of Indian Affairs, the primary agent of Congress in the admininistration of the trust responsibility, has used the trust doctrine as a means to develop a paternalistic control over the day-to-day affairs of Indian tribes and individuals. The trust responsibility calls for self-determination and self-government by Indian tribes. Federal-Indian trust law, as expressed both by Congress and the courts, calls for Federal protection, not Federal domination.

Plenary Power: Congressional Authority over Indian Affairs

The Constitution grants Congress broad power over Indian affairs. The scope of this power is extraordinary, and is perhaps equaled only by the power of the Federal Government over international relations. Congress' authority in Indian affairs is commonly referred to as 'plenary,' which means absolute or total.

Indians are expressly mentioned twice in the Constitution. "Indians not taxed" are excluded from the count for determining representatives to Congress. Far more importantly, Congress is expressly given power to "regulate Commerce with foreign Nations, and among the several States, and with the Indian Tribes." Congress has ratified many treaties with Indians; thus the treatymaking power and the power to spend money for the "general Welfare of the United States" have also been used to support Congress' authority over Indian affairs.

The Supreme Court, relying primarily on the commerce clause and the treatymaking power, has recognized that Congress under the Constitution has exclusive power over Indian affairs.

The plenary power over Indian affairs is not limited to federally recognized tribes, but rather extends to "all dependent Indian communities within its borders." There are several instances in which the trust realtionship has been terminated but later restored by Congress. The trust relationship may remain in effect, especially in areas relating to land, even though the Bureau of Indian Affairs has failed to designate a tribe as federally recognized. Thus Congress' power reaches all Indian tribes in the United States, including terminated and "nonfederally recognized" tribes; the question is whether, and to what extent, Congress has chosen to exercise that power in regard to a given tribe. The best recent example of a full congressional resumption of the Federal-tribal relationship is the Menominee Restoration Act of 1973, where Congress restored the terminated Menominee Tribe by exercising it plenary power over Indian affairs.

While Congress' plenary power over Indian affairs is extensive, ther are limits on the power. When tribal or individual property rights are taken away, the tribe or individual is entitled to be compensated in cash for the loss. In addition, Congress' plenary power over Indians is subject to other constitutional limitations upon congressional power, such as the Bill of Rights.

It is Congress, not the Bureau of Indian Affairs or any other administrative agency, which possesses this plenary power. Those agencies hold only such powers over Indians as Congress has granted to them. Courts, therefore, have struck down administrative action over Indians because the action was not within the scope of authority delegated by Congress to the agency, even though Congress itself clearly had the power to take the action in question.

Congressional action in furtherance of its plenary power over Indians is not violative of the Equal Protection and Due Process Clauses, which prohibit discrimination on the basis of race. The trust relationship, jurisdictional patterns in Indian country, and Federal programs for Indians are not unconstitutional 'reverse discrimination' because they result in a special status for Indians. The reason for this is that the United States' relationship with Indian tribes is political, not racial, in nature; plenary power is intergovernmental in character and exists between the United States and the tribes in their capacities as governments. The Supreme Court, in rejecting arguments based upon the Equal Protection and Due Process Clauses, has upheld a Federal hiring preference for Indians; affirmed the jurisdiction of tribal courts over tribal members; and upheld reservation tax immunity from State law.

Powers which spring from concepts of natural right and justice are premised on a measure of consent by the governed. That history of Federal dealings with the Indian people has much too often been rule based on power, rather than on consent of the governed.

Definition of Indian: Tribal Membership

Who is an Indian? Early judicial decisions held that an Indian is a person who is ethnically or legally part of his or her tribe. Recognition by the tribe, once given, was not easily lost. This Commission has found, for example, that off-reservation Indian people identify themselves in the context of their tribal affiliation. The tribe's power over its own membership is the starting point for any discussion of Indian identity.

But Congress can, and has, passed laws to define Indian status for some Federal purposes. Although no statute has laid down a general definition of 'Indian,' Congress has sometimes set standards to define Indian status for special purposes. Older legislation used various degrees of Indian blood for different tribes, but those standards were often arbitrary and conflicted with tribal provisions. Recent congressional legislation, however, has avoided these conflicts and has given recognition to the primary tribal interest in membership by defining 'Indian' as a member of an Indian tribe.

In the area of eligibility for Federal services, the Bureau of Indian Affairs and other Federal agencies must work within definitions given by Congress. For example, the Indian Reorganization Act of 1934 contains a definition of 'Indian' for the implementation of that Act. That definition includes all members of federally recognized Indian tribes regardless of degree of Indian blood.

Despite that statutory definition, the Bureau of Indian Affairs and the Indian Health Service for many years defined 'Indian' for purposes of employment preference as any person who was a member of a federally recognized Indian tribe and one-fourth or more Indian blood. This administrative criterion was challenged in court as being contrary to the definition in the IRA. The Government conceded in a final judgement that the statutory definition in the IRA controlled. Similarly, a recent Supreme Court case found that the BIA had acted improperly by denying welfare services to Indians living 'near' reservations while providing the benefits to those living 'on' reservations. Again, the reasoning was that the BIA was acting contrary to congressional direction in denying benefits to tribal members.

In most circumstances, then, a person is an Indian if that person's tribe recognized him or her as an Indian. That means that the tribe, as a political institution, has primary responsibility to determine tribal membership for purposed of voting in tribal elections, property distributions, exercise of treaty rights, Indian perference, and other rights arising from tribal membership. Many tribal provisions call for one-forth degree of blood of the particular tribe but tribal provisions vary widely. A few tribes require as much as one-half degree of tribal blood and a small number permit any descendant of a tribal member to be enrolled, regardless of the blood quantum. For tribal purposes, that tribal definition is final. Absent express congressional action, the Bureau of Indian Affairs has no power to alter tribal determinations.

Indian Treaties: Cornerstones of Indian Law

Indian treaties, which have played such a central role in the development of Indian law and policy, were negotiated during the 18th and 19th centuries. These legally binding agreements were made between governments, the United States on the one hand and the tribes on the other. The courts have treated the parties as substantial equals; both sides agreed to compromise, with the tribes giving up claims to vast areas of land. Treaties were negotiated in the field by members of the executive branch of the Government, and went into effect after being ratified by the Senate. Unless abrogated (i.e., breached or broken) by subsequent Federal statute in whole or in part, treaties remain fully in effect.

Indian treaties are superior to all State laws and are entitled to equal dignity with any Federal statute. They are the 'supreme law of the land.'

Treatymaking continued until 1871 when Congress passed legislation which brought future treatymaking with Indian tribes to an end. After 1871, no further treaties were negotiated but the United States continued to deal with Indian tribes in essentially the same manner through 'agreements' which are ratified by both the House and the Senate, Executive orders, and statutes.

Treaties, while an extremely important part of Federal policy toward Indians, were by no means the only method used to deal with Indian tribes. The Trade and Intercourse Acts, which regulate trade with the tribes and controlled the liquor traffic, were another major means by which Congress dealt with the tribes. Treaties, however, deserve special mention because of their importance in the development of Indian law, and because of their great signficance to American Indians today.

The courts have always interpreted treaties in a manner favorable to the tribes. The historical realities of brutal and inequitable relations with Indians, along with the serious language problems existing during the treaty negotiations, led to the development of three basic canons of treaty construction:

1. Ambiguous expressions in trieties must be resolved in favor of the Indians;
2. Treaties must be interpreted as the Indians themselves would have foreseen and understood them;
3. Treaties must be liberally construed in favor of the Indians.

By using these canons, the courts have given expansive readings of Indian treaties. For example, the word 'trust,' or similar language, was never used in the treaties, but the courts have implied the existence of a trust relationship in treaties. The treaty phrase "to be held as Indian lands are held" has been interpreted to include provision for hunting and fishing rights. Treaty provisions reserving the right to fish at "usual and accustomed places" have been held to reserve appropriate easement rights over non-Indian land to gain access to off-reservation sites. The Supreme Court held recently that general provisions for the protection of the Navajo Tribe served to bar the operation of State taxes upon Indians in Indian country.

The Winters doctrine, providing that the reservation of sufficient waters for tribal use is implicit in Indian treaties, has been developed and consistently affirmed by the Supreme Court. Under that doctrine, Indian water rights precede and preempt any other rights established by State law. The fishing rights decisions in the Northwest provide another example of how the canons of construction have protected basic treaty rights from encroachment by the States.

One of the most significant elements of Indian treaty law is that Indian treaties were not a grant of rights from the United States to the tribes, but rather a grant from the tribes to the United States. Thus, all sovereign powers of tribes are retained unless expressly granted away by the tribe in a treaty or expressly taken away from the tribe by Federal statute.

Indian treaties, then, are not to be read in a neutral way. The courts have found that the historical circumstances surrounding treaty negotiations require rules of construction which cut in favor of the tribes.

Indian treaties, like international treaties, can be abrogated by Congress. Questions of whether Congress actually has intended to abrogate treaties have arisen frequently. The issue often comes up when administrative officials argue that general Federal statutes, which do not mention Indian tribes, regulate hunting and fishing rights, water rights, mineral rights, jurisdiction, and rights to the retention of land. A crucial point is that only Congress has the power to abrogate Indian treaties or otherwise regulate Indian affairs: the administrative agency seeking to limit Indian rights must have specific delegated authority from Congress before it can abrogate a treaty or otherwise diminish Indian rights.

The courts have cut back on administrative action affecting treaty rights by requiring very explicit directions from Congress to the agency. Absent such a showing of congressional action, treaty rights remain intact; treaty rights cannot be abrogated "in a backhanded way." Although the law is not fully consistent in the area, the better reasoned cases hold that treaty rights cannot be eliminated by administrative action unless there is a specific congressional statute which identifies the specific affected Indian treaty rights and which states that it is the intent of Congress to abrogate such rights. No Supreme Court case in the last 50 years has upheld any asserted abrogation of an Indian treaty.

The principles discussed above were developed in the context of Indian treaties; if those principles were limited solely to treaties, many tribes would not benefit from them because many reservations were established by Federal action other than treaties. The courts have recognized, however, that treaties are but one method of dealing with tribes and that treaty law is generally applicable to agreements, statutes, and Executive orders dealing with Indians.

The trust relationship, for example, was first applied to the Cherokee treaty but has since been applied in numerous nontreaty situations. The rules of treaty construction apply not only to treaties but also to statutes. Hunting and fishing rights can be established by methods other than treaty. Similarly, the Supreme Court has ruled that exclusive tribal jurisdiction can be established by agreement or Executive order, as well as by treaty.

Indian treaties, therefore, are an important foundation of all Indian law. Most early court cases involved treaty tribes. Policy changed, however, and the United States began to deal with Indian tribes by other means, such as Executive orders, agreements, and statutes. When those nontreaty tribes came into court, the rules of construction governing treaties were applied.

While this discussion has focused on treaties as law, any discussion of treaties would be incomplete without mention of their symbolic and moral significance to the Indian people. Unlike almost all other documents in Anglo-American law, treaties are seen as moral statements which represent the "word of the nation" and the "sanctity of the public faith." An Indian treaty is "a bulwark against State encroachment.... It is a monument to past guilt; and efforts to change the law include, in themselves, evidence of continued uneasiness."

This Commission, in hearing after hearing, has seen that American Indians rightfully expect that this Nation will continue to abide by the solemn promises made in these old laws: The Constitution is an old law, too. Thus while treaties can be broken by Congress, such extreme action must be truly a last resort. As Justice Hugo Black put it: "Great Nations, like great men, should keep their word." Indian treaties are among the very few laws in our society which raise those kinds of issues.

Jurisdiction: Varying Rights and Responsibilities in Indian Country

'Jurisdiction' sounds like an arcane word for lawyers only. To reservation Indians, it is far more than that. Jurisdiction is a living reality which has a direct, dramatic effect on their day-to-day lives.

Sovereignty refers to the powers of a government. Jurisdiction, as used here, refers to the human conduct (subject matter jurisdiction) and to the geographic area (territorial jurisdiction) over which a government's sovereign powers can be exerted. The question is whether conduct in Indian country (which usually means all land within reservation boundaries) will be regulated by the legislatures and courts of the tibes themselves or by the State or Federal Government.

Tribal councils (tribal legislatures) and tribal courts posses original jurisdiction within Indian country. As a general rule the States have no jurisdiction over matters involving Indian tribes or Indian people in Indian country absent a Federal statute giving them jurisdiction. Accordingly, absent Federal authority to a State, all Indian reservations within a State are islands where the laws of the state cannot reach. Those islands are governed by the institutions of the tribes. To put it another way, the laws of Arizona have no effect for most purposes in New Mexico or Utah. Absent express Federal legislation, the laws of Arizona have no effect for most purposed on the Papago and Navajo reservations. Only Federal legislation can change that pattern.

For its part, the Federal Government possesses and exercises only that jurisdiction which the Congress expressly provides for, even though potentially, its plenary authority is all encompassing.

Jurisdiction is both criminal and civil. Criminal cases involve wrongs against the public, ranging from disorderly conduct to murder, which become the subject of prosecutions resulting in imprisonment or fine. If a legislature has jurisdiction, it can define criminal conduct in many areas which are especially sensitive to Indians, such as questions involving hunting and fishing rights. The existence of jurisdiction will determine whether crimes will be defined by tribal councils or by State legislatures or Congress. Questions of criminal jurisdiction will also resolve whether violations of such criminal laws will be handled by Indian or non-Indian judges, jurors, prosecutors, policemen, and jailers.

Criminal jurisdiction, then, will determine whether crimes in Indian country are tried in tribal courts by Indians; in the local State courts where hostility by non-Indians is often great; or in Federal courts which are often inconveniently distant from the reservations but where there is usually less antagonism against Indians. In some situations, two governments can have "concurrent" jurisdiction. That is, it is sometimes possible for a criminal defendant to be tried in either tribal or State court for alleged criminal conduct. In other situations, it is possible that a criminal defendant could be subject to the concurrent jurisdiction of either the tribal court of the Federal court. In most cases, when two courts have concurrent jurisdiction, the individual will be tried and punished in the court where the case is first prosecuted.

Civil, as opposed to criminal, jurisdiction involves private or individual disputes such as depts, automobile accidents, and disputes over leases. Governments also pass civil laws in critically important areas such as child custody, education, zoning, domestic relations, environmental planning, and alcoholism. Again, the civil jurisdictional issue is truly fundamental: whether these important laws affecting Indian country will be passed by tribal councils or by non-Indian legislatures. Simiilarly, the question arises as to which government's courts have jurisdiction to hear civil cases - tribal courts, State courts, or Federal courts. As with criminal jurisdiction, in a limited number of situations, there can be concurrent civil jurisdiction between two courts.

Jurisdiction to tax has been the subject of continuing litigation and deserves special mention. The States have sought to increase their revenues by taxing persons and activities on the reservations. An increasing number of tribes believe that tribal taxation jurisdiction is essential to the long range economic viability of tribal governments. The problem is twofold. For most purposes, reservations are immune from State tases; individual tribal members and struggling tribal businesses badly need those exemptions. On the other hand, tribes themselves have powers to tax persons and activities on the reservations. Future tribal economic self-sufficiency may well depend upon the continued existence of that power.

Jurisdiction is often a question of the specific geographic area which is covered by the sovereign powers of a given government. Usually Indian jurisdiction cases involve disputes within reservation boundaries. The technical term 'Indian country.' however, is properly used to determine the geographic limits on State jurisdiction. The term 'Indian country' is derived from 18 U.S.C., sec. 1151, which is a Federal criminal jurisdiction statute. The statutory definition of Indian country applies as well to questions of civil jurisdiction.

The Indian country statute has three separate parts. First, Indian country is defined as all lands within the limits of any Federal Indian reservation, "not withstanding the issuance of any patent." Land within reservation boundaries which has been opened to settlement by non-Indians is Indian country unless Congress intended to diminish the reservation. Thus, Indian country includes all land within the reservation boundaries, including 'checkerboarded' land - that is, those areas within Indian reservations where non-Indian land is interspersed with Indian land. Second, Indian country includes all dependent Indian communities within the borders of the United States. Third, Indian country includes all Indian trust allotments, even though they may not be within the boundaries of a reservation.

Normally, unless expressly limited by Federal legislation, Indian tribes have criminal and civil jurisdiction in Indian country. On the other hand, absent express Federal legislation, States do not have jurisdiction within Indian country. The reverse is true outside of Indian country: absent express Federal law to the contrary, Indians leaving Indian country have generally been subject to State law otherwise applicable to all citizens of the State.

Synthesis: Indian Tribes and People in America's Legal and Political System

Political science texts commonly state that there are four levels of government in the United States: the Federal Government, the State governments, the county governments, and local governments. In States where Indian country is located, that notion is incorrect and confusing. In fact, in those States there are two separate chains of government: the Federal Government and Indian tribes, on the one hand; and State, county, and local governments on the other. This is not to say that Indian tribes are instrumentalities or creations of the Federal Government. They are not. It is analytically essential, however, to recognize that Federal law, not State law, is preeminent in Indian country. Tribal powers spring from the tribe's own inherent sovereignty and can be diminished only by express Federal, not State, action.

From the early days of this Republic, local interests have placed the greatest pressures on Congress to limit the land bases and powers of tribal governments. In some instances, such as the Allotment Act, Public Law 280, and the Termination Acts, those pressures were notbaly successful.

But, when one considers the long historical sweep of Federal-tribal relations, the marvel is that tribes have retained so many of their essential governmental powers. Similarly, with the exception of Public Law 280, tribal governments have retained the great part of their immunity from State jurisdiction.

This is partly due to congressional actions such as the Indian Reorganization Act and, most particularly, the progressive legislation during the 1970's. Congress has truly been a trustee during those periods.

The station of American Indians in our society is also due to the classic opinions of the United States Supreme Court which developed the basic Indian law doctrines when the Cherokee Tribe came to that court of last resort in the 1830's. Those principles have since been reaffirmed and applied to other tribes and to other circumstances. Both of those doctrines - tribal sovereignty and the trust responsibility - remain vital and far-reaching today.

Federal policy cannot, of course, provide a full picture of life on the reservations, in the cities, or in those areas occupied by terminated and non-federally recognized tribes. It is a long way from Capital Hill, the White House, and the Supreme Court building to Indian country.

Even today, many tribes exercise relatively few powers of self-government. No tribe has exercised the full range of those powers. The tribes still feel the effects of the restrictive Federal policies laid down between 1871 and 1933.

But since the termination era abated during the late 1950's and especially during the 1970's, the definite trust of tribal policy has been toward a greater use of their powers of self-government. The terminated and non-federally recognized tribes have sought to develop their existing rights and have attempted to reestablish the full Federal-tribal relationship. The federally recognized tribes, taken as a whole, have moved forcefully and responsibly in the direction of developing their governmental systems. Tribal legislatures are adopting social programs, land use planning measures, and tax plans to provide for the future. Tribal courts are expanding their systems of justice. Thus the States usually cannot govern on the reservations, but the tribes are showing that they can do the job competently and fairly.

These developments hold the greatest promise for the tribes. They hold promise for the land, which has been there forever, and for the generations which will be there tomorrow. Ultimately, that promise can only be realized by American Indians themselves. But the distinctive doctrines of Federal Indian law and policy are fundamental tools which the tribes have used and are using to fulfill that promise.

REFERENCES

Cohen, Felix. Handbook of Federal Indian Law. Albuquerque: University of New Mexico Press, 1971.

Statutes

Antoine v. Washington, 420 U.S. 194 (1975).
Arizone v. California, 373 U.S. 546, 599-600 (1963).
Barta v. Oglala Sioux Tribe, 259 F. 2d 533 (8th cir. 1958).
Buster v. Wright, 135 F. 947 (8th cir. 1905).
Cherokee Intermarriage Cases, 203 U.S. 76 (1906).
Cherokee Nation v. Georgia, 30 U.S. (5 Pet.) 1 (1831).
Cherokee Nation v. Southern Kansas Ry., 135 U.S. 641, 654 (1890).
Choctaw Nation v. Oklahoma, 397 U.S. 620, 631 (1970).
Choctaw Nation v. United States, 318 U.S. 423, 431-432 (1943).
Colville Tribe v. State of Washington, 412 F. Supp. 651 (1976).
Conley v. Ballinger, 216 U.S. 84, 90 (1910).
Crain v. First National Bank, 324 F. 2d 532 (9th Cir. 1963).
DeCoteau v. District County Court, 420 U.S. 425 n.2 (1975).
Delaware Indians v. Cherokee Nation, 193 U.S. 127 (1904).
Draper v. United States, 164 U.S. 240 (1896).
Edye v. Robertson, 112 U.S. 580, 599 (1884).
F.P.C. v. Tuscarora Indian Nation, 362 U.S. 99 (1960).
Fisher v. District Court, 424 U.S. 382 (1976).
Hauenstein v. Lynham, 100 U.S. 483, 490 (1880).
Joint Tribal Council of the Passamaquoddy Tribe v. Morton, 528 F. 2d 370 (1st cir. 1975).
Lone Wolf v. Hitchock, 187 U.S. 553 (1908).
Manchester Band of Pomo Indians v. United States, 363 F. Supp. 1238 (N. D. Cal. 1973).
Maxey v. Wright, 105 F. 1003 (8th cir. 1900).
McBratney v. United States, 104 U.S. 621 (1882).
McClanahan v. State Tax Commission, 411 U.S. 164 (1973).
Menominee Tribe v. United States, 391 U.S. 404 (1968).
Mescalero Apache Tribe v. Jones, 411 U.S. 145, 148, 149, 150n. 15, 153 (1973).
Morton v. Mancari, 417 U.S. 535, 540, 552 (1974).
Morris v. Hitchcock, 24 D.C. 565 (1904).
Opliphant v. Schilie, 544 F. 2d 1007 (9th cir. 1976).
Patterson v. Council of Seneca Nation, 245 N.Y. 433, 157 N.E. 734 (1927).

Perrin v. United States, 232 U.S. 478 (1914).
Quechan Tribe v. Rowe, 531 F. 2d 408 (9th cir. 1976).
Reid v. Covert, 354 U.S. 1, 17 (1957).
Ruiz v. Morton, 415 U.S. 199 (1973).
Santa Rosa Band of Indians v. Kings Court, 532 F. 2d 655 (9th cir. 1975).
Seminole Nation v. United States, 316 U.S. 286, 296, 297 (1942).
Snohomish County v. Seattle Disposal Company, 70 Wash. 2d 688, 424 P. 2d 22 (1967).
Sohappy v. Smith, 529 F. 2d 570 (9th cir. 1976).
Talton v. Mayes, 163 U.S. 376 (1895).
Tulee v. Washington, 315 U.S. 681, 684, 685 (1942).
United States v. Ahtanum Irrigation District, 236 F. 2d 321 (9th cir. 1956).
United States v. Anteleope, 44 U.S.L.W. 4361 (April, 1977).
United States v. Blackfeet Tribal Court, 244 F. Supp. 474 (D. Mont. 1965).
United States v. Clevand, 503 F. 2d 1067 (9th cir. 1974).
United States v. Creek Nation, 295 U.S. 103 (1935).
United States v. Kagama, 118 U.S. 375 (1886).
United States v. Mason, 412 U.S. 391, 397 (1973).
United States v. Quiver, 241 U.S. 602 (1916).
United States v. Ramsey, 271 U.S. 467, 471 (1926).
United States v. Sandoval, 231 U.S. 228, 239 (1913).
United States v. Santa Fe R.R., 314 U.S. 339 (1942).
United States v. Shoshone Tribe, 304 U.S. 111, 116 (1938).
United States v. Walker River Irrigation District, 104 F. 2d 334 (9th cir. 1939).
United States v. Washington, 525 F. 2d 676 (9th cir. 1975).
United States v. Winans, 198 U.S. 371 (1905).
United States v. White, 508 F. 2d 453 (8th cir. 1974).
Wakefield v. Little Light, 276 Md. 333, 347 A. 2d 228 (1975).
Ward v. Race Horse, 163 U.S. 504, 516 (1896).
Warren Trading Post v. Arizona Tax Commission, 380 U.S. 685 (1965).
William v. Lee, 358 U.S. 217 (1959).
Winters v. United States, 207 U.S. 564 (1908).
Whiting v. United States, civ. No. 75-3007 (D.S.D. 1975).
Worcester v. Georgia, 31 U.S. (6 Pet.) 515, 559 (1832).

Chapter 6
Native American Crime in the United States

SIDNEY HARRING

The Native American is something of an enigma to this criminologist: while having a higher crime rate than any other racial or ethnic group in the United States, and indeed on of the highest measured crime rates in the world, they have been little studied by criminologist. While one can only speculate in the reasons for this one starting point may be the traditional 'social problems' approach of American criminology. Strongly identified with 'solving' urban social problems there has been a focus on urban, predominantly black 'street crime.' In addition, lines of academic boundaries put Native American's in the baliwick of anthropologists who, while concerned with the great poverty and other social problems in Indian communities, did not specifically develop a criminological literature on Native American crime. In addition there has been a tendency to focus attention disproportionately on the problem of alcoholism, seeing Native American crime as simply an extension of the alcohol problem, and not explained by the same sociological variables that explains black and white urban crime.

Besides, this approach is theoretically unsound. Marshall Clinard and Daniel Abbott make clear that any valid criminological theory must work in different societies:

> A truly comparative criminology must approach existing data and conduct new research by using theoretical frameworks, propositions, or models that can be tested across various societies. For an adequate comparative criminology it is essential to ascertain whether similar social processes account for crime in technologically developed and less developed societies (1973:1).

While Clinard and Abbott are specifically concerned with comparing African crime patterns to those in developed countries, their observation is equally true when making parallel comparisons within a single nation with different levels of development. Analysis of Native American crime can be expected to provide data for improving our theoretical understanding of American crime. Much that is known about Native American crime defies conventional criminological assumptions: for example Native American crime in rural areas is only slightly less than in urban areas on the average with the very highest rates found on a few individual rural reservations and small towns. Similarly, while low income levels are customarily associated with high crime rates, there is evidence that Native American crime rates increase as income rises (Harring, 1970). These little known crime patterns are every bit as American as the more well known urban white and black crime rates, and can be expected to be as much importance to criminologists.

This analysis will first analyze patterns of Native American crime to show clearly how it is different from other crime patterns in American society. Second, it will analyze patterns of law enforcement on Native American reservations, and against Native Americans off reservations. Finally, it will consider these patterns of crime and law enforcement in relation to the political and economic situation of Native Americans in the United States.

Native American Crime Patterns

It is some reflection of the position of Native Americans in the United States that their high crime rate went virtually unnoticed until the 1960s, with major textbooks in criminology either ignoring them, or putting their crime rate modestly above whites, but below the 'high' black crime rate (Sutherland, 1966). Anthropologist Omer Stewart (1964) first correctly outlined the patterns of Indian crime, pointing out that their arrest rate was three times the black rate and eight times the white rate, and that it was often higher on rural reservations than in the city. Charles Reason (1972), relying heavily on Stewart, found that more detailed statistical evidence largely confirmed Stewart's analysis, but correctly noted that the data was grossly inadequate to fully understand the situation. Reason's last observation is as true today as it was in 1972. In spite of the fact that the Bureau of Indian Affairs has collected volumes of data on Native American crime in the last ten years, these data are virtually unanalyzed: the Law Enforcement Division's Annual Report has not been published since 1976 because of a lack of funds.

Briefly stated, using data from the FBI's Uniform Crime Report, Native American's have an arrest rate about three times that of blacks and ten times that of whites. Put in terms of arrests per 1,000 population over age 14 these differences are ataggering: in 1968 there were 33 arrests per 1,000 whites, 122 per 1,000 blacks, and 366 per 1,000 Native Americans - meaning that the average Native American is arrested slightly oftener than once every three years, a level of exposure to the sanctions of the criminal justice system that no other group faces. This situation clearly continues at the present, although there is some indication that urban Native American arrests are declining as rural Native American arrests increase.

Nor can these high crime rates be dismissed as only minor, public order, alcohol-related arrests, although it is true that a greater proportion of Native American arrests are for these offenses. In 1976, 43 percent of all Native American arrests were for the two offenses 'drunkenness' and 'disorderly conduct.' This compares to 30 percent for whites and 18 percent for blacks. But about five percent of all Native American arrests are for violent crimes (homicide, rape, assaults...)- a rate lower than blacks and about that of whites, and about 15 percent for property crimes - far below blacks and slightly below whites. It is clear, in other words, that Native American's have a substantial crime problem, even without the artificially high levels of public order arrests.

These data must for now be taken only as the barest indications of the true pattern of Native American crime for the data is woefully inadequate. While American crime data in general is inadequate, Native American data suffers from unique problems that makes it far more inaccurate. For example, the FBI's Uniform Crime Reports are about 97 percent complete for standard metropolitan statistical areas, but only about 80 percent complete for rural areas where about 50 percent of all Native Americans live. To make this worse the reservation arrest data is simply not included in the FBI data at all. This means that while virtually all white and black arrests find their way into the FBI data up to half of all Native American arrests are automatically excluded. This means that in all the comparisons preceeding we were comparing virtually the entire white and black arrest data with about one-half of the Native American data. We do not know exactly how including all Native American data would change our conclusions.

Without a correction for different population bases this leads to a substantial 'undercount' in Native American crime of as much as 50 percent. This is without any reference to the commonly acknowledged 'underreporting' practices by both public and police that criminologists are now aware of. In effect we might say that Native Americans are undercounted twice in official statistics - once alongside every other group in America; and once because the reservations, where 50 percent of all Native Americans reside, do not report their arrest data to the FBI.

But data does exist for crimes committed on reservations. The Bureau of Indian Affairs police, and the tribal police of individual reservations keep crime statistics which have never been systematically analyzed by criminologists. While exact comparison is impossible since statistically the census bureau cannot keep track of the Native American population, we can say that these reservation police record fully as much crime as the FBI does: reservations reported 104,022 arrests in 1976. In the same year the FBI reported 104,797 Native American arrests, including only 18,753 in rural areas (where all reservations are). Since these 18,753 'official' arrests include numerous Indians arrested off reservation most of these data do not overlap with the 104,022 reservation arrests. Even if some undetermined proportion of the data does overlap it does not change the striking conclusion: the Uniform Crime Report includes only about one-half of the recorded Native American arrests.

Moreover, using these reservation data we can reveal a distortion of great theoretical importance in the FBI data. Of the 104,797 Native American arrests reported by the FBI in 1976, 81,386 were urban. When compared to the 18,753 rural arrests reported in the same data (the remainder are suburban) we are left with the unmistakable conclusion that Native American crime is primarily an urban phenomenon - especially when we note that the reservation population is slightly more than one-half of the urban population. In fact there are more than four official urban arrests for one rural arrest. In reality we can see that there are 104,022 additional rural arrests, those made by the various reservation police forces. Adjusting for population this means nothing less than that rural reservation Native Americans have an arrest rate at least as high as those in cities. Since urbanization and crime have been closely linked by sociologists since the domination of the 'Chicago School' in the 1920s this fact in itself contains important implications for criminological theory.

When we begin to analyze these reservation arrests we find that, relatively speaking, Native American crime is more serious on reservations than it is in the city. For example the rate of aggravated assaults on reservations in 1976 was 745 per 100,000 as compared to 128 per 100,000 for the entire rural United States - rougly six times the rate. The murder rate was three times the United States rural rate (21.4 per 100,000 as opposed to 8 per 100,000) and the rape rate about four times (93.4 as opposed to 25 per 100,000). For property crime, however, reflecting the urban pattern Native American's had a much lower rate than the rural population, generally about one-half the rural rate. The arrest rate for liquor related public order offenses was about the same on reservations as in the cities - about 40 percent although there are differences in categorization. Overall, this means that patterns of rural Native American crime are very similar to urban Native American crime with one important exception - while urban Native Americans are roughly as inclined to be biolent as urban whites are, rural Native Americans are far more violent.

This comparison of reservation and urban Native American crime rates can only be made in the roughest terms because the data is so imperfect they cannot be easily compared, but the importance of the information suggested by these data is too great to ignore. To make matters even more complex the data of the U. S. bureau of the Census is probably inferior to that of the police. The distinction between reservation and urban Native Americans is an artificial one, with a larger proportion of all Native Americans being both during the course of a year. Native American employment patterns are heavily dependant on seasonal work, particularly construction, or unskilled jobs that can simply be quit when it is time to move. Most urban Native Americans have close ties to reservations that includes some period of residence from time to time. The very highest Native American arrest rates are probably concealed as 'suburban' arrests in the FBI data - arrests in cities between 5,000 and 50,000 population. These cities would include a number of 'service centers' for reservations, the most famous of which is Gallup, New Mexico. Small local Native American populations are augmented daily by reservation dwellers. The arrest patterns are neither reservation, nor urban, but focus on the regulation of recreational behavior of shoppers who have completed their other business. Off-reservation population statistics are often gross under-counts of local conservative political forces determined to keep welfare-related costs down - a particularly great problem in the intensely conservative and anti-Native American rural West.

This comparison of on and off-reservation arrests, while important, does not even reflect the greatest variation in Native American arrest rates - that is found in an inter-reservation comparison. To my knowledge no such comparison has ever been published although the data has been available since the 1960s. BIA Division of Law Enforcement Reports contain only the roughest groupings of reservations by region. This data for 1968 was compiled from private correspondence with six regional offices of the BIA with the findings ranging from a low of 5.1 arrests per 1,000 population at Nambe Pueblo (one arrest out of a population of 195) to a high of 2,150.8 arrests per 1,000 at the Mescalero Apache Reservation.

A simple reading of this data provides evidence that any simple notion of Native American crime patterns must be dismissed. Tremendous variation is concealed in a single comparison of Native American and white arrest rates. The lowest six reservations had rates below the white arrest rate - all not incoincidentally Pueblo reservations. Similarly the seven reservations with the highest rates - over 750 arrests per 1,000, were all large reservations inhabited by either Plains Indians or Apaches. But these simple comparisons conceal more complex relationships. For example two Sioux reservations in North Dakota had middle-ranged rates of 221 and 301 respectively, while two others had very high rates of 860 and 990.3 per 1,000. Several Pueblo's had arrest rates as high as the middle-ranged Sioux rates - Santa Clara at 276.3; Picuris at 212.5; and San Juan at 191.1. At present we simply lack data for explaining the significance of this data. But these differences within the Native American arrest rate are fully as important as differences between Native American arrest patterns and those of other groups in determining the theoretical foundations of the high Native American arrest rate. Any analysis that simply groups Native Americans into one category without sensitivity to these tribal and reservation differences runs a grave risk of oversimplification and of concealing more fundamental patterns of relationships.

Despite the weaknesses of the statistics this data reveals something of the complexity of Native American crime patterns, and also reveals simply that it can be studies statistically given a large-scale effort to reconstruct the statistical evidence from the FBI's Uniform Crime Reports, from the Bureau of Indian Affairs' Division of Law Enforcement, and from some independant meausures to validate this data.

Patterns of Law Enforcement

Any student of Native Americans in the United States knows that law enforcement, on or off reservations, has a special history of hardship, racial oppression, and complexity. Young Menominee's several years ago jokingly told me that the Shawano County Jail was the 'home of the braves.' The irony of this reality when compared to the 'land of the free' is no joke.

The simplest beginning point is to note that off-reservation Native Americans are legally treated as anyone else, and are fully under the jurisdiction of whatever law enforcement authorities are appropriate. This means that urban arrests are made by any municipal police force, applying any criteria it wishes. Here well-documented patterns of racial discrimination are obviously relevant, but we do not know as much about the policing of 'Indian ghettos' as we do about the policing of black and Hispanic communities. We do know that Indian communities such as Minneapolis' 'Cedar Street' receive special attention of law enforcement personnel on the lookout for particular 'Indian problems.' The extent to which this is translated into racially discriminatory arrest policies is unknown, but certainly not unknowable. One study, analyzing sentencing data from a western state (Montana) discovered a clear pattern of discrimination against Native Americans in felony sentencing that I expect is repeated at every state in the criminal justice system (Hall & Simkus, 1975).

Similarly we do not have many good studies of the enforcement practices of the off-reservation small town 'service centers' where Native Americans do routine shopping and other business - places that may well have the highest numbers of arrests proportionately - Gallup and Farmington, New Mexico; Gordon, Nebraska; Rapid City, Winner, Yankton and Sisseton, South Dakota; Shawano, Wisconsin, for example. One such study shows that Navajo drinking patterns are clearly singled out for special attention by the police (Katel, 1980). Another focused on the magnitude of the 'Indian problem' in terms of the costs of arresting and jailing them for taxpayers in small South Dakota towns - in Winner, Native Americans accounted for 65 percent of all arrests, 255 out of 399; in Yankton, 14 out of 47 in one typical month; in Wagner, 15 of 19 in another typical month; in Sisseton between 51 percent and 80 percent annually; in Rapid City, 97 out of 340 in another typical month (Farber, 1957). Although somewhat dated these trends probably still continue.

Apparently the level of white racism near Native American reservations is very high. This is surely incorporated into law enforcement policy by the small, rural sheriff departments of the west. What protection that urban Native Americans have, afforded by relative anonymity and serious social problems requiring police attention, are lost in the conservative small towns of the West. The 'crime problem' and the 'Indian problem' are likely to become merged in local minds, and this should be reflected in the crime statistics. Again, this data is available, but must be collected by race on a county by county basis.

On the reservations themselves there exists a maze of jurisdictional problems, combining Federal, state and tribal authority in different measures according to reservation. In the past ten years there has been a marked tendency to put either the BIA or tribal police in charge of routine policing of most Western reservations, and to both strengthen and train those organizations. As of 1976 the BIA or tribal police provided policing services to 415,915 Native Americans (and an unspecified number of other residents) on 126 reservations covering 200,000 square miles. This service was provided by 149 permanent BIA officers, 47 temporary BIA officers, 91 contract officers, and 464 tribal officers - a total of 751 police officers (BIA, 1975). Since statistical data for these different types of officers is merged in the BIA reports, this process conceals important differences in the arrest patterns and discretionary powers of these various law enforcement agencies.

Tribal police are hired by the governing structure of the respective reservations while the BIA police are federal civil servants hired by the district offices of that agency. Clearly the trend is toward increasing the numbers of tribal police. The BIA, in the post-Wounded Knee II period, is trying to strengthen tribal authority, for reasons that will become clear in the following section.

We have established that arrest patterns on reservations are much like those off-reservation, with a larger percentage of 'drunk-related' arrests being the major difference. We have also suggested that racism on the part of off-reservation police is responsible for some part of the high Native American arrest rate. How then does one account for the fact that Native American police officers produce similar arrest patterns? Does this tend to argue against any racial biases in external arrest patterns?

We can begin to approach this problem by noting that, even when Native Americans organize their own tribal police we are not dealing with Native American law, but an Anglo-American law enforcement, directed at the Native American population, and often carried out by individuals who are Native Americans. This distinction can be developed on several levels, but one place to begin is with traditional Native American law.

No traditional Native American legal norms whatsoever are incorporated into the American criminal law - it is entirely of Europe origin and has been imposed from without and by force. The American Indians have a rich legal tradition as E. Adamson Hoebel (1954) and others have pointed out. This legal order, like that of other Native peoples aroung the world, was entirely replaced by the laws of colonial powers, often at very high social costs. We should not forget that the largest legal mass execution ever carried out in the United States was the hanging of 38 Santee Sioux warriors in Mankato, Minnesota after an unsuccessful 1863 uprising. They died chanting traditional death songs, but also knowing that warriors traditionally did not die on the gallows (Andrist, 1964).

Traditional Indian law had a strong sense of justice. Personal disputes were settled by appeals to tribal leaders, following established rules. Property was mostly communally held, although what personal property that existed was protected by tribal law. Punishment included personal ostracism, forced labor for the tribe or the victim, group pressure, but featured minimal use of force. Thomas Jefferson noted that: "crimes are very rare among them (Virginia Indians) (Cahn, 1969: 182).

It is easy for modern criminologists to dismiss the significance of this law, assuming it quaint and only appropriate for folk societies and not practical for complex societies. Nevertheless the experience of the Socialist countries with community based law, and the experiments financed by the Law Enforcement Assistance Administration (LEAA) to replicate them in the fact of the breakdown of "law and order' in cities in the United States, establishes, not only that the core of Native American law is sound in the modern period in any society, but also that its loss was a sorry one to the American legal tradition.

The BIA-imposed tribal legal codes were nothing less than naked attempts to enforce dominant moral standards by force, an important aspects of the overall assimilationist design. The first Indian penal code prohibited dancing, polygamy, practicing as a medicine man, prostitution and drunkeness. The only other crime mentioned was stealing but even the anti-theft provision was intended primarily to destroy traditional inheritance practices (Barsh & Henderson, 1978). Todays tribal legal codes commonly have nothing 'tribal' left to them. For example, not only does the Law and Order Code of the Crow Tribe have no remnants of traditional Crow Law , it actually abolishes traditional Crow tribal marriage and divorce. To make matters worse tribal authorities often enforce this law unfairly, providing tribal courts that were manifestly unjust - especially against opponents of the faction in power (Lawrence, 1972).

We can approach the tribal police from this same perspective - not only is tribal law not Native American in any sense of the word, but the tribal police have never been 'tribal.' Rather they were a U. S. Army (and later BIA) sponsored 'Indian' police, composed of white-directed Native Americans recruited to carry out U. S. Government Indian policy. The various tribes almost always strongly resisted white domination, and tribal structures often remained strongly anti-white for years after military conquest. This is proven by white policy toward Native Americans, the assault on tribalism, an attack on Native culture and social organizations expressly designed to end these remants of resistance. The development of alternative political structures, modeled on white structures, was a part of this overall plan, and the Indian police were but one component of it (Hagan, 1966; BIA, 1975; Barsh & Henderson, 1978).

This model is not only of historical relevance, well up into the 1960s the core of Indian policing was directly in the hands of the BIA and controlled, not on the reservations, but out of BIA field offices. Police policies had little to do with individual tribal policies, but were the bottom level of a policy that originated in Washington. 'Indian law' during this period was nothing but a BIA-enforced shell of white law, enforced by Native American patrolmen, often under the control of white officers. A good part of the key to understanding the current problems with the tribal police is simply that since 1890 when forty-three Indian police murdered the great Sioux Chief, Sitting Bull, they have not fully been able to transcend either their history nor their function (Ortiz, 1980; Johansen & Maestas, 1979). The police institution in white society has gone through a long process of legitimation that has yet to occur with tribal police organizations.

Since the 1960s a further problem has arisen for the tribal police. Many of the major tribes have experiences high levels of factional conflict, leading at their highest point to the American Indian Movement's (AIM) seizure of Wounded Knee, South Dakota, a hamlet on the Pine Ridge Sioux Reservation. This factionalism has a long history and has affected many tribes. At the risk of oversimplification there generally emerged two factions: the 'treaty' faction which accepted the domination of white society, and the 'traditional' faction which opposed most forms of modernization. This brief assessment of tribal factionalism aside, suffice it to say here that the tribal police are often closely associated with the 'treaty' faction and therefore are seen as the enemy of the 'traditionalist.' AIM members on the Pine Ridge reservation have accused the tribal police of being 'goon squads' for tribal leaders - a political police most interested in repression of the opposition. Traditionals on the Red Lake Reservation in Minnesota shot it out with tribal police and burned the police station and jail in a similar dispute (Johanses & Maestas, 1979; Akwesasne Notes, 1980).

While the significance of these events should not be overestimated, neither should they be ignored. The discovery of large energy reserves on Western reservations has sharpened these political distinctions, and greatly raised the political stakes involved. The prospect of huge incomes reversing a century of Native American poverty is attractive to many. Similarly, large scale energy development is properly seen as greatly undermining traditional Native American culture and potentially finally providing the whites with an economic based assimilation in the 1980s and 1990s that they failed to gain forcibly between the 1840s and 1950s. This strengthens the determination of the traditionals to resist. This puts great political pressure on tribal police, already strained to cope with the rising crime and social disorganization accompanying the 'energy boom.'

No analysis of the tribal police would be complete without noting that they have a singularly bad reputation as being among the worst police force in America, plagued by neopitism, poor training, high job turnover, low pay and brutality. This fact is universally recognized in the literature, and was the motivation behind the opening of a BIA-financed Indian police academy, first located in Roswell, New Mexico in 1969 and later moved to Brigham City, Utah in 1973. Here tribal police officers receive modern police training that includes training for special units designed to control mass protest.

This line of analysis would lead one to conclude that Native American on-reservation arrest patterns are similar to off-reservation patterns especially since the tribal police are simply applying another version of the same kind of law enforcement applied within American society in general. This generally is the case.

But again it must be noted that while we potentially have the data to test this hypothesis, it has not been done. The activities of the various tribal police forces can be studies and evaluated. Variations in arrest patterns between reservations can be explained by enforcement practices of different tribal police forces. It is likely, for example, that much of the variation between reservations can be explained by enforcement practices - rather than by actual differences in behavior. It is imperative that criminal behavior patterns be separated from enforcement practices in order to develop adequate theories of crime. This is especially important in compatative criminology - if these distinctive patterns cannot be distinquished we cannot really have a comparative criminology.

Toward a Theoretical Explanation of Native American Crime

While some scholars in the field of criminal justice have argued that the search for theories of crime caucasion is not important, sociologists continue to see research aimed at developing better theories as critically important. Among the methods used by sociologists studying crinimological theory is the comparative method, analyzing crime patterns cross-culturally. The potential theoretical importance of the study of Native American crime in the United States is that it is a major group that has a crime pattern sharply different from the predominant crime patterns in the society in general. Any adequate theory of American crime must be able to account for such important variance in crime patterns. Even more important for those studying world-wide crime patterns, Native Americans represent an important link between crime patterns in developed nations and crime patterns in Third World countries. Native American crime patterns can be studied comparatively both in relation to those of other groups, and also, very importantly, between different tribal or reservation groupings, as well as along traditional urban/rural lines.

At the outset, before reviewing theories of Native American crime, we can say that we currently lack the data for adequate study of Native American crime. We can also say that most theories of Native American crime are inadequate in that they sought only to explain the uniqueness of Native American crime as opposed to all other crime patterns, ignoring both great differences between tribal groupings and also patterns of similarity between Native American and non-Native American crime. Finally, some theories turn almost entirely on the single issue of alcohol abuse, overlooking both the fact that most alcohol abusers do not commit crimes, and that most white and black crimes involve some alcohol abuse as well.

Culture conflict: The major criminological theory that has received the most attention in relation to Native Americans is Sellin's culture conflict theory. White society imposes demands on Native American society that Native Americans find impossible to meet. They are expected to fully support themselves, but are not given the tools to do so. The result is a high incidence of deviant behavior. This is doubly high as a white legal system criminalizes traditional Native American behavior patterns (Sellin, 1938).

Poverty: Deviance and crime can be expected to follow from conditions of poverty in this explanation, and Native Americans, because they are the porrest racial grouping in American society, have the highest crime rate. This explanation emphasized that Native American crime patterns are much like other groups (Dozier, 1966).

Depressed Aggression: The Native American has severe problems in asserting status or power in a situation controlled by whites and dependent on the government for necessities of life. This fosters a great deal of hostility and resentment which must be suppressed. Drinking and expressive criminal acts provide a needed outlet (Lemert, 1958).

The reservation system: Native Americans exist as wards of the government. All decisions historically have been made for them and they were never in a position to learn social responsibility (Stewart, 1964).

Native Americans are aggressive, violent and irresponsible: Some anthropologists see criminal traits as inherent in Native American culture. These traits are then preserved by the reservation system, which becomes a breeding ground for violence and crime (Greenway, 1969).

Primitive World View: Several anthroplogists have argued that Native Americans have a 'primitive world view' - a culturally defined mental state that views the world very different from modern white society. Psychological tests designed to measure acculturation have demonstrated little differences between urban Native Americans and those in remote regions with littel white contact. This would indicate that psychological acculturation is not taking place, a factor likely to result in social disorganization and a high rate of crime (Hallowell, 1955; Ablon, 1965).

There are other explanations of this genre as well. There is also no shortage of critics. Craig MacAndrew and Robert Edgerton (1969) and Nancy O. Lurie (1971) have successfully demolished any illusion that Native American drink to solve an 'identity crisis,' a proposition, like Greenway's, which is inherently racist. Going beyond this criticism, we argue that each of these explanations, even if they have some measure of reality in explaining a single situation, cannot account for the full range of patterns of Native American criminality. The simple poverty thesis does not conform to the data: Native American crime appears to rise with income level (Hayner, 1942). Finally, these explanations, with the exception of Sellin's try to define Native American crime with highly specialized theories, quite distinct from theories of white crime and focusing on small portions of the totality of Native American experience in the United States.

The starting point for an explanation of Native American crime is to analyze the most important element of the Native American experience in America. These are, as outlined by anthropologist Joseph Jorgensen (1971; 1978), economic domination and political powerlessness. Protesting against explanations of current Native American society that focus on comparisons with traditional Native American society, Jorgensen focuses instead on the last one-hundred years of Native American/white relations. Using terminology borrowed from the sociology of development, Jorgensen likens the Native American situation to the metropolis -satellite economic relationship existing between developed and underdeveloped nations. This neo-colonial model is both a political and economic form, characterized by both political powerlessness and economic impoverishment. Changes in Native American society during the past one-hundred years are analyzed in terms of the dominant white political economy.

The phenomenon of neo-colonialims is only of the last three decades and refers to the transformation of formerly colonial societies from the direct political control of colonizing nations to local political elites, both trained by the former colonial powers, and also entirely dependent upon them for both political power and economic support. A neo-colonial society, then, reproduces the economic structure of a colonial society, but with a different political form, and often with extreme exonomic impoverishment (Leys, 1975). Within the last ten years American social scientists have come to recognise that Native American society is a classic example of neo-colonialism, with the BIA only recently handing over more than token power to tribal leaders (Ortiz, 1980; Lurie, 1972; Thomas, 1966a, 1966b; Ruffing, 1979). These tribal leaders, however, are actually reservation leaders, elected by a majority vote process patterned after American democracy, and having no relationship to traditional Native American democracy or traditional political institutions. The political options open to these reservation leaders are sharply circumscribed by both the BIA and dominant white political and economic institutions.

How do we move from this general political and economic statement to the social problem of high crime rates among Native Americans? This type of explanation locates the 'causes' of Native American crime in the same social and economic forces that shape white crime generally, although we note that the experiences of whites and Native Americans have been historically differnt - and, importantly, the different tribal and reservation groupings themselves have different experiences. Hence, we have some foundation for both intra-tribal crime pattern differences, as well as inter-reservation differences, and a framework for the study of these comparisons of official crime statistics. The neo-colonial experience and its relationship to criminal behavior can be empirically tested.

The relationship between neo-colonial political and economic patterns and Native American law enforcement is much simpler to develop than is the relationship to patterns of criminal behavior. The tribal police are a text-book model of colonial police force. Some kind of police force of the oppressed people has proved a historical necessity in the maintenance of colonial society. Not surprisingly many neo-colonial societies have been dominated by teh remnants of these forces, remade into the military and police forces of fledgling nations. This result can be expected since the colonial powers spent disproportionate effort developing these social control forces from within the controlled population. Similarly, a tribal police force was among the first of the 'Indian' institutions to emerge after white military victory. While the power of the tribal police in the American context simply cannot rise to the level that it has in Third World countries because American political institutions are both more powerful, and have a strong tradition of domination over the state's social control apparatus, the social importance of this social control apparatus is still fully as significant. Something of the outline of this significance can be seen in the role that tribal police have taken in factional struggle on reservations. It is no accident both that the dissidents on the Red Lake Reservation attacked the police station as opposed to other government buildings, and also no accident that the U. S. Prosecutor sought (and received) severe prison terms for those convicted (Akwesasne Notes, 1980).

The relationship between this conceededly political function and the social problem of a high Native American crime rate is more complex, but it is clear that there is no intrinsic reason why reservations should apply standards of public order that appear to parallel white society. The appropriate standards of social order on Native American reservations is an issue properly decided by Native Americans, with reference to traditional cultural values. This is not a process facilitated by an Indian Police Academy owned part and parcel by the BIA, as corrupt, discredited, and white dominated an agency as any have been.

While our data on the specific process of Native American crime is sketchy, and in need of much research, what we need to know here roughly parallels deficiencies in studying comparative criminology in developing countries. Study of the relationship between crime and economic development is still at an immature stage, and it is in this theoretical work that an explanation of Native American crime patterns will be found. Futher study of the questions raised here, in this kind of theoretical framework, can be expected to answer a great many questions about Native American crime. Reference to this literature already answers one key question: the rapid energy-based economic development of the reservations of the West can be expected to lead to a rapid rise in Native American crime rates, just as it has in Third World countries. This, for a group with already one of the highest measured crime rates in the world, in itself demands extensive further study. Many reservations face perhaps twenty years of extensive mineral exploitation that will leave their lands decimated, the air polluted, their population dependant on a few highly skilled jobs that no longer exits, water supplies exhausted - all for relatively little money that will not substantially benefit most members of the tribe.

We cannot separate social science from the history of oppression and economic exploitation that Native Americans have experienced in the United States. In a theory of crime that solidly links the 'high' Native American crime rate to the political and economic exploitation that has occurred, instead of some racist 'Indian problem' we can identify crime as another facet of that same package of exploitation, and focus our search for a solution, not on more and better BIA and tribal police, but on the transformtation of Native American society from a neo-colonial society to one in full control of its culture and its economic resources.

REFERENCES

Andrist, Ralph. The Long Death. New York: Macmillan, 1964.
Anthropology Resource Center. Native American and Energy Development. Cambridge, Mass., 1978.
Barsh, Russel, and J. Youngblood Henderson. "Tribal Courts, The Model Code, and the Police Idea in American Indian Policy," In American Indians and the Law, edited by Lawrence Rosen. New Brunswick: Transaction Books, 1978.
Cahn, Edgar S. Our Brother's Keeper. Cleveland: World, 1969.
Callaway, D. G. "The Effects of Power Production and Strip Mining on Local Navajo Populations," Lake Powell Research Bulletin, 22 (June, 1976).
Clifford, William. An Introduction to African Criminology. Nairobi: Oxford University Press, 1974.
Clinard, Marshall, and Daniel Abbott. Crime in Developing Countries. New York: Wiley Interscience, 1973.
Crow Tribe. The Law and Order Code of the Crow Tribe.
Dozier, Edward. "Problem Drinking Among American Indians," Quarterly Journal of Studies on Alcohol, 27 (March, 1966): 72-87.
Farber, W. O., et. al. "Indians, Law Enforcement and Local Government," Brookings: Institute of Indian Studies, State University of South Dakota, 37, 1957.
Greenway, John. "Will the Indians get Whitey," National Review, 21 (March 11, 1969): 223.
Guillemin, Jeanne. "American Indian Resistance and Protest." In Violence in America edited by Hugh D. Graham and Robert Gurr. Beverly Hills: Sage, 1979.
Hagan, William T. Indian Police and Judges. New Haven: Yale University Press, 1966.
Hall, Edwin, and Albert A. Simkus. "Inequality in the Types of Sentences Received by Native Americans and Whites," Criminology, 13 (2) (August, 1975): 199-222.
Hallowell, Alfred I. Culture and Experience. Philadelphia: University of Pennsylvania Press, 1955.
Hayner, Norman S. "Variability in the Criminal Behavior of American Indians," American Journal of Sociology, 47 (January, 1942): 602-613.
Harring, Sidney. "The Effect of Language Retention on the Indian Arrest Rate." Unpublished M. S. Thesis. University of Wisconsin, 1970.
Hobel, E. Adamson. The Law of Primitive Man. Cambridge, Mass.: Harvard University Press, 1954.
Johansen, Bruce, and Roberto Maestas. Wasi'Chu. New York: Monthly Review Press, 1979.
Jorgensen, Joseph. "A Century of Political, Economic Effects on Indian Society, 1880-1980." Journal of Ethnic Studies, 6, 1978.
-The Sun Dance Religion. Chicago: University of Chicago Press, 1972.

-"Indians and the Metropolis." In The American Indian in Urban Society edited by Jack Waddell and Michael Watson. Boston: Little, Brown, 1971.

Katel, Peter. "Sleeping it off in Gallup, NM," Corrections Magazine (August, 1980).

Keller, Charles. "The Indian Reservation," Humanity and Society, 4 (February, 1980).

Lemert, Edwin. "The Use of Alcohol in Three Salish Indian Tribes," Quarterly Journal of Studies on Alcohol, 19 (March, 1958): 90-107.

Lawrence, William J. "Tribal Injustice," North Dakota Law Review, XLVIII (Summer, 1972): 639-659.

Leys, Colin. Underdevelopment in Kenya. Berkeley: University of California Press, 1975.

Lurie, Nancy Oestreich. "Menominee Termination," Human Organization, 31 (3) (Fall, 1972): 257-270.

-"The World's Oldest On-Going Protest Demonstration," Pacific Historical Review, 40 (August, 1971): 311-332.

MacAndrew, Craig, and Robert Edgerton. Drunken Comportment, Chicago: Aldine, 1969.

Meister, Cary W. "The Misleading Nature of Data in the Bureau of the Census Subject Report on 1970 American Indian Population," Indian Historian, VII, 1978: 12-19.

Reasons, Charles. "Crime and the Native American," Race, Crime and Justice. Pacific Palisades, Calif.: Goodyear, 1972.

Ruffing, Lorraine. "The Navajo Nation," Review of Radical Political Economics, 11 (Summer, 1979).

Sellin, Thorsten. Culture, Conflict and Crime. Philadelphia: Social Science Research Council, 1938.

Stewart, Omer. "Questions Regarding American Indian Criminality," Human Organization, 23 (Spring, 1964): 61-66.

Sutherland, Edwin H., and Donald Cressey. Criminology. Philadelphia: Lippencott, 1966.

Thomas, Robert K. "Colonialism," New University Thought, 4, 1966: 37-44.

-"Powerless Politics," New University Thought, 4, 1966: 44-53.

Young, Mary. "The Indian Question Revisited," Marxist Perspective (Spring, 1978): 34-49.

U. S. Bureau of Indian Affairs, Division of Law Enforcement Service 'reports.' 1970-1976.

-Department of Justice, FBI's Uniform Crime Report, 1979.

Chapter 7
Indian Law Enforcement

DAVID WACHTEL

On March 6, 1978, the United States Supreme Court handed down a decision in the case of Oliphant v. Suquamish (435US919). Essentailly, the case established that Indian tribal courts do not have inherent criminal jurisdiction to try non-Indians and may not assume such jurisdiction unless given specific congressional authorization. The decision has subsequently caused much concern among tribal law enforcement agencies, tribal governments, and organizations that represent Indian concerns. One such organization, the National Congress of American Indians, in a letter to the President of the United States, dated May 15, 1978, expressed their apprehension towards this decision by stating that their decision "gives non-Indians an open invitation to go onto the reservation and do anything they please without fear of arrest or judicial reprisal." This apprehension is not universally shared by all forces concerned with Indian problems.

The difference of viewpoints concerning the effects of the Oliphant case on law and order on the reservation will be discussed later in this section. The concern expressed about this case has brought to the public light the whole matter of law enforcement and legal jurisdiction on the reservation. Therefore, I feel it is necessary to discuss several topics before analyzing the effect of this court decision. First, what is the history of law enforcement on Indian reservations? Second, what jurisdiction do Indian legal agencies have over non-Indians? Thirdly, what effect does termination have on the legal authorities of Indian police agencies?

For the purposes of this article the law enforcement agencies to be discussed is the Bureau of Indian Affairs (BIA) police. Some tribes have autonomous agencies charged with maintaining law and order within their territory. The Navajo Nation, for example, maintains its own police department with jurisdiction over most misdemeanors and tribal code violations. Serious felonies are the responsibility of the BIA police and the FBI, under the Major Crimes Act of 1885 and its subsequent revisions. The Navajo police have crime scene search and protection responsibilities but further investigation of the felony crime is done by one of the above named federal agencies. These autonomous police agencies are of interest for further research but the focus of my historical discussion of police forces on the reservations will be on the BIA police.

The mid-nineteenth century saw a major shift in the focus of non-Indian settlers of the territories who were in close proximity to the Indian tribes. When non-Indians first came into contact with native inhabitants they developed the policy of dealing with the tribes as sovereign nations. Whenever new settlers wanted some land occupied by Indians, they dealt with the tribe as a whole. This policy was discouraged in the annual report of Mr. Ely S. Parker, Commissioner of Indian Affairs, in 1869, when he stated: "because treaties have been made with them (Indians) generally for the extinguishment of their supposed absolute title to the land inhabited by them or over which they roam, they have been falsely impressed with the notion of national independence. It is time that this idea should be dispelled and the government cease the cruel force of thus dealing with its helpless and ignorant wards (Parker, 1869:6)." Up to this time it was the practice of the United States Government to use non-Indians, in particular military forces, to enforce order on the reservations.

In 1869, we find the beginning of the Indians as the agents of control and order on the reservation. Indian Agent Thomas Lightfoot, agent for the Iowa and Sac-Fox tribes of Nebraska, was the first agent to report the use of Indians as law enforcement officers. He reported to Commissioner Parker: "I have appointed a police, whose duty it is to report to me if they know of anything that is wrong (Lightfoot, 1869:356)." In 1872, Special Agent William F. M. Arny created a force of 130 Navajo mounted police. They were to retrieve stolen livestock and guard the borders of the Navajo Nation. This force, under the command of the powerful Chief Manuelito, was quite successful despite efforts to disband it by officials in Washington, D. C. (Arny, 1872:302).

Even though these two examples of Indian police agencies were important they did not injoy official sanction of the government officials in Washington, D. C. One of the reasons is that these forces dealt with internal matters and exercised control over native inhabitants. In 1874, Special Agent John Clum of the San Carlos Apache Reservation, added a new dimension to the development of police forces on Indian reservations. Prior to his force, the focus of policing on reservations was the native inhabitant. However, his force attempted to control both the Apache and non-Apache residents of the reservation. Clum wanted the military to relinquish control of the reservation and to leave the law enforcement duties to his police force, but he soon realized that he did not have the authority over the military segment he desired. Instead of arguing with the military leaders, he simply ignored their presence and established an initial force of four Apaches which grew to twenty-five Apache police under the leadership of a Virginian named Clay Beauford. This force was federally paid, unlike its predecessors, and was responsible for a major action that virtually established instant credibility for Indian police. In 1877, John Clum's force captured the war-chief, Geronimo, and fifty of his followers without firing a shot.

The success of Clum's force lead Commissioner Edward P. Smith to encourage Indian agents to establish Indian police forces. Thirty-nine out of sixty-two agents favored this concept; in fact, the Winnebagos, Santee and Red Cloud Sioux maintained separate police forces quite well (Priest, 1942).

Commissioner John Q. Smith, in 1876, in his annual report requested funds for these new law enforcement efforts. He felt that the Indians were being asked to exist in conditions white men could not. It was Smith's feeling that a paradox existed in that on one hand the Indians were obviously not civilized but on the other they were not allowed to create the necessary system of law and order to encourage civilization. He felt that one way to begin civilizing the Indians was to allow them to establish their own police force.

The recognition of the need for an Indian police force continued through the administrations of several commissioners of Indian Affairs. In 1879, Congress recognized the need for Indian police and appropriated funds for an Indian police force. The amount of thirty thousand dollars was allocated and a total of 480 police officers were to be employed. Even though these forces were not without their Indian and non-Indian critics, they continued to grow in size and legitimacy. During the 1883 session of Congress the authorized strength of the Indian police forces grew to 1,000 privates and 100 officers. This number represents the largest authorization of strength for the Indian police forces in the history of Congress.

As the size of the departments grew, it became apparent that new laws were needed to handle the increase of criminal activity on the various reservations. The first major Supreme Court decision to affect this area was decided in 1885. <u>Ex Parte Crow Dog</u> (109US556) established that federal courts did not have jurisdiction to handle cases where both the victim and offender were Indians and the crime occurred on an Indian reservation. The Supreme Court suggested that Congress legislate a solution to this problem. In response to this decision, Congress passed the Major Crimes Act of 1885, which gave federal courts and police jurisdiction over certain criminal offenses involving Indians on the reservation (Prucha, 1975).

It was not until 1908 that the beginning of a unified effort to control crime can be found. Until that time Indian police forces operated independently from any central control. In that year, Mr. William (Pussyfoot) Johnson was appointed as the Chief Special Officer by Commissioner Francis Leupp. Johnson created a force of deputies that were responsible for enforcing the liquor laws. This enforcement effort is worthy of research itself. Nonetheless, Johnson's force was extremely successful in reducing or eliminating bootlegging activity in, aroung and through, the Indian Territory of Oklahoma. However, when prohibition became law of the land the alcohol traffic was diverted to the now dry major urban centers. Once in these centers the bootleggers forgot about the market in Indian Territory. This caused Johnson to require his deputied to begin to enforce laws under the Major Crimes Act and this we find the roots of the modern force called the BIA police - a force with 350 employees.

The nature of law enforcement on Indian reservations has changed over the past century. Initially, the police forces were established to maintain law and order among the native inhabitants. The police kept the Indian agents appraised of any abnormal activity on the reservation. However, the modern Indian forces have the additional responsibility of protecting the inhabitants from external threats.

In order to have a better understanding of the origins of policing authority on reservations, it is necessary to discuss the question of Indian juristiction over non-Indians. The advocates of Indian jurisdiction over non-Indians base their arguments on several practical realities: (1) the size and economic ability of a particular tribe; (2) the tribal relationship with neighboring states and countries within which it is located; (3) demonstrated willingness or lack thereof of non-Indian governments to provide law and order with fair and impartial treatment of the Indian community; and (4) the physical proximity or isolation of the tribe to other government services.

In the case of Ex Parte Crow Dog the Supreme Court decided that non-Indian courts did not have the jurisdiction over Indians who committed crimes on reservation lands. The court stated that: "The United States was seeking to extend United States law, by argument and interference only...over aliens and strangers; over members of a community separated by race and tradition...from the authority and power which seeks to impose upon them the restraints often external and unknown code...; which judges them by a standard made by others and not for them (Crow Dog, 1883: 571)." This case, of course, precipitated the Major Crimes Act of 1885, which established the relationship between Indian offenders and the federal court system.

However, the question of Indian police powers over non-Indians was left unclear. "The Indian nations had always been considered as distinct, independent political communities, retaining their original natural rights, as undisputed possessors to the soil, from time immemorial, with the single exception of that imposed by the irresistable power (Marshall, 1831)." This was the feeling of Chief Justice John Marshall as expressed in 1831 when he was deciding the Cherokee 'removal' issue. At that time the only powers that had been removed from the tribes generally were related to international jurisdictions, such as the right to go to war and make treaties with other nations. The problem of law enforcement was not present because either the tribes had no contact with non-Indians or the military maintained the peace on the reservations. The Major Crimes Act establised the jurisdiction of federal courts over Indians on reservations. The question of non-Indians was never clarified beyond any specific treaty provisions. This was rectified through the Oliphant decision which will be discussed later (Worchester, 1975).

Another issue involved in the power of jurisdiction of federal and state courts and Indian policing powers is the issue of termination of tribal existence. Termination occurs through acts of Congress, treaty provisions, cessation of collective action and recognition. The early view was that tribal membership is legally incompatible with United States citizenship. This viewpoint led to a number of treaties and statutes that provided that a given tribe should be dissolved when its members became citizens of the United States. Once this dissolution occurred the tribe was to divide tribal funds and lands into allotments. The allotees were then removed from any special status and were subject to United States and local jurisdiction. The Supreme Court reinforced the view in the case of In Re Heff (196US488). In this case the Court decided that the Indian liquor laws did not apply to allotees since they were no longer tribal members. The defendant in this case was a Kickapoo Indian and the treaty discussed was the Treaty of June 28, 1862. This treaty provided that once members of the Kickapoo tribe became allotees they ceased to be members of the tribe and thus became citizens of the United States (Choen, 1977).

However, the Heff concept did not last long. In a later case entitled U. S. v. Nice (241US591) the court reversed itself by stating that allotment did not terminate tribal existence so as to remove the allotee from the scope of Indian liquor laws adopted pursuant to the congressional power to regulate commerce with the Indian tribes.

The present viewpoint is clear that neither allotment nor citizenship, nor both together, imply a termination of tribal existence in the absence of an express provision of a statute asserting a connection. These are factors to be considered in determining whether a given group has ceased to maintain tribal relations. Other factors can determine whether the tribal separation of a group from the main body of the tribe and the inactivity of participation in tribal resources and tribal government.

A case that upholds that viewpoint is the decision of Cherokee Trust Funds. This case held that those Cherokees who remained in North Carolina when the main body was removed to the Oklahoma Indian Territory thereby lost their tribal membership because of inactivity in tribal government. The Supreme Court felt the relationship of the group that remained in North Carolina to each other was merely social or business oriented. Also, no treaty was ever made between this band and the United States. The matter of termination is important because it brought these Indians within the jurisdiction of the state and local courts and outside of the Oliphant decision.

On March 6, 1978, the Supreme Court handed down its decision in Oliphant v. Suquamish. This case established that Indian tribal courts had no jurisdiction to try non-Indian criminal offenders. Many opinions have been expressed on the effect on Indian reservations. However, they seem to be divided into two basic camps; one group of experts feels the case merely reiterates previous precedent that establishes the jurisdiction of the Federal control agencies over non-Indian offenders who commit crimes against Indians on the reservations. Another group feels that the case is 'bad case law' and opens the reservation to non-Indian criminals.

A representative of the first group is Interior Department Solicitor Leo M. Krulitz. In his press release dated April 12, 1978, he stated that this case does not leave a void in criminal law enforcement on reservations. Krulitz further stated that: "Except where a state has acquired, by Act of Congress, jurisdiction over Indian country within its borders, Bureau of Indian Affairs police and tribal police commissioned by the Federal government may arrest non-Indians for offenses committed against Indians or their property in Indian country (Krulitz, 1978)." This group of experts felt that this case reiterates the conclusion that the United States has jurisdiction over crimes committed by non-Indians against the person or property of Indians on several previous occasions: <u>United States v. Ramsey</u> (271US467) ; <u>United States v. Pelican</u> (232US448).

In <u>Williams v. United States</u> (327US711) the Supreme Court clarified the question of who has jurisdiction over non-Indian criminal offenders by stating: "While the laws and courts of the state of Arizona may have jurisdiction over offenses committed on this reservation between persons who are not Indians the laws and courts of the United States, rather than those of Arizona, have jurisdiction over offenses committed there, as in this case, by one who is not an Indian against one who is an Indian (Williams, 1946:714)." Additionally, recently the Federal Court of Appeals for the Eight and Ninth Circuit held that offenses committed by non-Indians against Indians may not be prosecuted under state law: <u>United States v. Big Crow</u> (523F.2d955); <u>United States v. Cleveland</u> (503F.2d1067).

On the third page of a memorandum dated April 10, 1978, Solicitor Krulitz, in his letter to the Assistant Secretary of the Department of the Interior for Indian Affairs, summarized his opinion by stating: "The United States continues to have jurisdiction over Indian and non-Indian alike who violate the Federal laws that apply throughout the nation or who violate substantive criminal laws applicable to Indian country. Unless a state has acquired valid jurisdiction over the Indian country within its borders..(under federal statute, the federal government) continues to have exclusive jurisdiction over non-Indians who violate federal enclave law by committing a crime against an Indian or Indian property (Krulitz, 1978:3)."

Although the case law appears to be clear on who has jurisdiction it is important that case law discussions be seen in the light of protected judicial hearing rooms. A more pragmatic view can be seen in a letter from Mr. Forrest Gerard, Assistant Secretary of the Department of Interior for Indian Affairs to Mr. Benjamin Civiletti, Acting Attorney General during this time (March 15, 1978). In that letter, Mr. Gerard expressed some reservations about the practical effect of the case in question. He stated: "A prime reason for tribal action in this area has been as noted that the Federal Government which has jurisdiction over crimes by non-Indians against Indians has failed to exercise that authority and has repeatedly discouraged tribal officials from relying on the Federal Government to exercise its authority and provide protection under the Federal criminal code (Gerard, 1978:1)."

Assistant Secretary of the Interior for Indian Affairs, Mr. Gerard, sent a letter to all area Directors and Superintendents for the BIA police, dated March 8, 1978. In this letter he instructed all BIA law enforcement officers not to arrest non-Indians for tribal criminal offenses but to continue to arrest for federal offenses. He further stated that if BIA law enforcement officers carry a commission from the state of local non-Indian agency they may arrest for state criminal offenses. but must turn the offenser over to the appropriate non-tribal authority for prosecution. This is the cross-deputization model to be discussed later.

Acting Attorney General Civiletti, in a letter to all United States Attorneys, reminded the U. S. Attorneys that they have the responsibility to review all cases in respect to their effect on the peace and good order of the community. He also reminded them that if they reject the case it cannot be prosecuted elsewhere. An interesting question arises when you examine the so-called victimless crimes. The case of reckless driving, for example, has no Indian victim and therefore the Major Crime Act of 1885 does not apply. Mr. Civiletti encouraged tribal and BIA police to be deputized by non-Indian agencies, preferrably state agencies, so that they can respond to the offense legally. Another voice of support for the cross-deputization model of enforcement.

Obviously, there is confusion in the operational jurisdiction of the modern-day Indian police. It is our opinion that the actual effect of the Oliphant decision is somewhere between the NCAI's dire predictions and Attorney General Civiletti's belief that no effects will be felt by the Indian police. In response to a survey we conducted we found that the method of obtaining cross-deputization with local authorities is a common reaction to the Oliphant decision.

As Chief Myron Oats of the Chippewa-Cree tribal police stated, his department was not effected by this decision because all his officers have been cross-deputized with the County Sheriff's office. Chief Oats' response was typical and shows that the Oliphant decision was palatable since it could be minimized through cross-deputization. It must be noted that this court decision only limited tribal court jurisdiction and did not prevent the Indian police from taking offenders into custody. Chief Kendall W. Korems of the Fort Mojave police stated in his response to our survey that the Supreme Court did not rule that Indian officers were without power to take into custody non-Indians committing crimes. If the Oliphant case did not cause the confusing state of jurisdiction and police response where did this confusion originate?

It is our belief that the confusion stems from role-confusion on the part of the Indian police officers. We feel there is a fundamental difference in the role perception of non-Indian officers and their Indian counterparts. The difference may have begun with the first law enforcement agencies on the reservations but whereever it came from it appears to be present. The non-Indian officer sees his role as the protector of the community. They, generally, do not differentiate between offenders based on where they reside. It can be said that the professional non-Indian officer approaches his job in an objective, value-free context, or at least he or she should attempt to be as objective as possible. However, it seems that the Indian police officer has a different orientation.

Depending on the residence of the offender and his racial category the officer will respond in either the stereotypical, legalistic manner of his non-Indian counterpart or he may respond in the 'gatekeeper' role. That is, the officer may respond as his academy taught him to when the offender is a non-Indian but he may feel pressure to handle the case differently when the offender is Indian. The first reservation police departments were established to keep order within the confines of the reservation and to protect the native residents from external forces. There is no reason why this tradition has not been carried on by the modern officers. If our contention is correct the confusing state of police jurisdiction and responses to crimes can be understood.

The cross-deputization model may be the solution to the federal hesitancy mentioned by Mr. Gerard in his letter to Mr. Civiletti. After reviewing the responses to our survey and other documents it is our conclusion that the Oliphant decision, in fact, cleared some of the confusion and will lead to greater numbers of prosecutions by local jurisdictions. Once local officials see that they benefit tremendously from the cross-deputization of Indian officers they will most likely endorse this model. This is an important step since much of the confusion associated with reservation police existed long before the

Oliphant case. Indeed, reservation law enforcement can only benefit from legal mandates which tend to clarify their role.

Synopsis of the Oliphant v. Suquamish Decision

Oliphant v. Suquamish Indian Tribe No. 76-5729. Argued January 9, 1978 - Decided March 6, 1978.

Petitioner Mark David Oliphant was arrested by tribal authorities during the Suquamish's annual Chief Seattle Days celebration and charged with assulting a tribal officer and resisting arrest. Oliphnat applied for a writ of habeas corpus to the United States District Court for the Western District of Washington. The petitioner argued that the Suquamish Indian Provisional Court does not have criminal jurisdiction over non-Indians. The District Court disagreed with this argument and denied the petitions. On August 24, 1976, the Court of Appeals for the Ninth Circuit affirmed the denial of habeas corpus in the case of petitioner Oliphant. Certiorari, 431 U. S. 964, was granted to decide whether Indian tribal courts have criminal jurisdiction over non-Indians. It was found that they do not.

Respondents do not contend that their exercise of criminal jurisdiction over non-Indians stems from affirmative congressional authorization or treaty provision. Instead, respondents urge that such jurisdiction flows automatically from the 'Tribe's retained inherent powers of government over the Port Madison Indian Reservation.' Indian tribes are 'quasi-sovereign entitiles,' the Court of Appeals agreed and held that Indian tribes, though conquered and dependent, retain those powers of autonomous states that are neither inconsistent with their status nor expressly terminated by Congress. According to the Court of Appeals, criminal jurisdiction over anyone committing an offense on the reservation is a 'sine qua non' of such powers which means it is absolutely necessary.

The effort by Indian tribal courts to exercise criminal jurisdiction over non-Indians is a relatively new phenomenon, and where the effort has been made in the past, it has been held that the jurisdiction did not exist.

Beginning with the Trade and Intercourse Act of 1790, 1 Stat. 137, Congress assumed federal jurisdiction over offenses by non-Indians against Indians which would be punishable in the state or district if committed against a white. In 1817, Congress went one step further and extended federal enclave law to the Indian Country, the only exception was for any offense committed by one Indian against another (3 Stat. 383, 18 U.S.C. 1152).

It was in 1834 that Congress was first directly faced with the prospect of Indians trying non-Indians. In the Western Territory Bill, Congress proposed to create an Indian territory beyond the western directed destination of the settlers. The territory was to be governed by a confederation of Indian tribes and was expected ultimately to come a State of the Union. While the Bill would have created a political territory with board governing powers, Congress was careful not to give the tribes of the territory criminal jurisdiction over United States officials and citizens traveling through the area. The reasons were quite practical: officers, and persons in the service of the United States, and persons required to reside in the Indian country by treaty stipulation, must necessarily be placed under the protection, and subject to the laws of the United States. To persons merely traveling in the Indian country the same protection was extended. Congress' concern over criminal jurisdiction in this proposed Indian Territory contrasted markedly with its total failure to address criminal jurisdiction over non-Indians on other reservations, which frequently bordered non-Indian settlements. The contrast suggests that Congress shared the view of the Executive Branch and lower federal courts that Indian tribal courts were without jurisdiction to try non-Indians.

If tribal courts may try non-Indians, as respondents contend, those tribal courts are free to try non-Indians even for such major offenses as Congress may well have given the federal courts exclusive jurisdiction to try members of their own tribe committing the exact offense.

In 1891, the Court recognized that Congress' various actions and inactions in regulating criminal jurisdiction on Indian reservations demonstrated an intent to reserve jurisdiction over non-Indians for the federal courts. In, In re Mayfield, 141 U. S. 107, 115-116 (1891), the court noted that the policy of Congress had been to allow the inhabitants of the Indian country: "such power of self-government as was thought to be consistent with the safety of the white population with which they may have come in contact, and to encourage them as far as possible in raising themselves to our standard of civilization." The general object of the congressional statutes was to allow Indian nations criminal jurisdiction over all controversies between Indians, or where a member of the nation is the only party to the proceeding, and to reserve to the courts of the United States, jurisdiction over all actions to which its' own citizens are parties on either side.

In a 1960 Senate Report, that body expressly confirmed its assumption that Indian tribal courts are without inherent jurisdiction to try non-Indians, and must depend on the Federal Government for protection from intruders.

While in islotation the Treaty of Point Elliott, 12 Stat. 927 (1855), would appear to be silent as to tribal criminal jurisdiction over non-Indians, the addition of historical perspective casts substantial doubt upon the existence of such jurisdiction. In the Ninth article, for example, Suguamish acknowledged their dependence on the Government of the United States. The Indian nations were, from their situation, necessarily dependent on the United States for their protection from lawless and injurious intrusions into their country. By acknowledging their dependence on the United States, in the Treaty of Point Elliot, the Suquamish were in all probability recognizing that the United States would arrest and try non-Indian intruders who came within their reservation boundaries. Other provisions of the Treaty also point to the absence of tribal jurisdiction. Thus the tribe agreed not to shelter or conceal offenders against the laws of the United States, but to deliver them up to the authorities for trial. When read in conjunction with 18 U.S.C. 1152, which extends federal enclave law to non-Indian offenses on Indian reservations, this provision implies that the Suquamish are to promptly deliver up any non-Indian offender, rather than try and punish him themselves.

By themselves, these treaty provisions would probably not be sufficient to remove criminal jurisdiction over non-Indians if the tribe otherwise retained such jurisdiction. But an examination of our earlier precedents satisfies us that, even ignoring treaty provisions and congressional policy, Indians do not have criminal jurisdiction over non-Indians absent affirmative delegation of such power by Congress. Indian tribes do retain elements of quasi-sovereign authority after ceding their lands to the United States and announcing their dependence on the Federal Government.

Indian reservations are a part of the territory of the United States. Indian tribes hold and occupy the reservations with the assent of the United States, and under their authority. Upon incorporation into the territory of the Unites States, the Indian tribes thereby come under the territorial sovereignty of the United States and their exercise of separate power is constrained so as not to conflict with the interest of this overriding sovereignty. Their rights of complete sovereignty, as independent nations, are necessarily diminished.

From the formation of the Union and the adoption of the Bill of Rights, the United States has manifested an equally great solicitude that its citizens be protected by the United States from unwarranted intrusions on their personal liberty. The power of the United States to try and criminally punish is an important manifestation of the power to restrict personal liberty. By submitting to the over-riding sovereignty of the United States, Indian tribes therefore necessarily give up their power to try non-Indian citizens of the United States, except in a manner acceptable to Congress.

Finally, we are not aware of the prevalence of non-Indian crime on today's reservations which the tribes forcefully argue requires the ability to try non-Indians. But these are considerations for Congress to weigh in deciding whether Indian tribes should finally be authorized to try non-Indians. They have little relevance to the principles which lead us to conclude that Indian tribes do not have inherent jurisdiction to try and punish non-Indians.

REFERENCES

Arny, William F. M. Annual Report to the Commissioner of Indian Affairs. Washington: Bureau of Indian Affairs, 1872: 302.

Cohen, Felix. Handbook of Federal Indian Law. Washington: U. S. Government Printing Office, 1977.

Crow Dog. Ex Parte Crow Dog, 109 U. S. 556, 1883: 571.

Krulitz, Leo M. "News Release," Solicitor of the Department of Interior (April, 12, 1978):1.

Lightfoot, Thomas. Annual Report to the Commissioner of Indian Affairs. Washington: Bureau of Indian Affairs, 1869: 356.

Marshall, John. Cherokee Nation v. Georgia, 30 U. S. 1, 1831.

Parker, Ely S. Annual Report to the Commissioner of Indian Affairs. Washington: Bureau of Indian Affairs, 1869: 6.

Priest, Loring Benson. Uncle Sam's Step Children. New Brunswick: Rutgers University Press, 1942: 139.

Prucha, Francis P. Documents of United States Indian Policy. Lincoln: University of Nebraska Press, 1975: 162.

Williams. Williams v. U. S., 327 U. S. 711, 1946: 714.

Worchester, Donald. Forked Tongue & Broken Treaties. Caldwell, Idaho: Caxton Printers, 1975.

Chapter 8
Anomie and Violence among Native Americans

LAURENCE FRENCH

Much has been written on both minority violence and majority/minority relations yet seldom are the two combined into a comprehensive theoretical framework. This omission often tends to confuse the issue with many research articles contributing to existing negative, stereotypical portrayals of minorities. Consequently, America's unique minorities, notably blacks, Appalachian Mountain folks, Latinos and American Indians, are commonly viewed in terms of narrow ethnocentrism. They are seen as inherently violent people vis-a-vis the rest of the United States society. And of these groups the American Indian is alleged to be the most violent, having the highest personal-offense rate in the nation.

Moreover, Native Americans have long been depicted as being 'savages'; a people who freely engage in senseless, impulsive, and even sadistic violence. Another popular negative stereotype is that of the 'drunken Indian', an impression that no Indian can handle alcohol. Anyone closely associated with Indian groups realizes that these stereotypes have had a tremendous negative impact on Indian/white relations and even affects how some Native Americans have come to perceive themselves. In essence, these images contribute to a self-fulfilling prophecy whereby majority/minority relations come to facilitate these stereotypes. Hence, majority Indian policy and programs often end up exacerbating the 'Indian problem' instead of resolving or controlling it, as specified by the mandates, as such policies and programs.

A further fallacy is to generalize to an 'Indian type.' Officially the United States majority society recognized some 800,000 Native Americans while the actual figure perhaps exceeds 1,000,000. Indeed, there are 467 recognized Indian tribes and bands in this country with populations ranging from less than 100 to more than 100,000 (Navajo) natives, and speaking some

200 different tribal dialects and languages. Even phenotypes differ from group to group and from region to region. Social, physical, and linguistic differences aside, North America's indigenous people possess a similar psychocultural orientation, at least in their traditional, aboriginal heritage. It is a cultural philosophy tailored to the cooperative life style of these aboriginal societies, one where interpersonal and environmental harmony were important survival norms. Violence during aboriginal times, for all intents and purposes, was directed toward other tribes and bands who were considered to exist outside the realm of the particular tribe's world-orientation. This is why so many Indian tribal names translate to mean the 'principal people.' Prior to white contact, the 'harmony ethic' seemed sufficiently strong enough to maintain not only an Indian /nature balance but an intertribal balance as well. Massive social and personal disorganization and disruption were a direct consequence of white contact and conflict.

Perspectives on Minority Conflict

In the search for 'natural laws' governing social behavior Durkheim (1968), Tonnies (1957), and Sorokin (1928) built upon the St. Simon/Comte 'social evolution paradigm' ordering societies into two basic categories: folk and urban/technological. Durkheim labelled traditional societies as 'mechanical' and urban /technological ones as 'organic,' while Tonnies used the terms 'gemeinschaft' (folk) and gessellschaft' (urban/techological), and Sorokin posited his 'sensate' (folk) and 'ideational' (urban /technological) classification. These works, in turn, provided the basis for the race/relation considerations that emerged out of the 'Chicago School' during the first half of this century. Paramount among these theorists was Robert E. Park who studies in Europe and was greatly influenced by the work of Simmel. Park's 'race/relation cycle' gained further credence due to his varied field experience as both a newspaper reporter and as secretary to Booker T. Washington, the noted black educator.

Park developed a race/relations cycle which addressed itself to western colonialism where the competitive-oriented, colonializing forces represented the majority society, while the 'underdeveloped' cooperative-oriented, traditional cultures were assigned a minority status. Within this perspective, Park recognized that majority/minority relations are relevant to power and authority and do not necessarily reflect population characteristics per se. That is, the minority group may in fact be superior in numbers to the majority control group within that particular social environment.

Basically, Park contended that interracial adjustments resulting from colonialism usually progressed through four stages starting with initial 'contact,' followed by 'competition/conflict,' 'accommodation,' and eventual 'assimilation.' History tells us that many of these situations never progressed beyond the accommodative stage and relatively few colonial majority/minority encounters resulted in widespread assimilation. Even seemingly widely assimilated societies whose diverse populations were forged during colonial efforts (Hawaii, Cuba, Brazil...) are, in fact, quite factional along class, race, religious and subcultural lines.

Simmel (1955) and a student of his works, Lewis Coser (1956), elucidated the functions of social conflict. Much of this work not only seems applicable to majority/minority relations, but lends itself to the issues of cultural diversity and cultural conflict as well. Objective, or calculated, conflict, what Simmel termed 'realistic conflict,' is aggression directed toward tangible social objectives such as status, power, and resources. 'Non-realistic (subjective) conflict,' on the other hand, stems from social frustrations. In the former situation, conflict is seen as being a rational process directed toward the accomplishment of specific goals, while in the latter, aggression becomes an end in itself. Students of majority/minority relations would generally agree that realistic conflict is widely used either by the majority power elite or by those converting this power and authority (revolutionaries), while non-realistic conflict is most likely to affect the alienated marginals caught up in the transitional void generated by the majority/minority cultural gap.

Interestingly, these scholars claim that reciprocal animosity between cultural groups within a society tends to strengthen both groups' internal cohesion while at the same time maintaining the rigid class and/or caste lines and social distances (boundary maintenance) between these groups, hence creating a self-fulfilling prophecy which perpetuates and fuels itself. The basic proposition here is that out-group hostilities increase in-group cohesion. However, a corallary to this theorem is that the more rigid these in-group/out-group divisions within the society, the more serious will be the psycho-cultural ramifications experiences by those caught up in the majority/minority cultural gap - the alienated marginals.

Primary Conflict and American Indians

Perhaps the best way to review white (majority)/Indian (minority) relations and its relevance to 'primary conflict' is to use Park's race/relations paradigm to explain the nature of relations regarding the three critical steps in the cycle: contact/conflict, competition, and accommodation.

Contact/Conflict: The history of white/Indian contact is one of conflict going as far back as the mid-1500s with DeSoto's venture into what is now Florida, Georgia, North Carolina and Texas. And this conflict continues up to the present with grim reminders such as the occupation of Wounded Knee and Alcatraz, the invasion of the Bureau of Indian Affairs headquarters in Washington, D. C., and the presence of federal agents and troops on the Pine Ridge reservation during the turbulent 1960s and 1970s.

While these four centuries of contact and conflict were one of considerable violence on both sides, the nature of white colonial exploitation initiated most of the aggression. Much of it generated initially through deceit in the form of 'dishonorable treaties.' Indian wars and treaties started with Opechancanough's attack on the Jamestown settlement in 1622 and continued into the twentieth century with the American Indian Movement (AIM). (Costo, 1977; Deloria, 1974; Josephy, 1968).

Indeed, the history of white/Indian contact is salted with successful Indian counter-offenses waged against the white colonial powers. The Powhatan Confederacy of Algonquin Nations fought the British settlers at Jamestown and continued to battle whites in the New England area for a half century until finally outnumbered and overwhelmed by the 50,000 white settlers in the late 1600s. Similar exploits occureed in the southern colonies and in the southwest as well (Josephy, 1968).

Eventually, a pattern emerged whereby Native Americans were used as pawns in the European war of colonial attrition. French, Dutch and Spanish colonial powers often used unsuspecting Indian groups to fight their battles, all the time greatly diminishing their numbers in the process. Perhaps the French and Indian War best illustrates this phenomenon.

Here the Huron Tribe of the Four Tribe Iroquois confederacy, as well as many Algonquin tribes who sided with the French, were eventually devastated by the English-allied Five Nations Iroquois Confederation. This pattern was effective in ridding the eastern United States of most of its smaller tribes while forcing the stronger tribes into larger confederations.

General Harman's defeat in 1791 at the hands of the Shawnee-led Confederacy is indicative of the effectiveness of Native American combatants, but Indian victories were reversed eventually by the superior numbers and armament of the white forces. The Native Americans soon found that their best strategy was the hit-and-run tactics of guerrilla warfare, a method employed up until the 1924 Indian Citizenship Act and made famous by such fighters as Geronimo, Mangas, Nachez, and Chihuahua.

Slavery was yet another consequence of initial white/Indian contact. Contrary to popular belief, Indian slavery played an important role both in colonial trade and in the extermination of most of the southeastern tribes, and reduced dozens of tribes to five durable ones termed as the 'Civilized Tribes.' Indian slavery as a deliberate process of exploitation was used mostly by the British. It was a mechanism for generating inter-tribal hostilities and for upsetting other European competitors, notably the French and Spanish. Nash (1974) noted that Indian slavery was crucial to the development of Charleston, South Carolina, and that this slave trade involved all the colonies, Moreover, the Indian slave trade included all the horrors long associated with the worse image of slavery - beatings, killings, separation of families, and the like.

Indian slaves soon became a viable part of the trade scene along with deer skins and furs. This economic incentive proved highly successful in that intertribal hostilities in the South increased considerably. Certain tribes were more aggressive than others in the pursuit of Indian slaves for the British. But the effects of this process were felt, and both the Indian slave trade and the Indian population decreased proportionately; so that by 1780, the vast majority of the tribes within the English settlement were either extinct or had retreated westward into other Indian territory. Thus, nearly a century of Indian slave trade transpired before the Europeans realized that blacks were better suited for this role than were Indians (Perdue, 1979; Lauber, 1970).

A third type of contact/conflict situation involved genocide, the outrigth slaughter of the aboriginal population. Again there exists a long history of Indian genocide at the hands of whites, as Josephy illustrated using DeSoto's expedition as an example: "Lured in an errant fashion by constant rumors of great riches just ahead, the expedition members wandered for three years through the southeast, meeting Creeks, Cherokees, Chickasaws, Mobiles, and numberous other Indian groups, and leaving behind them a crimson trial of cruelty and pillage (Josephy, 1968 :295)."

Genocide was often accompanied with cruel tricks and deceit such as disease infested 'peace offerings' and the destruction of peaceful hunting camps that included the killing of the elderly, women, and children. These 'massacres' soon became commonplace involving both white and Indian combatants and both white and Indian victims. However, the superior numbers of the whites obviated any real threat to their survival. On the other hand, the massacres posed serious threats to Native American victims especially when entire villages, bands, and even tribes were destroyed through this genocidal tactic.

Competition/Conflict: Fraudulent treaties, Removal and Allotment were three powerful devices used to assure whites the upper hand in their competition with Indians over land, water, minerals and other valuable resources. The treaties speak for themselves as they have had such an impact that they are still being contested in federal courts today. Indeed, the current furor over broken treaties has resulted in two contravening movements. First, the Native American Rights Fund (NARF) was founded in order to aid Indian claimants to better present their cases before the white courts. This was followed shortly by white legislative attempts to neutralize the situation by nullifying all Indian treaties (see U. S. Congressional Bill 9951).

Forced Removal and General Allotment, in comparison, represent official white policy toward Native Americans prior to their being officially recognized as United States citizens. Removal was first articulated in our country's infancy with the 1802 Georgia Compact and the 1803 Louisiana Purchase. Yet it was not until a quarter century later, under a Jacksonian presidency, that these harsh policies were forged and implemented. Georgians wanted the Indians out of their state and to insure these ends traded their western territory (now Alabama and Mississippi) to the federal government in return for assurances that the U. S. would rid the state of its unwanted Indian population. The Louisiana Purchase provided a convenient dumping ground for these displaced southeastern Indians. However, during the quarter century between the Georgia Compact and Louisiana Purchase and Jackson's assuming the Presidency, the Five Civilized Tribes (Cherokee, Choctaw, Creek, Chickasaw, and Seminole), those not destroyed by slavery during the colonial era, adopted many attributes of their white neighbors and developed contemporary type societies (French, 1978).

By 1835, the work of Presidents Jefferson and Jackson was sealed with the infamous 'Removal Treaty' which forced these tribes west of the Mississippi River into the newly created 'Indian Territory.' Oklahoma, a special part of the Louisiana Purchase, was set aside for displaced Indians. As white migration pushed west, more tribes were forced off their ancestral land and sent to Indian Territory. Many of these were Plains Indians (Sheehan, 1973).

Allotment (Dawes Act of 1887) was the next significant federal policy designed to produce cultural genocide. Once removed to Indian Territory with the promise of a perpetual home-land, the Indians discovered yet another lie and, following the Civil War, the western half of this special territory was opened up to white settlers. This land now became known as the 'Oklahoma Territory' and white settlers began crowding out the Cheyenne, Arapaho, Commanche, and Kiowa Indians - Indians earlier forcefully resettled there. Subsequently, some seventy years following the initial 'Removal Treaty (1835), the Dawes (1887) and Curtis (1898) Acts spelled the end of Indian Territory, and with it autonomous tribalism. Like Removal, Allotment affected a large proportion of the Indian population and was not restricted merely to what later became the state of Oklahoma (Washburn, 1975).

Not only was communal ownership or tribal lands outlawed, Indians soon became the minority in what was once Indian Territory. Not all Native Americans were alloted land and those who were subsequently were forced off their land in white courts. In these courts an Indian's word was considered inferior to a white man's especially since Native Americans, as a group, had not yet been legally recognized as U. S. citizens. Overall, allotment was instrumental in reducing 'Indian Territory' within the United States (as it existed at the time) from the originally promised 140 million acres to a minuscule 289,920 acres. Clearly the combined Removal/Allotment policies were highly successful competitive devices for the majority society.

Accommodation/Conflict: Generally speaking, Native Americans accommodation, as Park described it in his race/relations cycle, coincided with Indian citizenhsip in 1924. Native Americans were still interned on federal reservations but their status changed in that now they were considered to be 'wards' and not 'enemy hostiles.' Moreover, the administration of these concentration camps was transferred from the U. S. Army to the Department of the Interior. For the most part these were merely administrative changes, but if anything, the Indians' new status as third class citizens entailed more intervention into their personal lives. Attempts now were made to control every aspect of their life with only token authority given to tribal leaders. Four federal policies contributed to this situation: (1) Reorganization, (2) Termination, (3) Relocation, and (4) Self-Determination.

Reorganization (Wheeler-Howard Reorganization Act of 1934) was the master plan for the current reservation system with its manifest policy of federal paternalism and adolescent accommodation. It consolidated a number of tested policies such as educational resocialization (boarding schools), internment, forced accommodation, and colonial administration, and incorporated these into a larger 'culture of poverty.' Remarkably, certain Indian groups thrived in spite of these conditions. Perhaps forced migration from their traditional homelands, a history of broken treaties, harsh attempts at destroying native languages and cultures proved to be counterproductive and initiated a strong desire among American Indians to preserve their respective cultures even in the face of adversary and cultural genocide (Boyce, 1970).

Nonetheless, the reservation system contributed to the creation of numerous social problems among Native Americans, the most significant being the creation of 'marginal Indians.' Here alcohol came to symbolize the magnitude of the problem. While the General Indian Intercourse Act of 1832 prohibited the sale of alcohol to Native Americans, this is only part of the story. More significantly, American Indians were denied the opportunity to adapt culturally to this phenomenon; and even after repeal in 1953, most reservation and urban Indian populations still do not have a culturally-relative perspective on alcohol. This is yet another example of how forced accommodation through federal paternalism generated cultural and psychological marginality for many Native Americans.

Reorganization allowed for the systematic federal colonalization of Native Americans by placing them under strict accommodative regulation and forcing them into the lowest social class in America, a position which placed them into a separate 'third class' status (Lumpenproletariate). Federal paternalism and its policy of adolescent accommodation, or conditional dependency, created a self-fulfilling prophecy thereby forcing Indian wards into an ambiguous social-cultural environment where they were seldom allowed to become autonomous individuals or responsible adults.

Clearly, the most significant product of federal paternalism was Indian marginality which, in turn, was the single most critical factor contributing to Indian social and health problems and Indian violence. Consequently, while captives of federal reservations, Indian wards were reminded constantly of the inferiority of being Indian, while at the same time being denied the opportunity to become fulfledged members of the larger society. Unlike most other groups, assimilation has not been made available to Native Americans.

Termination emerged in the early 1950s as an attempt to rid the federal government of its Indian wards. The classic example involved Wisconsin's Menominee Indians who were unfortunate enough to be one of the target groups used to test the effectiveness of this policy. The problem with termination was that it was rooted in the Protestant Ethic and not based on the Native American Harmony Ethic. It was absurd to assume that the transition from the chaotic reservation system to one based upon the white white business model would be smooth. Even if American Indians were enculturated along lines similar to those of the dominant white society, the Termination model was a near-failure from the start since it was designed to put Native Americans at a considerable disadvantage in the highly competitive corporate world. Not only were Indian groups treated, and taxed, as corporations, the federal government severed most economic ties with their ill-prepared wards; hence they failed to provide the numerous financial advantages given to most white-run businesses. This fact alone has raised serious questions concerning the ulterior motives of Termination.

Termination was followed by Relocation, a plan specifically designed to rid the reservation of the younger Indians leaving only the dying and last elderly generation, who once deceased, would bring an end to the United States reservation system. This program encouraged Native Americans, especially young adults, to leave the reservation and tribal environment for that of urban settings where educational and job prospects were supposedly better. Relocation first surfaced in the mid-1950s as the Indian Vocational Training Act (1956) and continues today under the Direct Employment and Adult Vocational Training Program. This program was no more successful than any of the others. Instead, perhaps more than any other, Relocation is most responsible for our large, urban Indian ghettoes. Here Native Americans found that once again a federally sponsored Indian program had led to false hopes - this time by replacing rural poverty with that of urban poverty and despair.

The most recent and current federally sponsored Indian program is that of 'Indian Self-Determination' - a policy developed in 1975. On the surface this program seemed designed to improve Native American programs by placing them in the larger competitive U. S. pool where local, state, and regional agencies vie for federal subsidies through funding grants. Knowledgeable tribal leaders, however, have fears that this is actually yet another attempt to eliminate federal support for Indian programs.

Secondary Conflict and the American Indian

Clearly, Indian marginality is the major cause of Indian violence today, and most Indian marginality is a direct result of cultural ambiguity - the process of being torn between two contravening cultural expectations without the possibility of fully belonging to either. Marginal Indians often resort to alcohol as a means of escapism and retreatism and, by the same token, are more prone toward personal violence. The problem is not merely a choice between the traditional harmony ethos and the majority Protestant ethic, since neither of these present viable solutions to the contemporary Indian situation. What must be remembered is that the Bureau of Indian Affairs (BIA) has operated in such a fashion as to perpetuate an accommodative, dependent system; but when young Indians learn of their rich, yet unobtainable, past heritage and the role the majority society played in white/Indian relations, they often experience an inner-rage and a personal ambivalence that forces them to withdraw further from the majority society or to join an anti-establishment (rebellion) or anti-tribal movement (AIM phenomenon).

During the time he is formulating his self-identity and planning for adulthood, the marginal Indian fully realized that he has not been adequately prepared for any viable social position in either his traditional culture or in the majority society. In essence, the marginal Indian is ascribed the social status of 'perpetual adolescence' with his behavior reinforced by the majority society through its policy of paternalistic dependency (rewards) and severe punitive sanctions (harsh prison terms). This process is similar to that described by Lemert (1951) in his 'secondary deviance' concept. He suggested that societal control mechanisms often operate in such a fashion that they create the same problems they are supposed to control and that they accomplish this end by overreacting to what they consider to be the cause of this unacceptable behavior (primary deviance), but what, in essence, is usually merely a symptom of a larger problem.

Clearly, 'secondary conflict' is basically a consequence of structural factors (primary conflict) contributing, in turn, to Indian marginality (adolescent accommodation and cultural ambiguity). The reservation and urban Indian ghetto environments are not healthy ones as the high incidents of violence-related deaths attest. Not only do Indians have the highest violence crime rate of any racial group in the United States, suicide, including child suicide, is also common to this group. Gone are the traditional ways, along with their prescriptive forms of tension-management (wars, hunts, cultural rituals, competitive games, etc.) forcing most contemporary Native Americans to be victims of their own aggression, whether it be in the form of retreatism (alcoholsim, mental and physical illness, suicides...) or rebellion (murder, assaults, alcohol-related accidents...).

No simple solutions seem evident since it is no easy task to change the societal values of either the majority or the minority cultures. The main point of this selection is the uselessness of blaming the Indians for their social plight. Any viable solutions to Indian violence will have to address itself to both the primary and secondary sources of cultural and personal conflict, but such programs must be culturally-relevant to the particular Indian group under consideration.

REFERENCES

Boyce, George. When the Navajos had too Many Sheep. San Francisco: Indian Historian Press, 1970.

Costo, Rupert, and Jeannette Henry. Indian Treaties. San Francisco: Indian Historian Press, 1977.

Coser, Lewis. The Functions of Social Conflict. New York: Free Press, 1956.

Deloria, Jr., Vine. Behind the Trail of Broken Treaties. New York: Delta, 1974.

Durkheim, Emile. The Rules of Sociological Methods. Glencoe, Ill.: Free Press, 1968.

French, Laurence. "Death of a Nation," American Indian Journal 4 (June, 1978): 2-9.

Josephy, Jr., Alvin. The Indian Heritage of America. New York: Alfred A. Knopf, 1968.

Lauber, Almon. Indian Slavery in Colonial Times. Williamstown, Mass.: Corner House, 1970.

Lemert, Edwin. Social Pathology. New York: McGraw Hill, 1951.

Nash, Gary. Red, White and Black. Englewood Cliffs, N. J.: Prentice Hall, 1974.

Park, Robert E. Race and Culture. New York: Free Press, 1950.

Perdue, Theda. Slavery and the Evolution of Cherokee Society: 1540-1866. Knoxville: University of Tennessee Press, 1979.

Sheehan, Bernard. Seeds of Extinction. New York: W. W. Norton, 1973.

Simmel, Georg. Conflict (K. Wolff, Ed.). New York: Free Press, 1955.

Sorokin, Pitirim. Contemporary Social Theories. New York: Harper & Row, 1928.

Tonnies, Ferdinand. Community and Society. East Lansing: Michigan State University Press, 1957.

Washburn, Wilcomb. An Assault on Indian Tribalism. Philadelphia: J. B. Lippincott, 1975.

Chapter 9

Indian Violence: The Cherokee Example

LAURENCE FRENCH and JIM HORNBUCKLE

American Indians have long been an enigma in America baffling white leaders with their endurance to survive in spite of centuries of attempted cultural genocide. Certainly, they seem to be one of the ethnic groups most resilient to acculturation and assimilation. This plus their aboriginal status makes them one of the most unique ethnic groups in America. Paradoxically, ethnic survival and dire social problems seem to go hand in hand. Poverty, alcoholism, health problems, suicides and homicides are social factors closely associated with Native Americans. Reasons (1972) found that the American Indian has the highest crime rate of any racial group in the United States. He suggests that this is due to 'cultural frustration' stating that: "while economic factors are important, anomie and cultural conflict theories provide a more substantive basis of understanding (Reasons, 1972: 325)." Yet this is only half the answer. In order to truly understand the reasons for seemingly excessive violence we must also look at the informal subcultural control structure of the particular Indian group under investigation.

In essence, a wide gulf exists between the Cherokees' traditional gemeinschaft-oriented culture and that of the geselschaft-oriented dominant white society (Tonnies, 1957). Ostensibly, the 'collective will' associated with the aboriginal culture no longer suffices as a viable control mechanism, although certain aspects have survived and provides some subcultural control mechanisms. Nonetheless, contemporary Cherokee culture seems to illustrate what Durkheim (1950) suggested when he talked of the transition from mechanical to organic solidarity, the former reflecting gemeinschaft of 'folk' cultures and the later depicting geselschaft or urban/technological societies. This transitional period should be accompanied with normlessness or anomie, he suggested, a situation brought about by the disintegration of traditional goals, values and folkways. Reservation systems, however, are unique social microcosms in that there is little effort to assimilate Native Americans into the larger dominant society. Some even suggest that Indian reservations maintain a control mechanism analogous to colonial accommodation whereby those colonized are deliberately kept in a perpetual state of marginality being denied both the full benefit of their own traditional heritage and full membership into the larger majority society. In this sense one could strongly argue that many of the problems facing reservation Indians are social/structural in nature and not due to inferior biological, psychological, or moral factors as has been suggested so often in the past.

Wolfgang and Feracuti (1967) drew condiserable attention to the idea of latent, informal control apparatus operating in subcultures where the dominant formal control apparatus provides little service to these people. Although they used the urban, impoverished, ethnic community to illustrate their thesis, a similar argument holds true for rural, isolated ethnic subcultures. Moreover, most American Indian groups have a rich traditional aboriginal cultural heritage, some of which has survived to the present, providing them with an established frame of reference regarding latent subcultural controls.

This selection addresses itself to the nature of violence among one of the unique Native American groups - the Eastern Cherokees. Here, violence is viewed within the combined 'cultural frustration/subcultural control' perspectives linking past cultural traditions with the contemporary social situation. We propose that most violence among Eastern Cherokees indeed involes both cultural frustration and latent subcultural control mechanisms which when combined generates a highly charged atmosphere conducive to spontaneous violence.

Indian reservations differ from other ethnic subcultures due to the subordinate status of its members. Clearly, federal paternalism is an important factor in their cultural frustration. Federal paternalism is a mode of forced accommodation wherey the superiority of the dominant social order is imposed through a rigid legal mechanism of control. Indian reservations are under the direction of the Secretary of the Interior. The Department of Interior, through its Bureau of Indian Affairs, has an agency located at each federal reservation. The Indian Agency, in turn, regulated tribal government, education and health services while other federal agencies, Health and Human Services (formerly HEW) and the Justice (Federal District Court and the Federal Bureau of Investigation) and Education Departments control other aspects of reservation life.

A consequence of this rigid control system is the emergence of an adolescence/accommodation situation where reservation Indians come to be viewed by the dominant control apparatus as being dependent children regardless of their actual physical age or tribal status. Hence, a self-fulfilling prophecy occurs where the mechanisms of social control generates a restrictive social environment highly conducive to psychological ambivalence and cultural marginality. By the same token, a semblance of the 'old ways,' that is, the traditional folk society, still survives within reservation subcultures and provides Indian members with varying degrees of 'Indianism.' This refers to the degree of ehtnic identity internalized by tribal members. An 'Indianism continuum' would have 'real Indians' at one end and 'white Indians' at the other. The inference here is that 'being Indian' refers to a state of mind. Nonetheless, physical characteristics do play a role here as well. Historically, mix-bloods were selected for preferential treatment by the white-dominated Indian agency and this practice apparently continued to date. A general rule of thumb for selecting tribal leaders was, "the whiter-the-better." Yet not all 'white Indians' are white looking as the vulgar terms 'Uncle Tomahawk' and 'Apple' attest. Like black 'Uncle Toms' these two terms are used to depict members of the racial group who are controlled by white interest groups. They are thought of as being Indian on the outside and white on the inside.

Although two distinctive role models are available on Indian reservations, those of the 'real' or traditional Indians and the 'white', or middle-class Indians, each comprised of only a small proportion of most Indian populations. Instead the majority of Native Americans today, living on or off the reservation, can be classified as being 'marginal Indians.' These people are torn between two worlds, the Indian and the white, with little chance of being fully accepted in either. By the time most American Indians reach adolescence and are seriously involved in their identity search, they find they are culturally deprived and denied many of the important attributes of both the Indian and white worlds. Again this is because reservation socialization is designed to 'regulate' and not to either retain the traditional Indian culture or assimilate the Indians into the larger dominant society. Thus the marginal Indian finds himself/herself with a foot in each world with little hope of succeeding in either. Some leave the reservation, usually migrating to urban Indian ghettoes, only to find themselves in a similar hopeless situation.

In the past, the traditionalists lived apart from both the middle-class and marginal Indians but more recently, with the American Indian Movement and other attempts to rekindle Indian pride, they have been the ones emulated most. Pan-Indianism, the movement toward developing a universal Indian ethnic image, is evident on most reservations and urban Indian ghettoes as well.

While many feel that 'Indian awareness, is the answer to the problem of cultural marginality quite the opposite may be true, especially during the transitional era which may involve a generation or more of Indians interested in recapturing their past heritage. Adolescent and adult marginal Indians seeking to reestablish their past heritage may instead encounter more bitterness and frustration when confronted with the actual extent of their cultural deprivation. It is no easy matter trying to re-socialize persons already molded in the adolescence/accommodative perspective. For one thing, it may be a near impossible task to transcend the reservation socialization process; consequently the current shift toward 'being Indian' may be more frustrating than trying to pass as white was for earlier generations of marginal Indians. At any rate, marginality seems to be a direct result of Indian dependency fostered by the government's policy of federal paternalism. This combination of effects coupled with the informal subcultural control process existing on most Indian reservations can produce an emotionally ladened atmosphere conducive to excessive frustration for some marginal individuals. This high tension situation would obviously create a similar problem for its marginal populations regardless of ethnic affiliation.

The Eastern Band of Cherokee Indians represents one of the most traditional elements of the old Cherokee Nation which once encompassed parts of six Southern states: Virginia, North and South Carolina, Tennessee, Georgia and Alabama. They were isolated by the Appalachian mountains and this made them less susceptible to outside influences. Thus when the other Cherokee villages were actively engaged in the development of the new Cherokee Nation during the late 1700s and early 1800s, the Appalachian Cherokees were opposed to these new changes (Reid, 1970). Subsequently when the Cherokees were forced off of their land in 1838, it was the Appalachian Cherokees who were spared the humiliation of 'Forced Removal' to Indian Territory west of the Mississippi River (Oklahoma). The 8,000 enrolled members today are, for the most part, descendants of the 1,000 or so Appalachian Cherokees who selected to remain behind. They came under federal reservation status in 1925 after much of their land was swindled by white speculators (Mooney, 1972). One of the most infamous persons to reap a fortune at the expense of the Eastern Cherokees was Wil Thomas, an individual so shrewd that he was made an adopted son of the tribal chief - Yonagusta (Bauer, 1968).

Currently some 6,000 Eastern Cherokees live on the 56,700 acre reservation while another 2,000 live adjacent to the 'Qualla Boundary,' as it is commonly called. At first glance, this many seem like sufficient acreage for a population this size, but it must be realized that most of this is rugged mountainous terrain of which only ten percent is suitable for agricultural purposes. Furthermore with the advent of the development of the Great Smoky National Park and tourism in Southern Appalachia, most of this farm land has since been utilized for the tourist industry (Tribal Report, 1976). Hence, the situation today is a highly charged one with the interests of tourism, supported by white dominated federal, state and local leaders in conjunction with the small Cherokee middle-class elite on the one hand, and the interests of the traditional full-bloods who want to preserve the old ways including many aspects of this aboriginal culture and the Cherokee language on the other. Caught in between are the majority of the Eastern Cherokees, many phenotypically Indian, who are exposed to both interest groups.

What makes matters worse is the fact that these interest models are diametrically opposed to each other. The Eastern Band, like all Indian reservations, is subjected to numerous federal, state, and local control agencies, all of which subscribe to the Protestant ethic. This social model placed considerable emphasis on individual achievement and responsibility. It is existential in nature. The traditional Cherokee society, in comparison, is a folk culture with its own 'harmony ethic' (Thomas, 1958). Many attributes of the harmony ethic have survived from aboriginal times and are evident among the more traditional full-bloods residing on the Eastern Band reservation. Avoidance and mutual obligation are the main tenets of the harmony ethic. Cherokees subscribing to this folk ethic go out of their way to avoid giving offense to other people. Hence, obligatory hospitality, public impassivity, the refusal or unwillingness to contradict, a reluctance to assume authority and a strong sense of individual autonomy regarding personal behavior best illustrated those Cherokees socialized within the harmony ethic (Kupferer, 1960). Obviously, it is phenomenological in nature.

For these Cherokee partly socialized in either the Protestant ethic or the harmony ethic, or both, cultural marginality and psychological ambivalence are the result. And this is precisely what the reservation policy of federal paternalism mandates - a manageable group of dependent wards. The Bureau of Indian Affairs' Social Service Agency at the Qualla Boundary reports the current situation as such:

> The problems encountered when an Indian attempts to move from extreme poverty and an agrarian way of life to a money economy are awesome. Added to this transition, the Cherokee feels keenly the on-slaught of the dominant Anglo-culture compounded by over eight million pleasure seeking tourists each year who invade his reservation and gawk at him (her) as the Native American. The astute Cherokee obliges for economic reasons and with tongue in cheek he dresses in feathers, dances, sells Indian-made artifacts (or Japanese-made Indian artifacts), prepares food, serves food, and generally entertains the visitors. It is, however, an affront to his way of life and although his economic situation is greatly improved, this rapid change in economy and culture has not been attained without a price - one of which is excessive use of alcohol and the resulting problems of broken families, children living away from their natural parents, crime and delinquency, etc. (Thomasson, 1975: 29).

Ms. Thomasson's statement sums up the Indian Agency's perception of the problems plaguing the Eastern Cherokees. Yet it is this same agency which encourages tourism and the resulting exploitation of the Cherokee. Granted they are the most visited Native American group in the United States today with over 8,000, 000 vistors each tourist season (April to October), but most of the profit goes to white businessmen who lease tribal land for their tourist enterprises. Only a small elite of middle-class Cherokee profit from the tourist industry. In fact, it is estimated that nearly 80 percent of the Indian families live below the poverty level. Our analysis of Indian violence focuses on this particular social environment.

In the past the most striking facet of the Cherokee culture was the suppression of any expression of overt hostility in interpersonal relations. Other aspects of this informal control process (harmony ethic) included a high value placed on independence, a resentment of authority, as well as a complementary hesitancy to command others and a reluctance to refuse requests made by relative and other Cherokee. These conditions alone would seem to be quite oppressive and frustrating. As it was, certain escape mechanisms were built into the aboriginal Cherokee culture. When a tribal member sought to affect the behavior of a peer, a 'neutral third agent' was selected as the intermediary who in turn would convey this message to the offending party. The third party technique also provided a vehicle for avoiding direct responsibility for offensive acts. A contemporary example is that alcohol is often credited as the cause of offensive behavior on the part of traditional Cherokee.

While overt aggression was not approved during the aboriginal culture, it was not forbidden altogether, but rather was directed toward acceptable avenues of experssion. The Cherokee year was divided into two seasons, summer and winter, each with its own approved form of aggressive behavior. Wars were initiated during the winter while stickball games dominated the summer season. This was a functional pattern since the early Cherokee economy was based on agriculture. They lived in permanent villages where everbody participated in the communal farm endeavor. This involved serious, arduous work which relied on a total cooperative commitment by all families. Perhaps this is the primary reason for their insistence on cooperation and avoidance of internal altercations. The cooperative farm, known as the 'Gadugi,' demanded the participation of all able-bodied adults postponing war parties until the winter season. Both activities, wars, and stickball, were highly ritualistic and aggressive providing adequate tension release for both males and females. And this system apparently fared well since the early Cherokee saw no need to maintain external control agencies such as legislative bodies, law enforcement officers, courts or correctional facilities.

All this was drastically altered with the advent of the Cherokee Nation, an experiment with the white man's way. Although the Cherokee Nation equalled that of the United States system, it was not allowed to exist and the Cherokee were forcefully removed by the United States Army to Indian Territory in 1838. Next came the reservation system with its policy of federal paternalism leading to adolescence/accommodation. Now the Cherokee, like other Native Americans, had to contend with both their native informal, folk cultural system and the formal enforced control apparatus of the reservation system. An excellent example of the latter being the General Indian Intercourse Act of 1832 outlawing the sale, possession or consumption of alcohol by Indians on federal reservations, which during its 121 years of enforcement probably contributed most to alcohol related social problems among Native Americans (Bahr, 1972).

It should be further stated that alcohol is a major problem facing all Native American groups and accounts for the vast majority of Indian health and social problems. Alcohol contributes to most Indian deaths with cirrhosis of the liver, sucicide and homicide being the three leading causes of death among members of this group (Frederick, 1973). Moreover, alcohol is involved in a high proportion of all assaultive and motor vehicle offenses as well. For the Cherokee and others within the Iroquoian linquistic group alcohol has come to represent a 'symptom' of their problems. Here alcohol is assigned the status of neutral third party allowing the alcohol victim to claim that it is not his/her fault but rather that of the alcohol. When viewing the general Iroquorian harmony ethic we find that this is a viable defense mechanism or excuse, however, this control technique fails to adequately operate once these problems reach the magnitude and proportion they have today. The problem then seems to be one of a lack of legitimate tension-release mechanism for the increasing proportion of marginal Indians. Looked at from a different perspective, it could also be said that the high stress factor associated with the reservation environment is also a major contributing factor.

Either of the factors discussed above, whether it be the deterioration of the traditional mechanisms of aggression release or the imposition of oppressive formal controls, would suffice in itself in generating a high tension social environment conducive to psychological ambivalence and cultural marginality. Imagine what happens when both disruptive factors operate simultaneously? Frustration is compounded, stemming from two unrelated sources, neither offering any legitimate avenues of expression. What results is sporadic eruptions of violence directed toward a convenient target of aggression - another Cherokee. Support of this contention is evident in the Tribal Health Report (1975) which indicated that the two most frequently reported health problems were laceration wounds with 1,067 cases in 1973 alone, and 2,645 other acts of violence reported for the same period. Moreover, nearly 1,500 mental disorders were also reported and these incidents are only those which are formally brought to the attention of the hospital staff. Most incidents are probably handled by 'medicine men' who still operate much as their anchestors did, and quite successfully too. These figures serve to illustrate the dynamics of the contravening controls and sanctions imposed upon the Qualla Cherokee. They seem caught between two systems, the modified aboriginal cultural heritage which seems to fulfill many of the needs of the small core of Cherokee-speaking traditionalists but is not available to the English-speaking marginals, and the dominant white society which fulfills most of the needs of the reservation staff, both whites and Indians, which again seems to exclude the marginal Indians. Consequently, they are being forced into this perpetual transitional state of marginality and the corresponding high tension accompanying this phenomenon.

A Profile of Violence on the Qualla Boundary

Case No. 1

Miss Q.
Crime: 1st Degree Murder
Age: late 20s
Race: Indian
Occupation: unemployed

Victim: Miss C.
Race: Indian
Relation to Offender: None

Probable Cause: Miss Q. confessed that when she found Miss C. with Mr. J. (Miss Q.'s boyfriend) she stabbed her twice in the chest with a switchblade.

Additional Information: Miss C.'s body was found near a graveyard.

Sentence: 6 years

Case No. 2

Mr. S.
Crime: 2nd Degree Murder
Age: early 30s
Race: Indian
Occupation: rock mason

Victim: Mr. U.
Race: Caucasian
Relation to Offender: None, neighbors

Probable Cause: Victim made comments about Mr. S. being

Indian. Mr. S. asked victim to leave his home; victim refused.

Additional Information: Three shots were fired, 1st through screen door, 2nd through floor, 3rd in victim's stomach. Victim bled to death. Mr. S. called the police and left with the gun - later turned himself in. Alcohol was involved.

Sentence: 6 months night time sentence.

<u>Case No. 3</u>

Mr. D.
  Crime: Voluntary Manslaughter
  Age: 20
  Race: Indian
  Occupation: unemployed

Victim: Mr. X
  Race: Indian
  Relation to Offender: None

Probable Cause: Mr. D. and friends were trying to pick up some girls. Victim drove up and began talking to the same girls. Victim made the comment that Mr. D's haircut looked as though he had been scalped. Mr. D. pulled out a knife and in a scuffle, victim fell on Mr. D.

Additional Information: Mr. X was cut across trachia and bled to death.

Sentence: 4 years.

<u>Case No. 4</u>

Mr. L.
  Crime: Voluntary Manslaughter
  Age: early 30s
  Race: Indian
  Occupation: unemployed

Victim: Mr. Y.
  Race: Indian (Seneca)
  Relation to Offender: None

Probable Cause: Seneca Indian and Cherokees were partying in a motel. Cherokee were asked to leave. They left and there was a knock at the door. Seneca Indian answered the door and was cut across the arm. Seneca Indians went out for revenge. They accused Mr. L.

(a Cherokee) of being the one who cut their friend. Seneca Indian jumped Mr. L. and was killed.

Additional Information: Mr. L. was hit with a blow that could have killed him because of an earlier injury. Alcohol was involved.

Sentence: 10 years - appealed.

Case No. 5

Mr. P.
Crime: Voluntary Manslaughter
Age: 20 years
Race: Indian
Occupation: unemployed

Victim: Mr. O.
Race: Indian
Relation to Offender: None, neighbors

Probable Cause: Mr. P. said Mr. O. lied to him.

Additional Information: Mr. P. was fishing at a pond with his father and uncle - drinking beer. Mr. P. saw Mr. O. coming up the road. Mr. P. picked a fight and Mr. O. was cut.

Sentence: Juvenile Correctional Institution - 4 years.

Case No. 6

Mr. H.
Crime: Assault with a Deadly Weapon
Age: 29
Race: Indian
Occupation: gas station operator

Victim: Mr. Z.
Race: Caucasian
Relation to Offender: None, neighbors.

Probable Cause: Mr. Z. went to Mr. H.'s trailer to tell Mr. H.'s girl frient to come home. Mr. H. got angry and started shooting in the air. Mr. Z. ran into a carwash. Mr. H. started shooting into the carwash.

Additional Information: The shots probably ricocheted off the walls of the carwash. Mr. Z. was hit in both the arm and leg.

Sentence: Probation

Case No. 7

Ms. W.
Crime: Assault on Officer
Age: 36
Race: Caucasian
Occupation: Motel operator

Victims: Mr. B. (Statepolice)
Mr. R. (Cherokee Policeman)
Race: Mr. B., caucasian
Mr. R., Indian
Relation to Offender: None

Probable Cause: Officers were arresting her boyfriend. She stated: "I'm going to kill you, you're not taking him."

Additional Information: Her boyfriend was an Indian. Ms. W. had a loaded gun but did not fire although she threaten to.

Sentence: Case pending at time of study.

Case No. 8

Mrs. I.
Crime: Murder - awaiting trial
Age: Mid 30s
Race: Indian
Occupation: unemployed

Victim: Mr. T., Mr. TT (Mr. T.'s borther) and Mr. F.
Race: Indians
Relation to Offender: None.

Probable Cause: Mrs. I. saw a car slow down in front of her house. She told her husband she thought someone was going to mess with their car and asked where the gun was. Car pulled up and stopped. Someone got out. Mrs. I shot Mr. T. twice, Mr. TT once and she beat Mr. F. with the blunt end of the gun.

Additional Information: Mrs. I. has not been drinking. Mr. TT. was killed. Mr. T. also apparently had beaten up Mrs. I.'s younger sister the day before. Mr. T was wounded and Mr. F. was assaulted. The victims had been drinking.

Sentence: Case pending at time of study.

Case No. 9

Mr. CC.
Crime: Involuntary Manslaughter
Age: 29
Occupation: Factory worker

Victim: Mr. SS.
Race: Indian
Relation to Offender: None, Drinking Buddy.

Probable Cause: Common women friends, drinking at a party.... These two men were with two women at a party. Police and community believe that the women probably killed Mr. SS and that Mr. CC took the blame for them.

Additonal Information: Victim was stabbed with a knife through the face, his eyes were slit and his back was cut and he had a fractured skull. He was also boiled in hot water in the bathtup. Victim was known as a bully.

Sentence: 18 months.

Case No. 10

Mr. E.
Crime: Involuntary Manslaughter
Age: 29
Race: Indian
Occupation: unemployed

Victim: Mr. G.
Race: Indian
Relation to Offender: Cousins

Probably Cause: Mr. E. caught Mr. G. in bed with his wife.

Additional Information: Mr. E. confessed he killed his cousin - with a knife.

Sentence: 2 years.

Case No. 11

Mr. M.
Crime: Voluntary Manslaughter
Age: 19

Race: Indian

Victim: Mr. A.
Race: Indian
Relation to Offender: None

Probable Cause: Unknown. Mr. M. beat Mr. A. with a baseball bat and a wooden board. Mr. M. was referred to a clinic for psychiatric evaluation and treatment.

Additional Information: Approximately 6 months after the incident, Mr. M. told authorities that on the night of Mr. A.'s death, he had forced him to have sexual intercourse with a third party (Mr. ZZ.) and then forced him to perform oral sex. Mr. A. then threatened Mr. M. saying he was going to cut off Mr. M's head if he did not cooperate

Sentence: 10 years.

Case No. 12

Mr. J.
Crime: Murder - awaiting trial
Age: Mid 30s
Race: Caucasian
Occupation: unemployed

Victims: Ms. K., and Ms. V.
Race: Indians
Relation to Offender: Ms. K. was Mr. J.'s girlfriend; Ms. V. was Ms. K.'s sister.

Probable Cause: Verbal altercation while drinking. Ms. K. attempted to stop Mr. J. from striking her sister. Mr. J. shot both of them.

Sentence: Case pending at time of study.

The cases paint a picture of subcultural violence, much of it victim-precipitated and most of it involving alcohol. Yet this data does not easily lend itself to secondary analysis, especially that associated with traditional criminological analysis, mainly because of the unique reservation cultural environment. To view this problem within the general United States criminal perspective would be to exercise a strong ethnocentric bias. The only viable explanation is a cultural one. Nonetheless, even five years of intensive investigation and observation does not guarantee an accurate conclusion. yet we feel that out assessment of this particular Native American group is perhaps more reliable than most.

Violence among the Qualla Cherokee is due mainly to intensive in-group tensions generated by the restrictive reservation environment. Marginal enculturation, limited social mobility, complex subcultural interaction and alcohol are all contributing factors. Most Cherokee are still unacceptable to their local white neighbors thereby limiting inter-group interaction while most of the millions of white tourist never directly interact with marginal Indians. Tourists often view Native Americans as if they were some photogenic curiosity maintaining a protective distance between themselves and their subjects. At the same time considerable social distance and enforced formality is maintained by the reservation agency thereby creating a social vacuum, for the single largest group of Cherokee - the marginal Indians. Excluded from both the traditional subculture and the elite middle-class contingency present on the reservation, the marginal Indians are forced into a stress-ridden environment, one which allows for little social or personal autonomy. Instead they are torn between these two cultures following the respective dictates of each whenever possible. But for the most part they must live in the chaotic world of their weak subculture, one based on retributive violence. There exist similarities between marginal reservation Indians and what Wolfgang and Ferracuti noticed among ghetto black communites. Here violence is a common factor resulting from the spontaneous eruption of frustration. Although alcohol lubricates these altercations it is also seen as a convenient and acceptable source of escapism.

Paradoxically, while few Native Americans have come to internalize any intrinsic moral or social significance to alcohol like the Jews, Italians, and Chinese, they have come to accept alcohol as a tension-reducing substitute which replaces the old traditional festivals, dances, wars, and stick-ball games. Consequently, when violence does occur, it often involves alcohol and is justified in terms of the old traditional blood-feud (Reid, 1970). This vendetta differs, however, from their aboriginal traditions in that it is often spontaneous and is carried out in the heat-of-passion while in aboriginal times alcohol was absent and retribution was a rational process involving all concerned parties (clans and families).

Solutions to this problem are not easy. Abstinence is not a viable response since alcohol merely reflects the symptom and not the cause of most Cherokee problems. Moreover, both the traditional and middle-class Cherokee drink as well and perhaps have as high a proportion of problem drinkers - however, their less conspicuous modes of consumptions ('bout drinking for the traditionalists and 'social drinking' for the middle-class Indians) obviates their easy detection and subsequently the negative stigma associated with Indian alcoholism. It is the public and violent nature of marginal Indian drinking that has upset so many Cherokee and whites alike. Consequently any viable solution will have to address itself to the tension-generating factors and the development of suitable avenues of legitimate tension-reducing techniques. Clearly, this study looks at only one aspect of Indian violence, an even larger proportion of Native Americans suffer from self-directed tension - a fact brought out by the magnitude of mental and physical health problems among these people. It is our suggestion that a successful tension-reducing model would greatly eliminate the prevalence of both overt and covert aggression among Native Americans.

REFERENCES

Bahr, Howard. Native Americans Today. New York: Harper and Row, 1972.

Bauer, Fred. Land of the North Carolina Cherokees. Brevard, N. C.: Buchanan Press, 1970.

Collier, Peter. When Shall They Rest. New York: Holt, Rinehart and Winston, 1973.

Coser, Lewis. The Functions of Social Conflict. New York: Free Press, 1966.

Dennis, L. American Indians. Editorial Research Report, 2, 1966.

Dollard, John, et. al. Frustration and Aggression. New Haven: Yale University Press, 1967.

Durkheim, Emile. Suicide (G. Simpson, ed.). New York: Free Press, 1967.

- The Rules of Sociological Methods (G. Catlin, ed.). New York: Free Press, 1950.

Gearing, Fred. Priests and Warriors. American Anthropological Association Monograph, 1962.

Frederick, C. Suicide, Homicide and Alcoholism Among American Indians. Washington: U. S. Government Printing Office (DHEW), 1973.

Gulick, John. Cherokees at the Crossroads. Chapel Hill: University of North Carolina Press, 1960.

Howard, R., and M. Lewis. Psychosomatics. New York: Viking Press, 1972.

Kupferer, Harriett. The Principal People. Washington: U. S. Government Printing Office, 1960.

La Farge, O. The Changing Indian. Norman: American Association on Indian Affairs Monograph, 1942.

Linton, Ralph. Acculturation in Seven American Indian Tribes. New York: Columbia University Press, 1940.

Malone, H. Cherokees of the Old South. Athens: University of Georgia Press, 1956.

Mazur, A., and L. Robertson. Biology and Social Behavior. New York: Free Press, 1972.

Merton, Robert K. Social Theory and Social Structure. New York: Free Press, 1968.

Mooney, James. Myths of the Cherokee. Nashville: Charles Elder, 1972.

Park, Robert E. Race and Culture. New York: Free Press, 1964.

Reasons, Charles. "Crime and the American Indian," Native Americans Today (H. Bahr, et. al., eds). New York: Harper and Row, 1972.

Reid, John. A Law of Blood. New York: New York University Press, 1970.

Sellin, Thorsten. Conflict and Crime. New York: Social Science Research Council Monograph, 1938.

Timberlake, Henry. Lieutenant Henry Timberlake's Memoirs, 1756 - 1765 (S. C. Williams, ed.). Marietta, Ga.: Continental Book Company, 1948.

Thomas, Robert K. "Eastern Cherokee Acculturation," Master's Thesis. Chapel Hill: University of North Carolina, 1958.

Thomasson, E. Tribal Health Report. Cherokee, N. C.: Tribal Report, 1975.

Toennies, F. Community and Society (I. C. Loomis, ed). East Lansing: Michigan State University Press, 1957.

Tibal Report: Annual Tribal Report. Cherokee, N. C.: Tribal Report, 1976.

Wallace, D., Jr. The Emergent Native American. Boston: Little, Brown and Company, 1972.

Wolff, P. "Ethnic Differences in Alcohol Sensitivity," Science, 175, 1973: 28-29.

Wolfgang, Marvin, and F. Ferracuti. The Subculture of Violence. London: Tavistock, 1967.

Chapter 10
American Indian Tribal Courts

SAMUEL J. BRAKEL

Tribal courts exist today on some 60 to 120 Indian reservations, depending on the definitions of 'courts' and 'reservations.' Most of these reservations, and the major ones in terms of area and population, are located in the northern plains and Rocky Mountain states, particularly Arizona, New Mexico, Montana, and the Dakotas. For a variety of historical reasons - some relatively recent - having to do with degree of acculturation or dispersal or simply with the smallness of the Indian tribes and bands in other parts of the country, the Indian people in these parts, even if still living on 'reservations' or otherwise designated Indian landholdings, are - with a few exceptions - subject to state court jurisdiction.

The theory behind the self-government power of the American Indian tribes, including the power to regulate their affairs through an adjudicative system, is that this power derives from an original sovereignty, which though limited through wars, treaties, constitutional language, and congressional action, has never been fully extinquished. Jurisdictional conflicts concerning this theory have occurred, and continue to exist, on two levels: federal versus tribal, and state versus tribal.

In the struggle between state and tribal power, the federal government - most frequently the federal courts, including the U. S. Supreme Court - has been cast in the role of protector of the vestiges of tribal sovereignty. Chief Justice Marshall, in two cases involving the Cherokee tribe decided in the early 1830s, became one of the earliest and primary architects of tribal sovereignty: in Cherokee Nation v. Georgia, the Court designated the Indian tribes 'domestic dependent nations,' and in Worsester v. Georgia, it held that the "laws of Georgia can have no force (in the Cherokee Nation)," thus first establishing the principle of federal protection of what was left of tribal autonomy.

The federal government, however, has not always followed

this principle with consistency and clarity. In fact, on the issue of tribal sovereignty, vacillation may be the most salient characteristic of federal policy. The Daves Act (or General Allotment Act) of 1887, which was aimed primarily at breaking up the reservation system; the Indian Reorganization Act of 1934, which reversed that policy; the announcement of the Termination Policy in 1953, and the repudiation of that policy in the late 1960s are general examples. On the specific issue of court jurisdiction, the Major Crimes Act of 1885 and the Indian Civil Rights Act of 1968 illustrate the federal policy of restricting the judicial powers of the tribe in the face of the broad language of, and philosophy behind, the Marshall cases and similar pronouncements.

The Major Crime Act was the congressional response to the problem of jurisdictional vacuum indicated in Ex Parte Crow Dog, a case in which the U. S. Supreme Court had reversed the federal district court conviction of an Indian charged with killing a fellow tribesman, on grounds that the laws of the United States did not apply to acts of Indians in Indian country. The act specified 7 major crimes that would fall within the jurisdiction of the federal courts if committed by Indians in Indian country. The list has since been extended to cover 13 crimes: murder; manslaughter; rape, carnal knowledge of any female, not his wife, who has not attained the age of 16 years; assault with intent to commit rape; incest; assault with intent to kill; assault with a dangerous weapon; assault resulting in serious bodily injury; arson; burglary; robbery and larceny. The federal statute uses the word 'exclusive' in listing the crimes that come within federal jurisdiction; arguments persist and are increasing that the tribes should retain concurrent power to handle these cases, although at present no tribe asserts this in practice. Operationally, federal jurisdiction over major crimes means an FBI presence on the reservation and sporadic litigation in federal courts usually far removed from the scene of the crime and the residences of the accuese, witnesses, and victims.

The 1968 Indian Civil Rights Act is the culmination of hearings conducted during the 1960s before the Senate Committee on the Judiciary, Subcommittee on Constitutional Rights. These hearings, which were held across the country and on location at (or near) Indian reservations as well as in Washington, focused on the constitutional rights of the American Indian and elicited considerable testimony from Indian witnesses to the effect that these rights were frequently denied by tribal courts and governments. The solution was seen to rest in the enactment of a bill of rights for Indians, modeled on the Bill or Rights of the United States Constitution. Two provisions of the act made concrete the limits to be placed upon and the principles to be followed by the tribes: (1) no tribe shall imprison a convicted offender in excess of six months or exact a fine of over $500, and (2) habeas corpus is available to any Indian who wants to test (in federal courts) the legality of his detention by a tribe.

Together, then, the Major Crimes Act and the Indian Civil Rights Act make drastic inroads on the juridical sovereignty of the tribes. Other, often self-imposed, limitations exist as well. In theory, the tribal courts are left with jurisdiction over all civil and criminal matters that occur within reservation boundaries with the exception of the 13 federal crimes as long as 'due process' is observed in criminal cases. The fact is, however, that many tribal courts have either ceded or never assumed jurisdiction over one or more of the following areas: probate, juvenile problems, domestic relations, housing issues, and like - matters in which special laws, expertise, or facilities were perceived to be needed but lacking. In general, moreover, the tribal courts - with a few rare exceptions - have refused to take jurisdiction over non-Indians who engage in illegal transactions or commit offenses on reservation property, despite the fact that a good argument can be made for their having this power and that non-Indians clearly can, and sometimes do, sue Indians in the tribal courts.

Perhaps the most significant fact about the origin and development of the tribal courts is that they are white American creations, and quite recent ones at that.

Historically, law, order, and justice in Indian societies were dispensed in widely varying ways, matching the wide variety in cultures and life-styles among the tribes. Much was left to private means of enforcement - appropriate action in many conflict situations being the responsibility of the family or clan. If resort to more public means was had, it might be to political (tribal) councils, soldier or hunter societies, secular or religious leaders, generally respected and/or elder individuals, or combinations of these. But there were no 'courts' and 'judges' in the sense of the 'independent' and 'exclusively adjudicative' institutions and personnel that Anglo-American ideals have them to be. Nor, of course, were there public jails, prosecutors and police, written codes and cases, civil-criminal distinctions, and other standard attributes of the Anglo-American justice system. Actions on the order of banishment, public ridicule, and restitution played large roles in traditional Indian dispute resolution and behavior control. Retaliatory (private) and retributive (public) death and mutilation were also known forms of 'punishment.'

The traditional law-ways of the vast majority of the Indian tribes, however, were lost - completely or nearly so - during the process of physical displacement and decimation which constitutes their history and by the subsequent generations of reservation life and exposure to white society. In the late 1800s the Bureau of Indian Affairs (BIA) created the Courts of Indian Offenses. The purpose of these courts, according to their BIA creators, was to promote acculturation and control on the reservations, which were faring badly in both respects. The judges of these courts were Indians appointed by and responsible to the BIA. They were usually 'assisted' (a term that denotes the questionable relationship that has carried over into the present) by an Indian police force. The Courts of Indian Offenses were most numerous in the early 1900s, when two thirds of all reservations were reported to have them. Throughout the course of their development, the BIA exerted a heavy influence on them.

Under the impetus of the Indian Reorganization Act of 1934 and the deemphasis of assimilation policies, reduction of the BIA role, and increased delegation of authority to the tribes themselves, the Courts of Indian Offenses began to give way to the modern-day tribal courts. Today the Courts of Offenses have been almost completely phased out and the tribal courts are dominant, although on a few reservations the transition either has not begun or is still in progress. The curcial aspect of this transition, theoretically if not always practially significant and salutary, is that under the tribal court system judges are appointed by, paid by, and responsible to the tribe (typically the tribal council) rather than to the BIA.

Political Context

The general political context in which the operations of the tribal courts must be described and assessed is one of a growing movement toward and a stridency about Indian self-rule and separation. A decade or two ago, white politicians and many Indian leaders were still talking about assimilation, termination of the reservation system, and readying the Indian for off-reservation life; today such language is political suicide. The present code words are 'self-determination' and 'retrocession' of landholdings, powers and rights taken from, or abandoned by, the tribes in past contacts with white society. Specifically, there is increasing support and clamor for the tribal courts to assume, to reassume, or to widen jurisdiction over matters of law and poeple which are currently outside their scope. The 1975 Senate hearings before the Subcommittee on Indian Affairs on the Indian Law Enforcement Improvement Act of 1975 reflect the current dominance of the sovereignty-retrocession perspective and the growing suspicion and hostility with which the status of, let alone any proposal for, tribal submission to state jurisdiction is viewed.

The political state of affairs puts a special burden on this report: a portion of the readership will be looking for quick, one-dimensional answers to complex and diffuse questions; a certain percentage is likely to take offense no matter what is described or concluded; others may derive undue satisfaction from seeing their preconceived views or prejudices confirmed. I have made an assiduous effort to be neutral in both the information-gathering and the reporting processes. I have tried to seek out and give significance to the views of the Indian people themselves, and not just those of the political leaders or institutional officials, but also the views of people who have no political or institutional stake in these matters. I have tried to make judgments based on ideas of fairness which I believe are shared generally, among Indians and non-Indians, modernists or traditionalists, lawyers and nonlawyers. I have sought to avoid the paternalistic view that only white ways and institutions are desirable and relevant, as well as the opposite view that Indians ought to be left to their own devices no matter what the consequences. For example, in this report I have refrained from faulting the tribal courts for failure to meet 'constitutional' requirements of providing counsel. Instead, I have made an attempt to assess whether and under what circumstances the help of counsel - professional or otherwise - would be relevant or important in the tribal court setting.

Finally, there is the problem of generalization. To generalize is always hazardous, but to avoid generalization means to avoid communication. It may be pointed out that the observations and experiences on 10 reservations cannot speak entirely satisfactorily for the situation on 60-100 other reservations. Even among the reservations visited, there are differences that defy generalization; nonetheless, a certain commonality of experience permits assessments whose applicability extends to the reservation court system in general. In any event, since this report contains much specific description to go along with its generalizations, a basis is provided for an independent judgement of the force and credibility of the broader conclusions.

Reservation Life

For the outsider visiting an Indian reservation, the first and overwhelming impression is that the living conditions and way of life are far from enviable. Most of the Indians have concentrated themselves in a number of small towns or settlements, where they live in ranshackle wooden homes or huts or, more and more these days, new cheap and sterile prefabs. Typically, the remaining stretches of reservation land - often vast areas - are unused (unusable?) and uninhabited (uninhabitable?). Litter in the form of useless furniture, authomobile parts, even rusting hulks of abandoned cars, and other rubble often clutters the 'backyards' or lines the town streets, many of which remain unpaved. Scruffy, seemingly ownerless dogs roam the streets. Often there is a small better-kept part of town with more substantial homes and watered lawns. This is where the BIA and tribal officials live, with their office building - often newly constructed - generally located in the same area. This is not, however, where and how the average reservation resident lives.

While some individuals and families on the reservations have retained a dignified and more or less traditional way of life, and others have made a 'successful' transition to a more modern and acculturated life-style, the majority of the reservation people appear to be trapped in a cultural no-man's-land that is debilitating and demoralizing in its effect on the 'inhabitants.' Traditional pursuits such as hunting and fishing no longer occupy significant numbers of people. Cattle or sheep herding, farming, or working in arts and crafts sustain relatively few. The number of people who can be employed in tribal industries such as lumber or mining is limited. And while some Indians still live idealized, if subsistence, lives in individual 'hogans' or communal 'pueblos,' many more have succumbed to the pressures of 'urbanization,' becoming residents of the typically drab and depressing reservation towns. Life there is sedentary and house-bound; in socioeconomic terms it is at best marginal. More often than not the opportunities that still exist for living the 'traditional,' productive life appear to be rigorously avoided. On many reservations where the rivers and lakes are still filled with fish, one is often hard pressed to find people fishing for sport, let alone for sustenance or commerce. On another level - trivial, but nonetheless telling - instead of walking the short distances within reservation towns that would be easy on bright winter or ward summer days, the Indians drive about in their ubiquitous pick-up trucks or in gas-guzzling, smoking old sedans.

Life on the reservation is not healthy either. Apart from the statistics on the subject, considerable evidence of alcoholism can hardly escape the most casual observer. Many Indians are afflicted with birth defects or suffer from serious dietary imbalances. With startling regularity, one sees individuals who walk with a limp or who are grossly overweight. One can detect a streak of self-destructiveness among the Indian people without having to resort to suicide statistics. In Montana, for example, where it is the lugubrious but perhaps effective practice to erect commemorative corsses along the highways at spots where car accidents have resulted in fatalities, the message hits home with the driver about every 20 or 30 miles. But near Browning, on the Blackfeet Reservation in northwestern Montana, there are stretches of raod where the message comes as often as some 10 or 12 times per 20 or 30 miles - bad roads and drinking forming a lethal combination. Drinking itself is, of course, a form of self-destructiveness; for anyone who doubts that, a trip to any reservation and the sourroudning towns is recommended. Many of these small towns in sparsely populated areas present scenes that are a good match for the skid-row areas of major metropolitan centers. The Navajo situation is particularly striking, since the reservation proper is dry by law. But on going into Gallup, Farmington, or any of several other border towns, one discovers that the prohibition law on the reservation is at best ineffective and probably worse - actually counterproductive - in that under these circumstances the Indians are 'forced' to drive 10 to 20 miles of treacherous highway to find a bar or package store and then to drive back afterward. For those who can take their drink without frills, there is a place called the Navajo Inn only about 1.5 miles (i.e., 20 miles closer than Gallup) from Window Roach, the reservation capital, which makes up in convenience for what it lacks in class. There, at all hours of the day and night, including the middle of the afternoon in the broiling sun, people in all stages of inebriation, including stupor, wander in and out of the bar, cross the highway, stand or sit around in clumps or by themselves among the rocks and sand, or lie on the ground as if dead. Most of these people appear to be hardcore alcoholics whose lives have in large part been lived in a state of severe addiction. The Navajo tribe has tried - so far unsuccessfully - to have the place closed down, on grounds that it is a public nuisance, a health hazard, and an embarrassment to the Navajo Nation. What has been accomplished is the erection of a highway sign warning motorists euphemistically of 'pedestrians' - ' alcoholics crossing' is what it really means.

There are many other subtle and less subtle signs of stagnation and decay on the reservation. For those who like to rail against various 'isms' - actual or imagined - it is difficult to think of a better case against 'colonialism,' 'welfarism,' or 'paternalism' than the real physical and psychological plight of so many of the reservation people.

This background on reservation life is crucial for evaluating the tribal court phenomenon. The implications are various: positively, an awareness of general reservation conditions can help toward understanding court problems and issues; negatively, it can reinforce the cycle of guilt over the origin and perpetuation of these ocnditions and thus block objective assessment of the courts' operations. Finally, one could dispute the negative characterization of reservation life, or challenge the right to make such an 'objective' characterization. One could argue, for example, that life in many off-reservation areas is equally unappealing and that many people, though by no means all, choose to live where they live. Many reservation Indians in particular have tried life elsewhere - usually a big city - and having found it at least equally wanting have returned to the reservation. It is important not to ignore the subjective and relative in any talk about the quality of life. Still, from spending time on the reservations talking and dealing with the Indian people, one is struck forcibly with the impression that for many Indians - subjectively - life is unsatisfactory and unrewarding and often bleak and hopeless. The so-called objective indicators - the alcoholism, education, employment, health, and suicide statistics also speak subjectively.

Indian Justice Versus White Justice

The notion that there are such things as 'Indian justice' and 'white justice' is too simple and too general to be meaningful. This dichotomy implies a number of equally invalid sub-dichotomies. Some of the main contrasts are the following:

Indian justice is to white justice as
impartiality is to prejudice
humanism is to legalism
mediation is to adjudication

To talk about white justice is unhelpful, primarily because of the tremendous diversity in justice operations in the United States. How the system works varies widely in accordance with conspicuous differences in goegraphy or demography and also in accordance with factors that are less easily identified or understood.

The only brand of white justice that can be meaningfully compared with Indian justice is the rural system operating closest to the reservations, and presumably the one that would be operating on the reservations themselves if it were not for the tribal systems. The stereotype of white justice, based mainly on the experience of urban justice and popularized in the media by observers of the urban scene, has least applicability to rural justice operations.

The term 'Indian justice,' on the other hand, may be taken to imply that some indigenous, traditional Indian justice arrangement exist. That is not the case. Historically and presently, the justice dispensed in the tribal courts represents nothing more or less than an effort to copy white man's precepts and white man's institutions.

<u>Impartiality Versus Prejudice:</u> One reason given in support of the tribal court system is that Indians would encounter serious prejudice in the outside courts. This consideration leaves one with the curious question of what amount of prejudice justifies what degree of inadequacy in a separate system.

It is true that many Indians believe that they would receive prejudicial treatment in state and county courts. In some areas, this perception is stronger than in others. Interestingly, however, Indians who live under state or county jurisdictions appear less likely to view white prejudice as a problem than those whose experience has been limited to the tribal courts. Whatever their actual experience, most Indian respondents regard the problem of prejudice as a passing one: "Things used to be bad, but they are better now."

In the brief fieldwork for this study, no evidence was uncovered that Indians received adverse treatment in white courts. Whatever the past patterns may have been, anti-Indian prejudice does not appear to be pervasive or systematic in the white courts. The real problem is how to deal with the Indians' negative expectations of white justice.

Politics and rhetoric aside, the Indians' perception of their tribal court system is no more favorable, even on the issue of prejudice. They feel that a considerable amount of prejudice finds its way into the tribal courts. There are countless charges that the tribal judges show favoritism toward council members or their interests, law-enforcement personnel or their friends and relatives, and other 'influential groups.' Such charges are credible concerning courts in which the judges have insufficient training, stature, support, or experience to be able to insulate themselves from tribal cliques and dissensions.

Humanism Versus Lagalism: The rhetoric in support of tribal courts often sets up a contrast between the excessively formal and sterilely technical white courts and the informal and personal tribal courts. As 'native institutions,' the tribal courts are presumed to be more understanding, more humane than the legalistic white courts. This has not been borne out in observations.

In this study and others, white justice - practicularly in rural areas - has been found in many respects to be quite informal and personal. In the state and county courts on or near the reservations, the treatment of both Indians and non-Indians was far from legalistic. Typically, a personalized discretion was exercised, in which the circumstances of the case, the situation of the accused and his or her family, and other particulars were considered in deciding whether to charge, what to charge, how to conduct the proceedings, how to communicate tribal rights, whether to accept guilty pleas and waivers of counsel, what standards of decorum to adhere to in trial testimony, and what disposition to make.

For example, in Oklahoma, the county magistrate refused a youth's guilty plea on a narcotics charge, in part because the police evidence was shaky. In North Carolina, the district judge delivered a compromise verdict in a driving-while-intoxicated case against an Indian man who had not been in much trouble before, but he threw the book at an Indian woman who had been a repeat offender of the traffic and narcotics laws. In North Dakota, a state judge questioned individual defendants thoroughly to find out if they had understood their rights before going on with the case, and a county court judge interrupted custody proceedings to talk for 15 minutes privately in chambers to determine what the Indian child wanted. In Utah, a defense counsel's thorough cross-examination of the prosecution witnesses in J. P. proceedings before a jury of four brought out the full facts of the arrest and booking process.

In the tribal courts, one finds the surface features of an informal and individualized justice: the tribal judges usually know the people who appear before them; there is little or no case law restricting their discretionary power; except on the Navajo Reservation, court procedure and decorum are quite loose; in the small percentage of contested cases, a wide latitude is permitted with regard to testimony. That, however, is about as far as it goes; underneath there are strong pressures toward a legalistic approach.

First, the tribal judges are insecure. With little formal education, let alone formal legal training, they are at a great disadvantage in dealing with the legal and social complexities of the cases brought before them. This results in a high rate of summary - typically legalistic - dispositions, in an almost invariable acceptance of quilty pleas, and in the standard imposition of fines or jail sentences. Any other type of processing or disposition is the exception. It is rare for judges to exercise their discretion imaginatively, and it is rare for the individual facts to be developed fully and subjected to adversary, or in any case detailed, scrutiny.

It is also typical for the tribal judges to deal summarily with the relatively few civil cases that reach the tribal courts. Here, the lack of knowledge on the part of the judges leads to peculiar legalism: the grandiose proclamation against the Housing Authority, for example, or the ex parte injunction against the postal clerk, when neither case involved contesting parties or contestable issues or resulted in forms of relief that had much chance of being enforced or even comprehended. In another case the very judge who issued an officious decree on landownership dismissed it as meaningless when one of the parties tried to take it seriously.

In addition to being professionally inadequate, the tribal judges are politically and socially insecure. They are appointed and paid by the tribal councils and sometimes removed by the councils at whim. The reservation tradition is for the councils to influence or control, often overtly, all phases of reservation business. It may be an encouraging sign that today the judges recognize and acknowledge the problem of council influence in judicial affairs and presumably try to deal with it. Still, there are too many complaints about interference and favoritism to believe that they deal with it very successfully. One way in which judges accommodate council pressures is through legalism. They are reported to invoke and sustain claims of sovereign immunity in cases that involve the illegal activity of council members. Or charges against council members or their families are dismissed on some other pretext. For example, one report alleged that when a council member was arrested for attempted armed robbery on the Navajo Reservation, the judge dismissed the case at arraignment on the grounds that the police had not given the defendant a copy of the warrant for arrest in jail. While political pressures and improprieties are not limited to the Indian tribal courts, in the tribal courts, from all accounts, political influence is perceived to be so pervasive and systematic as to constitute the norm.

Being a part of a closed society in which family and clan affiliations exert a powerful influence, tribal judges are very vulnerable to social pressures. People inevitably suspect that social pressures are exerted in judicial matters even when they are not. The judge has few protections against such pressures: the status of his position is not high enough to place him above social squabbles; and he lacks the educational or legal expertise that would compensate for precarious status or enable him to deal with, or effectively disquise a yielding to, improper influence. As a result, the reservation Indians do not perceive the institution of the tribal court to have much, if any, 'social' independence.

The problem posed or the suspicion aroused by blood relationship is unavoidable in any close-knit society. Most tribal judges are aware that they should disqualify themselves in cases in which clan or family relation is a factor, but they rarely do. Their reason, which is plausible enough, is that everyone is related to everyone else and that if they took the disqualification option seriously they would be disqualifying themselves all the time. That response, of course, fails to satisfy the parties who come out on the losing end in these situations. It may also be seen as an indictment of the tribal court concept.

Mediation Versus Adjudication: On some imaginary jurisprudentil scale, the tribal courts are often put at one mediatory, harmony-seeking extreme and the outside court system at the adjudicatory, accusatory opposite extreme. Comparisons of this kind have their origin in legal-anthropological literature and thought, in which 'primitive' (or simply non-Western) justice systems are examined against the background of the contemporary American courts. There is indeed some historical basis for such a contrast in American Indian traditions and Anglo-American practices. This view, however, does not square with the present -day realities of the Indian tribal courts or with the expectations of the reservation inhabitants.

The so-called traditional goals of mediation and harmony do not appear to weigh in the routine thoughts and actions of the tribal judges, the parties before the tribal courts, or the reservation residents. If one solicited it, most judges and even some politically oriented residents could engage in rhetoric about such concepts, but mediation and harmony are not part of their operational langauge, much less of their practices.

Instead, talk on the subjects of justice and crime took a conventional, unsophisticated, law-and-order form. Judges, council members, and residents spoke about being tougher on troblemakers. They complained about some defendants getting off with a slap on the wrist and about the lack of independence on the part of the courts. On the other hand, defendants complained about high bail and high fines, about the police orientation of judges, about judges' invariably being harsh and punitive, and so forth. When one got around to discussing underlying problems, it was in terms of low salaries for judicial and law enforcement personnel, inadequate physical facilities, tribal politics and factionalism, family jealousies, unemployment, and alcoholism. In other words, verbalizations about justice on the reservations were not different from those elsewhere. In fact, the Indian judges and police often sounded more Anglo than the Anglos, which is understandable in that they have no model other than the Anglo system to emulate.

The practices matched the talk: diversionary (noncriminal, mediatory) handling of criminal of criminal matters was, except in a few systems such as the Navajo's, virtually unheard of. Even the most marginally criminal cases were typically processed in straight law-and-order fashion. These included liquor violations, public drunkenness, vagrancy, nonsupport, illicit cohabitation - some of which cannot or can no longer be handled as criminal matters in white courts. Dispositions like probation, working off the penalty, and delay of conviction upon the accused's being given a chance to 'go straight' were rare in the tribal courts. Even restitution or the resolution of criminal and civil disputes in one proceeding - practices in tradtional Indian cultures - were uncommon occurrences. Again with the exception of the Navajo code, the tribal codes made little provision for diversionary solutions, which meant that no encouragement or incentive was given to law-enforcement and judicial personnel to experiment with such possibilities. Even among the Navajo judges, noncriminal dispositions were rare despite tribal code inducements. It is possible that they did not believe in them or that the lack of personnel, programs or physical facilities for 'divertible' offenders influenced them. On the other hand, the mere existence of a detoxification center (Standing Rock) or a nursing home (Blackfeet Reservation) did not guarantee that they would be used.

In the tribal courts, the judges rarely attempted to effect reconciliations between disputants or to establish harmony among reservation factions. In general, they made summary dispositions of the cases before reaching the merits. Often, as a result, the parties were left confused and unhappy. When the merits were reached or when all disputants were present, the judges could not prevent acrimonious exchanges from taking place during and after the proceedings. They were often unable to control the parties, and they lacked sufficient authority - real or perceived - to render the porceedings and the outcomes legitimate in the eyes of the litigants. The loser in any court is likely to emerge unhappy, but here the litigants lack of confidence in - and sometimes contempt for - the tribal court process is a different and more serious problem.

One factor that works against a mediatory or reconciliatory role for the court is that the judges are identified with law and order. Many tribal courts have no prosecutor, and the judge himself serves as such; some judges have formerly been tribal police officers; and the reservation people are aware of these facts. The overall picture, then is that the characteristics of an accusatory system mainly concerned with obtaining convictions, which are usually attributed to the white courts, are more applicable to the tribal courts.

The tendency in the white courts, on the other hand, was not to fully prosecute Indian defendants or hand down jail sentences against them. When interviewed, one district judge even indulged in the popular line that when an Indian 'borrowed' a car and 'forgot' to return it one could not really call it car theft. Other white law-enforcement officials invoked the alcoholism or different 'moral' standards in support of the Indians' lesser accountability and of their own dispositional leniency. Rightly or wrongly, personnel in the white justice system commonly viewed Indians as people with special subcultural attributes and hence with special claims to conciliatory treatment. This is not necessarily always healthy. Resentment about excessive paternalism was found among both whites and Indians outside the law-enforcement system. They singled out the federal system in particular for severe criticism of its treatment (or nontreatment) of major crimes among Indians. Many reasons besides paternalism account for this lack of vigorous federal involvement. One thing is clear, however, the perception of white justice as being excessively accusatory is inaccurate with respect to the treatment of Indian and non-Indian defendants alike.

Cultural Survival Versus Cultural Demise: Persons who favor the continued operation of the tribal courts often associate the survival of the courts with the survival of tribal culture in general, and vice-versa. The demise of the courts, they say, would spell the demise of Indian culture. While it appears to be logical and has immediate appeal, this either - or, all-or-nothing stance should be considered more closely.

It is implied that if one does not support one tribal institution one is anti-Indian, that if one does not recognize a total political-cultural autonomy for the Indians one must favor a total melting-pot assimilation. All claims of separate autonomy are regarded as natural; any movement toward integration is regarded as imposed and artificial. Such an extreme position is not helpful in discussing Indian affairs and problems in general or in assessing the workability of the tribal courts.

Whatever historical or moral arguments one may muster to the contrary, whatever ancient doctrines of 'residual' sovereignty or present-day claims to white reparations may exist, it appears anomalous in the latter part of the twentieth century that one small ethnic group should be separated from the judicial system that extends to all other citizens of the United States. The burden of persuasion for separatist ideas should fall on the proponents of separatism. In the case for separate tribal courts, instead of advancing the usual political and mystical arguments, proponents should show that the courts have concrete operational advantages.

The present performance of the tribal courts can hardly be said to indicate the vitality of Indian tribal culture. Terminating their operation does not mean the end of Indian culture, realistically defined. Finally, in contrast with tribal leaders or spokesmen, the average reservation resident has little interest in seeing the tribal court system maintained or expanded.

Indian Courts Versus Indian Culture: In both conception and operation, the tribal courts are little more than pale copies of the white system. All remedies to their operational problems are directed toward making them better copies. This leaves only 'localism' as a justification for their existence - that is, the desire for and convenience of locally controlled institutions. Local control, however, must be exercised responsibly: there must be mechanisms to check abuse of power and to promote optimum use of talent. In my view, official authority would be best utilized and personal power on the reservations would be best checked within the normal integrated setting of, and with the mechanisms available under, state and county jurisdiction. In twentieth-century America, the integrated approach is the only realistic and the only acceptable approach (for Indians as well as non-Indians). Integration into the larger judicial system does not necessarily threaten the preservation of the elements of Indian culture that are capable of being preserved or the revival of those that are worthy of being revived any more than the perpetuation of a dependent and often inauthentic tribalism would guarantee them.

Even the most favored of the tribal courts are burdened by inexperienced and unprofessional judges, administrative and procedural irregularity, substantively inadequate fact finding, and insufficient exploration of the legal content or social implications of cases. To these, one must add the problems of perceived partiality toward particular political or social factions and, in the less favored courts, perhaps the reality of discrimination, in addition, or the outright abdication of juridical responsibilities. Even on the more 'progressive' reservations, public confidence in the tribal courts is at best meager. Efforts to improve the courts are toward making them more like white courts or, worse, like a stereotype of white courts. White academics and professionals provide training sessions for Indian judges; often inexperienced white lawyers and advisors expand or revise the tribal codes; Congress passes an Indian Bill of Rights that is modeled on the United States Constitution; the federal courts are acquiring a broader jurisdiction in Indian criminal affairs; white judges or lawyers are being hired to sit on the 'tribal courts'; Indian judges begin to wear black robes; courtrooms are built or remodeled to resemble 'real' (i.e., white) courts; and so on. What relation do these practices have to Indian culture?

It requires no great leap of logic to arrive at the view that all this is a roundabout way of achieving what can be achieved more directly through the 'solution' of integration. That is not to say that extending state and county jurisdiction to the reservations would be without trauma or without the need for special formulas to assure Indian participation and representation; many Indians have negative perceptions of white justice; white officials are entrenched in most law-enforcement positions; and the Indians are at a great educational disadvantage. Nevertheless, integration is the only approach with real promise; it is inevitable in the long run, and it is not necessarily out of tune with the current trends (as opposed to the rhetoric) in Indian life and culture. The model of Indian justice for the 1970s and the future is not the Dakota, Montana, or even the Arizona (Navajo) one, but rather the Oklahoma model.

All steps taken to preserve the tribal courts or the reservation system can only be rearguard actions. The reservations, with their courts and other institutions, are destined to disappear in time. The only question is, When? The true motivations behind, and justification for, Indian separatism are psychological. As in the black movement in this country, separatist thetoric may be useful in restoring a sense of personal (or 'cultural,' if one insists) identity and worth to the members of an ethnic minority that has a history of being suppressed, exploited, and kept dependent. That is its total role. To recognize that does not mean that one should become an accomplice in the creation or perpetuation of artificial, separatist institutions. The time appears to be ripe to expose the temporary, psychological purposes of these institutions and to inform the Indians of more permanent, functional alternatives. It is time to acknowledge that Indian reservations do not preserve Indian culture. They are little more than depressed areas for marginal and dependent societies of Indians, whites, and mixed-bloods. They are sociological nurseries to which those who find life difficult outside can always return, places of more or less voluntary detention for the ones who have never left, zoos for white tourists, and laboratories for academics. Tribal courts do not exemplify an Indian culture worth preserving; they are imitations of white institutions, beset by aggravated versions of the problems of white institutions and characterized in part by the preservation in power of a few individuals whose own 'Indianness' and whose concern for the Indian people are often suspect.

Indian Courts Versus the Indian People: It is difficult to ascertain what the Indian people want. Many of them are quite cynical about reservation life and reservation institutions, including the tribal courts. On the other hand, they are ignorant of or equally cynical about, if not fearful of, the alternatives. The Indians who have had some experience in the outside world and with white institutions usually express mixed feelings about their experiences. The current emphasis on 'Indianness' and autonomy only complicates the picture for them. Those who have had no experience with white institutions also are influenced by the prevailing separatist rhetoric.

Few would argue the point that the reservation people should be left to choose for themselves. If they are to choose, however, they must be informed of the facts; and the misconceptions about the differences between Indian and non-Indian life and practives must be dispelled.

For example, the ideas that tribal institutions and courts are genuinely Indian, that they benefit the Indian people, and that Indians unanimously endorse and support them are all largely mythical. Equally groundless is the idea that contemporary nontribal institutions are unsuitable for Indians, although with sufficient propaganda it could become a self-fulfilling prophecy. Sometimes persons who are willing to acknowledge the systemic problems of tribal existence and tribal institutions and the dissatisfaction of Indian individuals with them are apt to put the issue in terms of the need to sustain 'tribal rights' over 'individual rights' in the long-term interest of Indian individuals. The argument is unconvincing in view of the almost certain disappearance of tribalism and separatism in the long term.

The tribal courts do not work well, and necessary improvements would require much time and involve many difficulties. To perpetuate them at all runs counter to the evolutionary trends in the Indians' relation to the dominant culture in this country. Therefore, it would be more realistic to abandon the system altogether and to deal with Indian civil and criminal problems in the regular county and state court systems. Existing integrated arrangements appear to work well enough. Integrated justice systems, however, could be improved by the employment of Indians in nonprofessional, advisory capacities in the whole range of law-enforcement and justice-administration posts until such time that more than the present few could participate fully as professional equals. There is no historical basis for the fear that putting the Indian people under the regualr justice systems will hasten the demise of their culture and traditions.

REFERENCES

Cherokee Nation v. Georgia, 9 U.S. (5 Pet.) 178 (1831).
Ex Parte Crow Dog, 109 U.S. 556 (1883).
Worcester v. Georgia, 10 U.S. (6 Pet.) 214 (1832).

Part 3

Indian Treatment Issues

Chapter 11
Indian Alcoholism

LAURENCE FRENCH and JIM HORNBUCKLE

This selection will approach alcoholism amomg Native Americans from a psychocultural perspective, which isolates Native American alcoholism from alcoholism in society in general. At times, this approach may appear to be at odds with more conventional etiologies and popular methods of treating alcoholism that are advocated by psychologist, psychiatrists, social workers, and medical personnel. Nevertheless, this approach fits the current multidisciplinary framework recommended by the National Institute on Alcohol Abuse and Alcoholism (NIAAA) (Keller, 1974).

Major Health Problem

From a psychocultural perspective, alcoholism is regarded as a 'symptom' of other social, cultural, and personal problems. Cultural sanctions and socially acceptable drinking patterns are factors relevant to individual alcohol abuse and alcoholism. The role of alcohol in the social, physical, psychological, economic, and cultural disruption experienced by Native Americans, historically as well as currently, is well documented. Alcoholism has become the single most serious health problem accounting for the three leading causes of death among Native Americans: cirrhosis of the liver, sucicide, and homicide. This compares with cardiovascular illness, cancer, and accidents as the leading causes of death in the United States overall (Frederick, 1973).

Although alcoholism is the most serious health problem for Native Americans, alcohol in itself is not necessarily the major contributing factor in what are typically called alcohol-related diseases, such as cirrhosis. Even these serious and terminal health problems are seen by many as not directly attributable to a single cause such as alcohol but rather as more closely associated with social patterns of behavior. In certain cultures, for example, alcohol is consumed without food. Thus, cirrhosis may be brought on through dietary neglect. In the same way, many other nonalcohol-related physical and mental health problems that plague Native Americans reflect a combination of factors rather than a single causal-lineal relationship between isolated factors.

Alcohol is a factor in 75 to 80 percent of all Native American suicides and about 90 percent of all homicides. The Federal Bureau of Investigation's Uniform Crime Reports (1958-80) support these statistics, indicating that Native Americans have the highest conviction rate for crimes of violence. Their conviction rate is twice that of blacks and Hispanics and three times that of whites. Not all Native Americans who drink are involved in violent crime, however. The rate of other alcohol-related offenses such as public drunkenness is eight times that of blacks and Hispanics and over twenty times that of whites.

The following, from the final report on alcohol and drug abuse prepared for the American Indian Policy Review Commission, is a clear statement of the alcohol problem among Native Americans:

> The streamrolling effect of the 'civilized society' upon the Indian people has wreaked a havoc which extends far beyond that of loss of material possessions. The American Indian and Alaska Native are caught in a world wherein they are trying to find out who they are and where they fit in. The land which was once their 'mother,' giving them food and clothing, was taken. Their spiritual strengths were decried as pagan, and familial ties were broken. Their own forms of education, i.e., that of legends, how to live, how to respect themselves and others, were torn asunder by the 'white society's' reading, writing and arithmetic. No culture could, or can be, expected to be thrust into a world different from its own and adapt without problems of cultural shock.... The Indian people of today are proud of their heritage and are fighting to maximize its influence upon their lives in a dominant white world. Many have succeeded. Many have not.... (The) destructive use of alcohol and drugs among Native Americans and Alaska Native individuals, families and communities is inextricably interwoven into all aspects of their lives and any effort to alleviate the problem must be comprehensive in scope and with the full commitment of the Indian people (Snake, 1976).

The chairman of the task force that prepared this report is from Nebraska, a state whose Native American population is 1 percent of the total state population. However, Native Americans account for 7 percent of all serious criminal arrests and 25 percent of all public drunkenness arrests in that state.

Etiologies

Alcohol abuse and alcoholism is one of the nation's most serious health problems and one of the most difficult illnessess to cure. That alcohol cannot be banned was shown by the ill-fated Volstead Act, better known as Prohibition, which attempted to enforce the Eighteenth Amendment. The amendment was universally abused throughout the country and finally repealed nearly fourteen years later in 1933. In spite of this emotional and costly national crisis, the medical profession, politicians, religious leaders, and the criminal justice apparatus took another forty years to agree that alcohol abuse and alcoholism is a health problem rather than a moral issue or criminal offense.

Nevertheless, alcohol-related offenses still account for the bulk of arrests nationwide, most of which are for nuisance misdemeanors such as public drunkenness. Society pays for this in terms of police and correctional time and adjudication of the public drunk, a costly process with little preventive or rehabilitative purpose. More significant is the proportion of serious violent offenses in which alcohol is a contributing factor. These include a large number of all homicides, suicides, aggravated assaults, rapes, spouse and child abuse, and vehicle accidents. In spite of the recently proclaimed awareness of a new era of 'alcohol enlightenment,' however, professionals and practitioners continue to be stalemated at the rhetorical level, making few serious efforts to ascertain the underlying reasons for alcohol abuse.

It has come to light that drug abuse, especially polydrug abuse involving alcohol and other mind-altering substances, is common among the legal, political, and medical professions. Accordingly, both the American Bar Association and American Medical Association (ABA;AMA) have been reluctant to pay more than cursory attention to the alcohol problem since neither profession wants its dirty linen washed in public. A self-serving cycle has emerged in which physicians, lawyers, and politicians staunchly protect their members who suffer from alcohol and drug abuse. Public disclosure of professional deviance is strongly discouraged by these organizations. Some would argue that this factor alone explains why the issue of alcoholism has been so vehemently ignored by these two professions.

A decade of studies and debate led to appeals from two prominent scholars and their associates, Jellinek and Chafetz, who asked for a realistic medical assessment of alcohol abuse and alcoholism. Both provided an international view of the treatment of alcoholism, indicating that the United States lagged behind a number of more progressive nations in Europe, Africa, North and South America, Asia, and the South Pacific (Chafetz,

1970).

Jellinek also suggested a way to classify alcoholism as a disease that is used widely toady in analyzing alcoholism and drinking patterns among Native Americans:

> 1. Alpha alcoholism characterizes people attracted to alcohol psychologically, who exceed the norm but retain the ability to control their drinking and even to abstain.
> 2. Beta alcoholism results in physical complications that are related to alcohol, such as cirrhosis of the liver, gastritis, or polyneuropathy.
> 3. Gamma alcoholism is a result of progressive beta symptoms with increased tissue tolerance to alcohol and adaptive cell metabolism.
> 4. Delta alcoholism results in an inability to abstain from drinking as opposed to a loss of control.
> 5. Epsilon alcoholism is periodic heavy consumption of alcohol or 'bout' drinking (Jellineck, 1960).

In 1970, Congress created the National Institute on Alcohol Abuse and Alcoholism (NIAAA). A concerted effort was made to explore the cause and extent of alcohol abuse in the United States. These efforst eventually led to an acceptance of the 'medical view' of alcohol abuse by the American Medical Association. In the 1973 issue of the AMA publication, Manual on Alcoholism this organization now posited:

> ...alcoholism and its complications extend into every facet of our existence - certainly including medicine. It is unfortunate that we must acknowledge that most members of the medical profession - with notable and commendable exceptions - have failed to accomplish a great deal in the treatment of alcoholics, or to apply themselves constructively to the alcoholic's problem. They have been unduly slow in recognizing alcoholims as an illness and, in practice, have tended to dismiss alcoholic patients as hopeless or, at best, unpleasant and unrewarding. In spite of voluminous literature published every year on the subject, major advances in the field have seemed disappointingly slow (Wolman, 1973).

The significance of the manual lies in its concise analysis of alcohol abuse and its warning to the medical profession that alcoholism reflects acomplicated interplay of physiological, psychological, and sociological factors. The manual readily discredits popular myths about alcoholism, stating that:

1. Alcohol by itself does not cause alcoholism.

2. Alcoholism does not result from drinking a particular beverage.
3. Alcoholism is not an allergic manifestation.
4. Alcoholism is not the result of an alcoholic personality.

The AMA now cites metabolic disturbances, endocrine deficiencies, glandular dysfunctions, and alcohol apperstat, as well as acetylcholine and receptor-site imbalances, as common physiological factors contributing to alcoholism. In addition, they acknowledge a number of psychological factors, such as self-destructiveness, parental relationships, and learned responses, and a number of sociological factors, such as abstinence, ambivalence, and permissiveness. They conclude that alcoholism stems not from a single cause, but from a complicated interplay of physiological, psychological, and sociological causes.

In _Alcohol and Health_, a special report from the United States Department of Health, Education, and Welfare (as it was then known), Chafetz warns that society has paid insufficient attention to an obvious fact:

> Certain cultures use alcoholic beverages and are little troubled with alcoholic problems, while others suffer major alcoholic disturbances as a consequence of their drinking. Since all societies and cultures have problems, many groups have obviously developed ways of coping with the pains of life in a nonalcoholic manner and, presumably, in ways that have less destructive personal and social consequences.... We have tried Prohibition, and it failed. We have tried campaigns of slogans, and they have failed. We have tried educational programs based on fear, and they have failed. Therefore, I suggest we learn from other experience and cultures (Chafetz, 1974).

It would be foolhardy to assume that a new irreversible milestone in alcohol awareness has been reached, however, especially since the search for implistic, innate etiologies is as common today as it has ever been. In the scientific community, the neopositivists are now rallying around 'sociolbiology.' Physiologists again claim they can isolate the causes of alcohol abuse and alcoholism by determining genetic, neurological, and endocrinologic malfunctions that, they allege, lead to biological susceptibility, and hence, alcohol pathologies.

It is unfortunate that a considerable proportion of neopositivist research addresses the alleged connection between racial differences and susceptibility to alcohol. This has grave consequences for Native Americans, the racial group most seriously afflicted by alcohol problems. Ironically, certain influenctial members of the scientific, political, and religious communities strongly subscribe to the idea of Native American inferiority and use the Native American experience with alcohol to support this opinion.

Federal policies clearly embody a double standard toward Native American alcoholism. The General Indian Intercourse Act, which was passed 86 years prior to the Volstead Act, prohibited the sale or use of alcohol by Native Americans for over 120 years (1832-1953), preventing them from developing acceptable drinking norms. This forced abstinence exacerbated the situation. Many Native Americans felt compelled to challenge this double standard, only complicating matters by getting themselves in trouble with the law. Overall, enforced selective prohibition did more to nourish the stereotype of the 'drunken Indian' than to remedy the situation. A self-fulfilling prophecy was created whereby the more Native Americans drank, and thus violated the law, the more the federal government justified its harsh policies toward them, setting an example for state and local governments as well.

Disruptive Federal Policies

To understand Native American alcoholism, it is crucial to understand the disruptive events brought about by policies mandated by the federal government. These policies are of two types: those concerned with outright physical genocide and those concerned with cultural genocide, that is, policies designed to destroy the 'aboriginal' or tribal culture. These policies have their roots in the colonial era of this country and extend to the present day. A quick succession of federal policies, following the Revolutionary War, dictating the nature of this country's programs for Native Americans include the following.

Wars with various Native American tribes were common as European countries sought to establish colonies in North America. The policy of attrition and genocide continued until President Grant's 'Peace Policy' in 1870, after which Native Americans had to be officially declared 'renegades' before being pursued as hostiles.

Removal was a policy begun in 1835 that sought to displace major Native American populations to 'Indian Territory' west of the Mississippi River.

Allotment (Dawes Act, 1887) was designed to undermine tribal authority and aboriginal culture. Land held by Native American tribes was divided into indiviudally owned farmsteads, and all 'excess' tribal land was opened up to white settlers. The 1898 Curtis Act complemented allotment by outlawing tribal governments, schools, churches, courts, and so forth.

The Indian Reorganization Act, also known as the Wheeler-Howard Act of 1934, attempted to repair the damage from the combined effects of removal and allotment. Native Americans were allowed once again to hold their land in tribal collectives, known as reservations. Nevertheless, Native Americans were denied land rights on their own reservations, and tribal land was soon leased out to white farmers and ranchers by the Bureau of Indian Affairs (BIA). Reorganization did much to create the dire health and social conditions on reservations, and many Native Americans contend that this form of federal paternalism creates a dangerous dependency for the reservations' residents.

Termination (P.L. 280) in 1953 and relocation in 1954 were part of the postwar effort to remove the federal government from the 'Indian business,' During the anticommunism era of McCarthy, tribalism was seen by many as a threatening form of communal living and thus a form of anti-Americanism. Termination was designed to transform Native American reservations from a communistic orientation to a capitalistic one. Reservations were to have corporate status, with each enrolled member regarded as a stockholder. Reservations were to be taxed on their property and profits. Relocation, on the other hand, attempted to attract young Native Americans away from the reservation and into urban areas where better educational and employment opportunities supposedly existed. Currently, about half the total Native American population of the United States resides off the reservation. The promise of a better life did not materialize, and many urban Native American communities are actually ghettos.

Self-determination (1975) is the current federal policy, which attempts to 'mainstream' Native Americans into the larger society. Many Native Americans do not want to be mainstreamed or otherwise assimilated, however, and they regard this latest federal policy as merely an extension of termination.

The nation is still polarized over the Native American issue. Native Americans themselves are torn between radical action and passive accommodation on reservations. Supporters of the American Indian Movement (AIM) have often divided reservation communities, causing a resurgence of interest in reservation politics, old treaties, land and water rights, and class-action suits. Radicals who win take over the reins of tribal power and attempt to change the status quo. Radicals who lose their battles with the status quo find the reservation a difficult place to live and often migrate to Native American ghettos in the cities. These urban populations are often more alienated than their counterparts on the reservation.

The visibility and publicity given AIM and other similar Native American action groups have created a powerful white backlash, which has led to actions such as H. R. 9054, introduced by Congressman Cunningham (Washington State), calling for the federal government to deem all Native American treaties illegal. This action would eventually exonerate the federal government of any past, present, or future legal obligations regarding Native American preference, treaties, or other special programs. This would make the plan of the 1975 Indian Self-Determination Act to abruptly discontinue existing Native American programs a certainty. This would force many marginal Native Americans into an even more tenuous cultural situation, one likely to enhance their anomie and consequently, their alcohol abuse and alcoholism.

The use and abuse of alcohol is strongly linked to cultual environments. Groups that prescribe legitimate avenues for the use of alcohol have fewer problems than groups in which either these controls are lacking or abstinence is the norm. Rivers and Rivers (1975) combined aspects of Blacker's and others' arguments in concluding that the rate of alcoholism will be low in a group or society where drinking customs, values, and sanctions are well established, agreed upon by all, and characterized by prescriptions for moderate drinking and proscriptions against excessive drinking.

Given that culture is now considered the single most significant factor concerning general patterns of alcohol use and abuse, it is clear that Native Americans have been severely handicapped in their adjustment to alcohol use. They have not been allowed to develop acceptable drinking norms. As a result of the General Indian Intercourse Act, the philosophy of abstinence still dominates relations between whites and Native Americans even though this law was repealed in 1953. In addition, 3½ centuries of disastrous federal policy toward Native Americans, ranging from outright genocide to current termination policies, have wreaked havoc with traditional Native American culture.

Native Americans have been forced to modify their tribal ways time and again, and each time more and more members are pushed out to the fringe of their traditional culture. Cultural marginality and escapism through alcohol have become major Native American problems. Any viable alcoholism treatment program for Native Americans must take these factors into consideration. Recently, NIAAA has begun to provide special programs for Native Americans, staffed primarily by Native Americans, which have achieved notable results in a relatively short period of time. Although this is a significant step forward, the recent trend has been to forfeit Native American programs for other alcoholism programs. In terms of the magnitude of the Native American problem with alcohol in the United States and of the professed mandate of NIAAA, this cutback in funding appears to make no sense. Some suggest, however, that it does make sense from a political prespective. As was concluded at the 'First National Congerence on the Native American Alcohol Phenomenon,' held at the University of California, Berkeley, May 1977, this country is far from finding any viable solution to Native American alcoholism at this time.

As it is, a small, elite group of regulators determines federal policy according to its cultural perspective, which, in this country, is the Protestant Ethic, while at the same time they maintain rigid physical and social distance between themselves and the individuals they regulate. Policies and programs fail because Native Americans are stripped of their cultural identity and denied access to their people's ways and hence their own psychological security. What results is a federal paternalism that creates adolescent wards torn between the arbitrary expectations of adult responsibility and those of childhood dependency.

To make Native Americans learn white ways at the expense of their own traditions leads to conflict that is often internalized and concealed through alcohol abuse. It is rarely that such conflict erupts in aggressive productivity, as is seen in the writings of Deloria and Dial and Eliades. But for more Native Americans, the result is massive aggression against the self, as shown in alcoholism, mental and physical health problems, suicide, or in aggression against others, as in assault or homicide. There is little doubt that the most well-adjusted Native Americans are those who are proud of their heritage (Deloria, 1968; Dial, 1975).

Cultural Circumstances

To be viable, a therapeutic model must encourage Native American clients to become more responsible in culturally relevant terms. According to the Harmony Ethos, a world view that encompasses all Native American cultures, such responsibility generally involves a personal commitment to Mother Earth, Father Sky, other tribal members (generalized others), and kin (significant others). In order to ascertain the nature of a client's drinking problem, however, a therapist must first understand the cultural circumstances surrounding the client's marginality.

Native Americans can be placed on a cultural continuum with 'aboriginal traditionalism' situated at the extreme right and 'white assimilation' at the extreme left:

white assimilation		aboriginal traditionalism
(middle class)	(marginal)	(traditional)

In turn, the continuum can be subdivided into three social classifications, each with its own psychocultural perspective and, correspondingly, its own unique drinking pathology, which taken together are similar to conventional analyses, notably those of Jellinek and Cahn (French, 1976).

Traditional Native Americans: Traditional Native Americans are also referred to as 'full bloods,' 'real Indians,' and 'conservatives.' Altogether, it is estimated that about 25 percent of the nation's 800,000 Native Americans fall into this category. Their psychological perspective is the most traditional, meaning that, of all Native Americans, they most strongly adhere to a phenomenological world view in which humans are seen as only one component among many in the scheme of nature. The natural environment (Mother Earth and Father Sky) - not humans - is seen as being the Superior Froce. Traditionalists feel that their destiny is intricately and intimately related to and dependent upon other natural phenomena. This is their given world, one where life, like nature, occurs in cycles. Traditionalists feel they are compelled to cooperate not only with their fellow Native American cohorts but with all aspects of their natural environment.

Natural cycles have must to do with the behavior of traditionalists, which involves cycles of 'passivity' punctuated with ritualistic sequences of extreme behavior. Based on prescribed activities, considerable personal license is sanctioned, including even otherwise criminal or taboo acts, as a way for traditionalists to manage tension. Such behavior is allowed in terms of Native American culture, which assigns the blame for these so-called indiscretions to neutral third persons or objects, one of which is alcohol. Within this perspective, a traditionalist can engage in bout drinking at prescribed intervals and still be considered responsible according to the group's own standards. Since the dominant white society has denied Native Americans most culturally prescribed avenues to manage tension, alcohol has come to represent a convenient method of ritualistic escapism for traditionalists (Neihardt, 1932; Radin, 1920).

Middle-Class Native Americans: Although middle-class Native Americans constitute the smallest proportion of American Indians in the United States, estimated at less than 15 percent, they are the most influential in terms of society's interactions with their minority group. In other words, they are most favored by white society and most likely to hold important positions within the white-dominated Native American regulatroy structure. They are referred to by other Native Americans as 'white Indians,''apples'(red on the outside and white on the inside),'five-dollar Indians' (enrollment cost for whites to claim to be Indian and hence claim Indian land), and 'Uncle Tomahawks,' all considered derogatory. They subscribe to the norms of the larger social order and are openly rewarded for their loyalty. A common practice of the Bureau of Indian Affairs (BIA) is to groom middle-class Native Americans, usually individuals who look white, for middle-level managerial positions on the reservation. These people include pseudo-Native Americans, commonly called 'five-dollar Indians,' who paid government officials during the allotment era to include their names on the offical federal Native American rolls thus qualifying them and their subsequent generations to enjoy land once set aside exclusively for Native Americans.

Many of these pseudo-Native Americans were in turn absorbed into the BIA hierarchy and passed off as 'Native American Leaders.' The middle class also includes 'apples,' individuals who are phenotypically Native American but who act as if they are white. In general, middle-class Native Americans subscribe to the Protestant Ethic, and those who have drinking problems usually manifest symptoms similar to their white counterparts (French, 1977).

Marginal Native Americans: The remaining 60 percent of the United States Native American population can be classified as 'marginal,' torn between their traditional cultural heritage and the dictates of the larger white society. Within this category, the 'reservation marginals' fall to the right while the 'urban marginals' fall to the left. In general, reservation marginals have better access to knowledge of their traditional heritage, a situation not always shared by their urban counterparts. Another group of marginals is the rural, nonreservation population such as the Lumbee of North Carolina. They represent remnants of eastern tribes decimated by the colonial slave trade, wars, and removal.

Many marginals suffer from the dilemma of looking 'Native American' and wanting to be 'Native American' but not knowing the exact nature of their traditional cultural heritage. For these, Pan Indianism offers a partial solution. Pan Indianism attempts to provide a general Indian ethnic image, one that can be shared by the some five hundred separate Native American tribes and bands in the United States. Access to either the traditional or the middle-class categories is seriously restricted for most of these individuals, however, perpetuating their cultural marginality. Their psychocultural perspective is one of frustration and ambiguity, creating a situation in which alcohol provides a convenient, yet unacceptable, method of escape.

Conclusions

In terms of Jellinek's classification, traditionalists manifest either epsilon or beta alcoholims. It is important to remember that drinking by traditionalists is tolerated in terms of their cultural milieu. Moreover, this drinking usually occurs in the presence of others. Using Cahn's (1970) 'eclectic classification,' it could be said that traditionalists consume large quantities of alcohol at rapid rates for concentrated periods, accompanied by intermediate cycles of abstinence. Blame is usually transferred to a neutral object, often alcohol itself. It is rare for outsiders to see intoxicated traditionalists since their visibility is restricted and their privacy protected by an intimate network, thus minimizing any stigma attrached to this behavior.

Middle-class Native Americans with drinking problems manifest symptoms similar to their white counterparts. Thus alpha, beta, gamma, delta, and epsilon alcoholism may apply to these individuals.

The drinking patterns of marginal Native Amerians fall between these two models. Marginals drink heavily in public at a greater frequency than their traditional counterparts, resulting in serious health, legal, economic, and social problems. Violence, either toward self or others, arrest, and jail often accompany these situations. Although done in the company of others, this drinking lacks the acceptable sanctions associated with most tradtional bout drinking. Their consumption of large quantities of alcohol at one time, more often as well as more publicly than traditionalists, leads to a dire situation for marginal Native American alcoholics. Many of them fall into Jellinek's gamma and delta categories and often experience serious health problems, such as cirrhosis of the live and diabetes.

It is important that individuals who work with Native American alcoholism, rather they are Native American or not, be aware of the larger social, political, and cultural issues involved. They must also be aware of their own subjective involvement in life and the limitations of their own values. It does little good to have a middle-class therapist tell a marginal Native American male client that he would be all right if only he would follow the therapist's prescribed role model, one usually based upon the therapist's own frame of reference. Life is more complex than that.

REFERENCES

Cahn, Sidney. The Treatment of Alcoholism. New York: Oxford University Press, 1970.

Chafetz, Morris, et. al. Alcoholism and Society. New York: Oxford University Press, 1970.

Chafetz, Morris. "Prevention of Alcoholism in the United States," Alcohol and Health. Rockville, Md.: U. S. Government Printing Office, 1974: 167-168.

Deloria, Jr,. Vine. Custer Died for your Sins. New York: Avon Books, 1968.

Dial, Adolph, and David K. Eliades. The Only Land I Know. San-Francisco: Indian Historian Press, 1975.

Frederick, Calvin. Suicide, Homicide and Alcoholism among American Indians. Rockvillw, Md.: U. S. Government Printing Office, 1973: 2-3.

French, Laurence, and Renitia Bertoluzzi. "The Drunken Indian Stereotype and the Eastern Cherokee," Appalachian Journal, 2 (Summer, 1976): 332-334.

French, Laurence, and Jim Hornbuckle. "An Analysis of Indian Violence," American Indian Quarterly, 3 (Winter, 1977); 335-356.

Jellinek, E. M. The Disease Concept of Alcoholism. New Haven: Hillhouse Press, 1960.

Keller, Mark. Alcohol and Health. Rockville, Md.: U. S. Government Printing Office, 1974 (HSM-72-9099).

Neihardt, John. Black Elk Speaks. New York: William Morrow & Company, 1932.

Radin, Paul. "The Autobiography of a Winnebago Indian," University of California Publication in American Archaeology and

Ethnology, 16 (April, 1920): 1-91.

Rivers, P. Clayton, and Linda Rivers. Psycho-Social Aspects of Alcoholims. Lincoln: University of Nebraska Extension Division, 1975: 49.

Snake, Rubin. Report on Alcohol and Drug Abuse (Indian Task Force II). Washington: U. S. Government Printing Office, 1976: 13.

Wolman, Walter. Manual on Alcoholims. Chicago: American Medical Association, 1973: 1.

Chapter 12
Contemporary Indian Justice and Correctional Treatment

LAURENCE FRENCH

Native American justice is currently embroiled in controversy and this dilemma seems to be exacerbated by the two popular, yet contravening, perceptions of this phenomenon. People tend to examine Native American justice from either the aboriginal customary judicial perspective or from the white adversary judicial perspective. Neither perspective accurately portrays a realistic picture of the situation. Clearly, the only viable perspective to Native American justice seems to be a synthesis of these two orientations.

The 'harmonious/aboriginal thesis'and its focus on traditional tribal law offers valuable insight into the Native American cultural folkways and customs as they existed both prior to, and during the early stages of white contact. But it is foolhardy to pretend that the aboriginal system exists in its pure form anywhere in the United States today or for that matter, that this system can be reconstituted. Perhaps a contemporary Sioux saying best reflects this cultural time bridge: "The days of the buffalo are gone forever."

By the same token, the 'competitive/white antithesis' and its focus on formal, adversary law tends to obviate viable Native American cultural attributes which have survived or have evolved over time. Clearly, many of the attributes of the Native American 'harmony ethic' are contrary to those prescribed by the Western 'Protestant ethic.' And there is little doubt to the fact that the U. S. criminal justice system has a narrow, ethnocentric biased perspective, one that tends to view American Indians as well as other racial, ethnic, sex, age and class groups as 'outsiders' to the dominant normative structure.

Medcalf (1978), in her challenging book - Law and Identity, articulated this dilemma by pointing out the legal Catch-22 Native Americans often find themselves in terms of government-directed, legal policy. She portrayed the law as a mechanism of legal control and, consequently, minority suppression, contending that this remains the ulterior function of so-called 'sympathetic' liberals, as well.

Here she weaves an intricate discussion linking the philosophical ideals of John Locke, notably its American liberal adaptation, to U. S. policy which, on the surface, seems to be manifestly directed toward helping the American Indian find his place within the larger dominant social order. Particular focus is place on the 1968 (Titles II-VII) Native Bill of Rights. Her argument is clear - legal solutions to Indian problems are superficial, if not suspect, at best: "To think of other human beings in terms of rights is to rob them of much of their humanity, because it reduces humanity to the bare essentials.... to reduce human relationships to rights and responsibilities, one against the other, is to render human relationships an 'irreducible minimum' just short of nothing at all (Medcalf, 1978:125)."

However, Medcalf made the common error of jumping from an effective critique of the 'competitive/white antithesis' to that of the 'harmonious/aboriginal thesis' somehow giving the impression that the latter is the real solution to the Indian dilemma: "Reexamination of the Indian Civil Rights Act, which extends constitutional guarantees to all individual members as against the tribe, provides an example. Such constitutional guarantees assume the prior absence of individual rights. But Native Americans must have had traditional ways of relating to each other and to their 'governments.' Why then institute individual rights against the tribal government (Medcalf, 1978: 125)?"

The American Bar Foundation has recently taken the opposite position. In its report, American Indian Tribal Courts, Brakel (1978) argued that tribal courts and tribal justice are white American creations and that the Indians have a difficult time administering white-type justice to their people. The study even went on to condemn the reservation system claiming that: "They are little more than depressed areas for marginal and dependent societies of Indians, whites, and mixed-bloods. They are sociological nurseries to which those who find life difficult outside can always return, places of more or less voluntary detention for the ones who have never left, zoos for white tourists, and laboratories for academics (Brakel, 1978: 102)."

Thus, while this report stressed many of the same points Medcalf did in her book, Brakel argued in favor of a greater reliance upon the 'competitive/white antithesis': "The tribal courts do not work well, and necessary improvements would require much time and involve many difficulties. To perpetuate them at all runs counter to the evoluntionary trends in the Indians' relation to the dominant culture in this country. Therefore, it would be more realistic to abandon the system altogether and to deal with civil and criminal problems in the regular county and state court systems (Brakel, 1978: 103)."

PanIndianism: The Native American Synthesis

The genesis of contemporary Native American movements extends back to the years following the Second World War when young Indian servicemen organized the National Congress of American Indians (NCAI). While other white-sponsored Indian advocacy movements preceded the NCAI, this was the first viable Indian-sponsored program. Later, a more radical-oriented Indian group emerged in the early 1960's. This was a reaction to what young Native Americans, during the turbulent 1960's, felt to be the ineffectiveness of the NCAI. The National Indian Youth Council (NIYC) challenged the now middle aged membership of the NCAI while at the same time following the trend of other discontented youth of the time. NIYC fostered the more radical AIM (American Indian Movement) faction much like the SDS fostered the 'weathermen.'

These growth problems aside, Indian movements were instrumental in promoting a positive universal Indian image - an image that did much to dispel the old negative stereotypes long promoted in movies, in books and on television. This phenomenon soon became known as the Pan-Plains Indian movement. Not only did Native Americans seek out a common ethnic image, they now strived for self-sufficiency and self-determination. It was within this protest environment that young Indian scholars began to consolidate their efforts so as to best serve their people.

Correspondingly, a number of Indian-run, Indian interest groups and organizations emerged. In 1964 the American Indian Historical Society became incorporated and has served from that time as the Native American academic honor society disseminating Indian news and scholarly works through its press (Indian Historian Press) and its publications (Wassaja, Indian Historian, Wee Wish Tree, as well as many books by Native Americans).

Other Indian organizations soon followed suit: the Mohawk Nation's, Akwesasne Notes; the Institute for the Development of Indian Law's, American Indian Journal; the American Indian Faculty and Staff Association at the University of Oklahoma and its influence in the development of the American Indian Law Review; and the Native American Rights Fund and its National Indian Law Library Catalogue and Announcements.

Moreover, Indian scholars like Vine Deloria, Jr., Bea Medicine, Rupert Costo, Adolph Dial and others did much to disseminate this information to the general public through professional, academic and public meetings, assemblies and media events. They served notice to the rest of the Nation and the world that the popular negative stereotypes of American Indians as being simplistic, primitive and savage entities would no longer be tolerated. Hence, the 1960's and 1970's saw an increase in Indian attorneys, scholars, medical doctors, administrators and the like. This was the Indian response and the emergence of contemporary Pan Indianism.

Native American Correctional Survival

Native American correctional survival is the basic philosophy of the special, Federally supported, Swift Bird project, the Indian-run, minimum security prison located in South Dakota designed to serve Plains Indian inmates. The concept actually stems from the Indian survival school philosophy which has its roots in the Red School House in St. Paul, Minnesota.

Basically, the Indian survival philosophy works on the assumption that much of the contemporary Indian problems are grounded in 'marginality,' the process of being caught between two worlds (the traditional Indian and the white dominant cultures) with little hope of fully belonging to either (Park, 1950; Sellin, 1938). Indian survival attempts to strengthen the Native American's self-image, what they refer to as their 'Indianism.' Once this task has been accomplished emphasis is then given to learning the basic skills necessary to survive in both of these cultural worlds.

Until cultural building and other preventive programs emerge, the 'Native American synthesis' will have to continue to focus upon its current ex post facto, resocialization programs. Presently, two Native American correctional orientations offer programs which fit the Native American systhesis perspective: (1) Indian correctional institutions exclusively for Native American Clients, and (2) Native American prison survival schools for Indian clients incarcerated within larger inmate populations.

The Institute for the Development of Indian Law described the problems with typical State and Federal prisons in relation to Indian clients as such:

> The prison environment, in which a disproportionate number of Native Americans find themselves, given the selective and discriminatory law enforcement system, is one which they find especially hostile and alien. Indians are greatly overrepresented in prison populations, yet often lack a voice in their operation (Kickinbird, 1978: 19).

The Native American Rights Fund (NARF) initiated changes that would attempt to resolve some of these problems articulated by Kickinbird. They first initiated action within the State prison system through the Federal courts and later helped to develop the first Indian-run correctional facility for Indian clients - the Cheyenne River, Swift Bird project.

Indian Corrections: Swift Bird Facility

In their first significant criminal suit, the Native American Rights Fund was instrumental in bringing about needed changes in the Nebraska prison system. Here, NARF successfully argued a class action suit for the Indian inmates, filed in U. S. Disrict Court against the director of the Nebraska Correctional Services Department (October, 1974).

A summary of the charges are as follows:

> Plaintiffs who comprise the class of Indian inmates incarcerated in the Nebraska Penal and Correctional Complex sued (the) defendant...claiming certain deprivations of rights secured to them under the First and Fourteenth Amendments.... Specifically, plaintiffs claimed that officials refused to permit an Indian Cultural Club; that access to Indian religion, including the Native American Church was denied to them; and that they were discriminated against in various ways in the rehabilitation process including work release, work assignments and the failure to provide Indian counselors and instructors (Indian Inmates of the Nebraska Penitentiary v. Vitek, No. 72-L-156, D.Neb., Order of October 31, 1974).

The suit resulted in the court ordering a number of changes including allowing Indian inmates to wear their hair long in traditional hairstyles, for official recognition of an Indian spiritual cultural club including the construction of sweat lodges and the use of medicine men for services. This order also included the Native American Church but the Nebraska Department of Correctional Services has 'stonewalled' all attempts to implement this element of the court order (see Public Law 95-341/August, 1978).

Moreover, it was decreed that the Nebraska correctional department would formulate an affirmative action plan designed to hire Indian personnel at their facilities and that the Nebraska penal and correctional complex was to provide accredited courses relevant to Indian culture and Indian studies for their Native American clients.

Indeed, this was a victory over past penal policies directed toward Indian cultural genocide, the process of destroying Indian culture for the purpose of forced assimilation. Indian inmates in Nebraska now have an opportunity to retain aspects of their cultural heritage, and to even strengthen it, while incarcerated. More importantly, this suit was the forerunner of the Cheyenne River Swift Bird Project - the prototype of Indian-run correctional facilities slated to be developed across the Nation.

This alternative Indian rehabilitation center was the product of Indian and white faculty and students at the University of Nebraska working in conjunction with NARF staff. The director of the facility, Rick Williams (Lacota Sioux) was a student at the University of Nebraska when the idea was conceived. Following his graduation, he served an apprenticeship with NARF under the direction of Walter Echo-Hawk, one of the NARF attorneys involved in the Nebraska Penal suit.

The Swift Bird facility is a voluntary pre-release Indian-run correctional facility designed to serve Native American clients from five northern Plains states (South and North Dakota, Nebraska, Minnesota and Montana) as well as the Federal Bureau of Prisons. The concept of Swift Bird is to provide individualized 'cultural reprogramming' for short-term Indian clients convicted and sentenced in either Federal court and/or in the courts of the participating states.

According to the Swift Bird mandate these volunteers: "Shall be dealt with humanely, with efforts directed toward their rehabilitation and return to the community as safely and promptly as practicable (Echo Hawk, 1977: 13)." Native American cultural and spiritual treatment are important considerations with the Swift Bird comprehensive classification and rehabilitation program effort.

As mentioned earlier, this orientation is similar to that employed by Native American 'alternative' and 'survival' schools. The basic premise here is that a person has to feel good about himself and who they are before they can become fully responsible and autonomous members of society. Alternative and survival schools orientations stress the positive attributes of being Indian, reinforcing the Pan Indian and particular cultural orientation of the client's home world environment, while at the same time providing the necessary skills needed to survive in the dominant white culture.

The Cheyenne River (South Dakota) Swift Bird facility was opened in the Fall of 1979 and only time will tell if it is successful. Perhaps the greatest obstacle to this program is the contravening jurisdictions involved and the lack of a clear legal mandate for the clients they serve. All clients (up to 70) must be admitted on a voluntary basis under a contractual agreement made between the Seift Bird staff and the sending institutions. Thus, the sending units have ultimate jurisdiction and legal custody over their clients while they are at Swift-Bird. The Native American prison survival concept has equal relevance to Indian clients incarcerated in State and Federal penal facilities. It tries to provide the essence of the Native American resocialization within both types of correctional environments.

Indian Prison Survival Schools

Indian prison survival schools have a serious mandate in that they must overcome the damage already done by the prisonization and reservation processes. Consequently, the Indian survival curriculum must consider certain cultural attributes unique to Native American clients. This involves the important first phase of Indian survival school programs - the development of a sense of Indian self-worth (the opposite of trying to 'white-wash' Indian clients). The next phase involves learning the basic skills necessary to cope within both the Indian and white worlds. Indeed, this is a challenging endeavor for any person and more so for those already suffering the stigma of incarceration.

The 'Indianism' process involves teaching the marginal Indian his cultural roots, Pan Indianism and the tenet of the 'harmony ethos.' Here, the client is exposed to the Indian orientation and encouraged to adopt a native-oriented cognitive style. Native American learning strategies include teaching native custom, rituals and languages, all designed to enhance the person's self-awareness and to provide a positive, 'cultural proactive' status resulting from incarceration. A consequence of this educational process is the shared collective Pan Indian identity.

Once these attributes are internalized, the marginal Indian can begin to reassess his/her past failures and ascertain why he/she is plagued by alcohol, violence and/or incarceration. Moreover, it is at this level of awareness that conventional treatment modalities can be introduced into the cultural program. And the introduction of popular counseling and/or experiential group modalities into the program does not provide an alien element since consensual treatment itself has a long aboriginal tradition, existing within Native American groups centuries prior to group psychotherapy, T-groups, encounter groups, network therapy and the like came into vogue within Western societies.

The final institutional stage of the Indian survival program is dedicated to teaching Indian inmates how to cope beyond their subculture and make it in the larger, white-dominated society as well. The teachers in both phases of the Indian prison survival school program should be comprised of both Indians and non-Indians. Traditional Indian inmates make excellent teachers in both phases. These individuals, unlike their marginal counterparts, seem to have a better sense of their cultural identity including the relevant rituals, the language and the like, hence seem to maintain a strong sense of their 'Indianism' even when incarcerated. This is the basic format of the Indian prison survival school.

In conclusion, it is interesting to note that Native Americans have long been expected to understand both cultural world views(harmony and Protestant ethos) while members of the dominant culture, especially those involved in legal and social service delivery (prosecutors, judges, law enforcement officers, defense attorneys, correctional, social service and health personnel, psychologists, psychiatrists, teachers...) usually do not feel compelled to have to try and understand American Indian cultures. The 'Native American systhesis' allows for this cross-cultural educational exchange between Indians and non-Indians while neither the 'harmonious/aboriginal thesis' nor the 'competitive/white antithesis' considers this form of reciprocity being viable. Cultural survival according to the 'Native American synthesis,' is a two-way process. The perspective also recognized the value in the preservation of one's unique cultural heritage, therefore, makes a distinction between forced accommodation/assimilation or other attempts to obviate attributes of Native American cultures and the reality of cultural pluralism.

REFERENCES

Brakel, Samuel. American Indian Tribal Courts. Chicago: American Bar Foundation, 1978.

Cohen, Felix. Federal Indian Law. Albuquerque: University of New Mexico Press, 1971.

Echo-Hawk, Walter. Cheyenne River Swift Bird Project. Boulder: Native American Rights Fund (October, 1977).

Frederick, Calvin. Suicide, Homicide and Alcoholism among American Indians. Rockville, Md.: U. S. Department of Health, Education and Welfard, 1973.

Kickingbird, Kathy, et. al. "Treatment of Native Americans in the Criminal Justice System," Manuscript awaiting publication.

Medcalf, Linda. Law and Identity. Beverly Hills: Sage, 1978.

Park, Robert E. Race and Culture. New York: Free Press, 1950.

Reasons, Charles. "Crime and the American Indian," Native Americans Today (H. Bahr, et. al., eds). New York: Harper & Row, 1972.

Sellin, Thorsten. Conflict and Crime. New York: Social Science Research Council, 1938.

Chapter 13
Native American Prison Survival Schools

LAURENCE FRENCH

Clearly, Native Americans represent America's most perplexed group, plagued with high unemployment, serious health problems and a high crime rate. The paradox of cultural conflict and psychological ambivalence leads to a high proportion of 'marginal' Indians, those caught up between their traditional (minority) heritage and the demands of the larger white (majority) society. Indeed, it is this unique majority/minority relationship which is the basis of most of these problems. United States Indian policy has forced the Native American from one federal program philosophy to another, increasing marginality each time.

Social solutions to the problems of marginality, on the other hand, have been basically symptom-oriented with little effort made to change the social conditions which cause marginality and its consequences: crime, alcoholism, poor health and early death. Subsequently, arrest and eventually prison often become the lot of the 'contemporary warrior'. This paper looks at the phenomena of Indian marginality and the contemporary warrior attempting to find a realistic, viable solution to the high incident of incarceration among young male Indian adults. Our perspective attempts to integrate two yet unrelated current innovative educational ideas - Indian survival schools and andragogy (adult education).

Social and Personal Disorganization

The focus of this inquiry is restricted to the northern Plains Indians although it is quite feasible that it has far greater implications within the larger Native American Indian population. Clearly, the following discussion concerning Indian social and personal disorganization applies to all Indian groups in the country.

Most Indian marginality is a direct result of cultural ambiguity, the process of being torn between two contravening cultural expectations without the possibility of fully belonging to either. These Native Americans often resort to alcohol as a means of escapism and retreatism and, by the same token, are more prone to personal violence. The problem is not merely a choice between the traditional harmony ethos and the majority Protestant ethic, since neither of these present viable solutions to the contemporary Indian situation. What must be remembered is that the Bureau of Indian Affairs (BIA) has operated in such a fashion as to perpetuate an accommodative, dependent reservation and urban ghetto environment rather than one of self-sufficiency and independence. And when young Native Americans learn of their rich, yet unobtainable, past heritage and the role of deceit the majority society played in White/Indian relations, this often serves to exacerbate their inner rage and personal ambivalence forcing them to further withdraw from the majority society or to join an anti-establishment and anti-tribal movement (the AIM phenomenon). By the time they are formulating their self-identify and planning for adulthood, the marginal Indian fully realizes that he has not been adequately prepared for any viable social position in either his traditional culture or in the majority United States society. In essence, the marginal Indian is ascribed the social status of 'perpetual adolescence' with this behavior reinforced by the majority society through its policy of paternalistic dependency (rewards) and severe punitive sanctions (harsh prison terms).

Alcohol and violence have come to represent the contemporary lifestyle of the marginal Indian. Reasons (1972) found that Native Americans have the highest alcohol-related crime rate of any racial group in the United States. In his analysis of national arrest rates, he found that the Indian arrest rate was eight times that of blacks and over twenty times that of whites. Another study (Frederick, 1973) by the National Institute of Mental Health found that the leading causes of Indian death are alcohol related and often violent. The three leading causes of death among Native Americans are cirrhosis of the liver, suicide, and homicide. This compares with cardiovascular illness, cancer, and accidents for the United States in general. Most of the violence involves Indian offenders and Indian victims, occurring in the heat of passion or in despair, clear indicators of the high tension and ambiguous situation confronting marginal Indians in contemporary American society (French, 1976, 1977, 1978).

The Contemporary Warrior

The Sioux warrior image was honed only after they were

forced from their traditional home in Minnesota. Until then they were considered to be a lesser threat than were their more aggressive contemporaries east of the Missouri - the Iroquois. According to Holder (1974), the ancestors of the contemporary Sioux originally occupied country north and east of the Missouri River as far as the Great Lakes. These western, or Prairie, Sioux later became the Plains Sioux. It was these fierce and respected warriors who dominated the northern plains along with their Algonquian neighbors - the Cheyenne. Prior to their adaptation to horse transportation the Sioux did not have such an admirable reputation. Indeed, their name is a French transformation of the Chippewa term for the meaning 'Lesser Adders'. The Iroquois were the 'True Adders' and they were the ones who forced the Sioux from the Great Lakes region across the Missouri and subsequently into their significant place in history.

A successful record as a warrior was the principal requisite for the ultimate status as a respected elder. And to be a successful warrior the male Sioux had to be brave, have fortitude, be generous, and acquire wisdom. These virtues suggest a life-process which generates its own psychological orientation. Bravery was the most important virtue for both males and females within the Plains-Sioux society. It also meant courting death for male warriors. Counting coupe and dog soldiering were two ways of testing one's bravery. Counting coupe was the practice of approaching the enemy and leaving evidence of your ability to have killed him although not doing so. It was a powerful psychological tool for the warrior since the enemy lived to fear the warrior who counted coupe upon him. In a similar vein, dog soldiering was yet another psychological test of bravery. Here the warrior bound himself to a fixed object on the battlefield taking on the enemy from this restricted stance. Fortitude is a corollary virtue stressing physical endurance and stoicism. The Sun Dance was the most significant ritual designed to test a warrior's fortitude, yet this virtue governed much of the Sioux's public (secondary) behavior as it continues to do even today among a large portion of the population.

These virtues and rituals have never died and since Wounded Knee II (1973) the warrior image has been rekindled among young Sioux men. Obviously, the warrior ways have changed markedly from those of the pre-reservation days. The warrior psychology, however, has not changed that drastically, and equally significant is the fact that the contemporary warrior's role is not a new one. It is an adaptation which was made at the conclusion of the Indian wars in the 1890s when the Sioux and other northern Plains Indians were forced upon reservations and their mobility greatly curtailed. Even then, tests of life experiences became important aspects of the warrior status and the warrior psychology. Now alcohol, fighting, and other forms of aggressive behavior provide the challenges needed to test the warrior. Within this environment, the successful warrior is one who tests these challenges, including jail and prison, and survives. And if he survives, he is eligible to become an elder (Radin, 1920; Neihardt, 1932; Bryde, 1971).

Marginality increases the probability of Native American failure. Subsequently, we have young adult males ready to test their warrior role with alcohol, altercations, jail, and even prison, with fewer and fewer succeeding. Instead, alcohol, jail and prison initially intended as means toward an end, now become ends in themselves for many Indians, denying them the coveted status of 'respected elder'. Indeed, few of these 'losers' even make it to senior citizen status. The role of prison survival schools is to provide viable intervention which can successfully tap the Native American's unique psycho-cultural orientation.

Cultural Relativity and Androgogy

Indian education has long been an area of interest to American educators, but with most endeavors meeting little success. The harsh boarding school era resulted in merely increasing marginality and restricting the use of the native language among these children (Kupferer, 1960). The other alternative, forcing the Indian child to cope within the majority (Protestant ethic) schools, is equally devasting often forcing native students into a greater state of 'failure' (Thomas, 1971). These failures have led to the emergence of a separate school of thought dedicated to the study of language and education (Cohen, 1969; Cole, 1972; Cook, 1973; Cazden, 1972).

The failure of cultural pedagogy does not necessarily spell failure for cultural andragogy. Quite the contrary, adult education seems to be a more realistic environment for Indian education, especially those elements of education which deal with life-experiences. These schools exist today among Native American groups and are known as 'survival schools' (French, 1977). The Indian survival school is based on principles which are the antithesis of the earlier boarding school concept which attempted to 'white-wash' native students. This philosophy is in line somewhat with Burger's (1968) concept, ethno-pedagogy, where the role of the teacher is that of bicultural change agent. Moreover, Indian survival schools subscribe to yet another of Burger's tenets, the use of an instructional model which relates the minority subcultural value system to that of the dominant values of the majority society. The idea here is to teach natives, youth and adult alike, to accept their 'Indianism;' including their cultural roots and heritage, customs and language; and then to teach them how to cope within the larger majority society. While this philosophy is an interesting one, not enough time has passed to test its effectiveness.

Even if this is a viable epistemological methodology it still needs to be adapted to the principles of andragogy and made culturally relevant. Knowles (1973) alerted educators to certain fundamental differences existing between the teaching/learning process involving children and those relevant to the adult student. Traditional teaching techniques, such as the Socratic method, unfoldment, apperception and behaviorism, designed to teach and socialize the child, do not necessarily lend themselves to the adult educational environment. Indeed, these and other educational techniques are seriously challenged by many adult educators and adult psychologists.

Andragogy seems to be sensitive to complex social-psychological factors, stressing certain distinguishing factors: self-concept, experience, readiness, time perspective and the adult's orientation toward learning. Given these criteria, Knowles suggests that adult learners are more self-directed than their less mature counterpart (primary and secondary and most college undergraduate) and more inclined to draw on their own life experiences. Furthermore, adult learners are likely to have more specific motivational incentives and hence be more aware of the time factors involved in their education pursuit (end oriented). And regarding orientation, adult learners more often prefer problem-centered information, that which they can associate with their own life experience, rather than subject-centered instruction.

The question now is how do these issues fit the Native American 'harmony ethic', the Indian survival school philosophy and the contemporary warrior image? The harmony ethic views man as being subordinate to Nature, thus fitting the interactionistic perspective, model-of-man while both the humanistic and behavioristic perspectives have their roots in the Protestant ethos, with the former subscribing to a philosophy of innate-rationality and the latter seeing other-directed behaviorial change occurring within controlled environments.

Given these differences it would be foolhardy to use WASP-oriented therapy and/or instruction techniques (humanistic, behavioristic) with Native Americans. Even then culturally-relevant interactionistic therapy and/or instructional techniques with native populations must be made relevant to their particular tribal group and/or directed toward the more general concept of pan-Indianism. 'Indianism' must be stressed in these programs. Most non-Indian 'western' programs focus on 'white-washing' natives, derrogating their native heritage and subsequently forcing them to abandon their traditional ways.

Attempting to teach individuals the secondary (public) skills necessary to survive in our Western-styled, individually-oriented society without first considering their traditional cultural heritage only serves to exacerbate their marginality and hence increase both their psychological ambiguity and social disorganization. Unfortunately, symptomology is the most common form of treatment reaction within the Protestant ethic. Consequently, Indians are often pigeon-holed according to their health or social symptoms, being labeled as alcoholics, diabetics, felons or the like and not treated as separate psycho-cultural entities. By focusing on their problems (symptoms) and not on the causes of the problems, many marginal Indians are forced into a 'heavy guilt trip'. Here the label becomes a significant part of their identity creating a self-fulfilling prophecy.

Indian survival schools not only work on improving the natives self-perception but do so within a culturally-relevant orientation. Indian self-perception is linked to the cooperative Harmony Ethic and its particular religious ethos (Mother Earth/Father Sky). Marginal Indians are taught their cultural ways including language (language, thought, and reality), customs, and rituals. Pan-Indianism is offered as a model for those persons not certain of their particular lost heritage. Here English, the Native American Church, and more general Indian attributes (long hair and common dress and jewelry) come into play. Regardless of which approach is taken, the desired end is the same - teaching marginal Indians to be proud of themselves and instilling strong psychological roots concerning their cultural-heritage.

Prison Indian Survival Schools

The idea of adapting the Indian survival school concept to institutionalized Indians emerged in 1974 when NARF (Native American Rights Fund) won its first major prison discrimination case (against Nebraska's Department of Corrections). This class action suit won Indian inmates the right to wear their hair in traditional fashion, to have cultural events at the institutions, and to build and use sweat lodges in their religious ceremonies. Shortly thereafter NARF was instrumental in establishing a special Indian correctional facility on the Cheyenne River (Swift Bird) reservation in South Dakota. Nevertheless, merely thinking about a project such as this is not enough and even if this particular project proves to be successful, it is designed to serve only a handful of Indian inmates from five northern Plains states (Nebraska, Minnesota, North and South Dakota and Montana).

What is needed is a viable program, one that could be used in existing 'majority-run' prisons as well as in special Indian institutions. For the program to be viable it must draw on the principles of andragogy - culturally relevant andragogy.

Indian prison survival schools must overcome the damage already done by imprisonment as well as overcome the basic social causes of psycho-cultural ambiguity which got the marginal Indian in prison in the first place. Consequently, the Indian survival curriculum must consider certain special cultural attributes of andragogy, notable the student's (inmate's) cognitive style, learning strategy, self-awareness, life-process, and human development. This involves the important first phase of Indian survival school programs - developing a sense of Indian self-worth. The next phase involves learning the basic skills necessary to cope, within both the Indian and White worlds.

'Indianism' involves an intricate process of teaching the marginal Indian his cultural roots and the tenets of the harmony ethic. Here the client is exposed to the Indian psycho-cultural orientation and encouraged to adopt a native-oriented cognitive style. Native American learning strategies include teaching native customs, rituals, and language, all designed to enhance the Indian's self-awareness enough to sustain him through life. A consequence of this educational process is the shared or collective personality identity of Native Americans and the corresponding cooperative primary (family, peer) and group (kin, clan) social networks.

Once these psycho-cultural attributes are internalized, the marginal Indian can begin to reassess his past failures and ascertain why he is plagued by alcohol, violence, and incarceration. Now and only now can conventional treatment modalities such as group therapy be used. Indeed, group therapy is not an alien existential device, but rather one which has a long tribal tradition. Consensual treatment has a long aboriginal history, existing centuries before group psycho-therapy, T-groups and network therapy came into vogue (after World War II) in western societies.

The next, and final, stage in the prison Indian survival school program is to teach the Indian inmate how to cope not only within the Indian culture, but to exist within the larger non-Indian (majority) society as well. But while the first phase utilizes a culturally-relevant, interactionistic andragogy model, this latter phase draws on all three models. Remedial skills are best taught through the behavioristic perspective, while group sessions lend themselves to the interactionistic orientation. And highly creative Indians (artists, crafts-people, poets, writers, and spirited individuals) can benefit greatly from the humanistic instructional model.

Once the incarcerated Indian male adult learns these survival skills he should be able to better cope in the complex dual-cultural environment he and his family face in contemporary America. It is interesting to note that Native Americans have always been expected to understand both worlds (protestant and harmony) while majority professionals; including psychologists, psychiatrists, teachers, professors, prosecutors, judges, law enforcement officers, defense attorneys and correctional, social service and health personnel usually do not feel compelled to have to try and understand American Indian cultures. This is merely a program philosophy and only time will tell if it is feasible to implement prison Indian survival schools or if others will allow its implementation. The biggest obstacles to these programs come from the majority society. This is nothing new. History already tells us that all the majority-determined Indian policies have failed. Hopefully, this program and other Indian-initiated, self-determination programs will at least be given a chance to work.

REFERENCES

Bryde, J.F., Modern Indian Psychology. Vermillion: University of South Dakota, Institute of Indian Studies, 1971.

Cazden, C.B., 'Dialect Differences and Bilingualism,' Child Language and Education. New York: Holt, Rinehart & Winston, 1972.

Clemmer, D., The Prison Community. New York: Holt, Rinehart & Winston, 1940.

Cohen, R.A., 'Conceptual Styles, Cultural Conflict, and Non-verbal Tests of Intelligence,' American Anthropologist, Vol. 71, 1969.

Cole, M. & J. Gay, 'Culture and Memory,' American Anthropologist, Vol. 74, No. 5, 1972.

Cook, J.A., 'Language and Socialization,' Class, Codes and Control (B. Bernstein). Boston: Routledge and Kegan Paul, 1973.

French, L., 'Social Problems Among Cherokee Females,' American Journal of Psychoanalysis, Vol. XXXVI, No. 2, 1976.

French, L. & J. Hornbuckle, 'Cultural Clash in our Educational System,' Indian Historian, Vol. 10, No. 4 (Fall), 1977.

French, L., 'The Perversion of Incarceration,' Corrective and Social Psychiatry, Vol. 24, No. 1, 1978.

French, L. & J. Hornbuckle, 'An Analysis of Indian Violence,' American Indian Quarterly, Vol. 3, No. 4 (Winter), 1978c.

Frederick, C., Suicide, Homicide and Alcoholism among American Indians. Rockville, Md.: National Institute of Mental Health (DREW + ADM 74-42), 1973.

Gearing, F.O., 'A Cultural Theory of Education,' Educational Patterns and Cultural Configurations (Roberts, J.I. & S.K. Akinsanys). New York: David McKay, 1976.

Hassrick, R.B., The Sioux. Norman: University of Oklahoma Press, 1964.

Holder, P., The Hoe and the Horse on the Plains. Lincoln: University of Nebraska Press, 1970.

Knowles, M., The Adult Learner. Houston: Gulf, 1973.

Kupferer, H.J., 'The Principal People, 1960,' Anthropological Paper, No. 78 (Bulletin 1960), Smithsonial Institution, Bureau of American Ethnology, 1966.

Neihardt, J., Black Elk Speaks. New York: Morrow, 1932.

Radin, P., 'The Autobiography of a Winnebago Indian,' University of California Publication in American Archaeology and Ethnology, 16, (April, 1920).

Reasons, C., 'Crime and the American Indian,' Native Americans Today (Bahr, et al). New York: Harper & Row, 1972.

Thomas, R.K. & A.L. Wahrhaftig, 'Indians, Hillbillies and the Education Problem,' Anthropological Perspectives on Education (M.L. Wax et al). New York: Basic Books, 1971.

Wax, M.L. et al Formal Education in an American Indian Community. Society for the Study of Social Problems (Monograph + 1), 1964.

Chapter 14
Counseling Native Americans

LAURENCE FRENCH

Multicultural and cross-cultural counseling have made tremendous inroads within the past two decades yet much still needs to be done especially in the area of integrating theory, research and counseling techniques. This selection addresses the issue of Indian counseling, attempting to link contemporary counseling techniques with unique Indian cultural attributes.

The Genesis of Contemporary Counseling Psychology

Contemporary counseling emerged, for the most part, out of the post Second World War era when group therapy became popular. Indeed, the main reason for this movement was an economic one, yet certain intrinsic values emerged from this technique in itself. Perhaps, the most significant latent function was the 'theraputic environment' group counseling created. At any rate, insightful psychologists and psychiatrists such as Moreno, Sullivan, Rogers and Lewin readily saw the utility of this phenomenon molding it into unique counseling modalities of which contemporary counseling technique are based (Binder, 1976; Shaffer, 1974; Yalom, 1975).

The group therapy movement also proved to be a convenient vehicle for the expression of internal dissention within the ranks of the psychoanalytic school. Not only did Freud's students reinterpret and contribute to his works on personality and the techniques he popularized for the treatment of personality disorders - psychoanalysis - many of these scholars and clinicians openly challenged elements of the Freudian perspective as well as each others treatment philosophies. Consequently, C. G. Jung, Karl Abraham, Alfred Adler, Karen Horney, Erich Fromm, A. H. Maslow and Harry Stack Sullivan became leaders of their own particular psychoanalytic schools.

This internal divisiveness within psychiatry was exacerbated by the challenge from the growing behavior camp - that which developed around the works of Ivan Pavlov, John Watson, Hermann Ebbinghaus, E. L. Thorndike and, later, B. F. Skinner. The strength of the behaviorists lie both in their long tradition, which they trace to Aristotilian 'associationism,' and their strong ties to 'positivism' - the scientific perspective. Clearly, the war-time acceleration computer technology greatly benefitted the behavioral school. Soon behaviorism branched into experimental, cognitive, and treatment camps each utilizing this new technology in their quest for better knowledge regarding the complexities associated with human behavior, and doing so through process and memory retention and recall as well as prescribing scientific methods for modifying these behavioral modes.

Contemporary counseling psychology draws from both the psychoanalytic and behavioristic perspectives. The major contributors, however, were scholars like Moreno, Sullivan, Lewin and Rogers who were able to integrate the group therapy element into innovative counseling frameworks.

Jacob L. Moreno was one of the first to explore with group therapy opening his Theater of Spontaneity in Vienna in 1921. He came to the United States in 1925 and it was here he developed his concept of 'psychodrama.' These early experiments with creative and cathartic self-expression perhaps illustrates the first use of groups for the specific purpose of creating a therapeutic environment. Indeed, Moreno's influence is so strong in this area, he is often credited with developing 'group psychotherapy' (Shaffer, 1974). These psycho- and socio-dramatic processes oftem employed the group more as an audience than as co-counselees. Nevertheless, these processes did occur within a group context and, equally significant, they focused upon the here-and-now, yet another critical group counseling concept.

Harry Stack Sullivan did much to link psychiatry with social psychology, notably the 'symbolic interactionists.' Drawing on the earlier works of George Herbert Mead (1934), Charles H. Cooley (1902) and W. I. Thomas (1951), Sullivan expanded Freudian psychoanalysis to involve the 'primary groups' where significant socialization occurs. He intergrated the symbolic interactionistic concepts, 'generalized other' and 'significant other,' into the psychiatric realm consequently developing his own term which he used to depict the major agent of socialization - the 'mothering one.' As a medically-trained psychiatrist, Sullivan did much to encourage others to forge inter-disciplinary pursuits in their quest for viable behavioral treatment modalities. Moreover, he introduced the primary group as an effective means for group therapy (Sullivan, 1955).

Clearly, the transition from group-psychotherapy to group counseling emerged out of the T-Group and Laboratory Method initiated by Kurt Lewin in 1946, which, incidently, was a response to interracial sensitivity among white public servants and officials. Lewin's contributions to counseling psychology also included popularizing the Gestaltan method, a technique he adopted in Germany under the direction of Wertheimer and his colleagues, Kohler and Kaffka. The Gestaltans posited a holistic approach to human perception contending that humans perceive their particular realities directly as a whole and not as clusters of sensations (bundles and association hypotheses) as was commonly believed previously. Equally significant is the Gestaltan view of 'closure' - the tendency for people to perceive reality within limited cognitive boundaries. The psychological phenomenon is now commonly referred to as "psychic or personality space" and plays an important role in both individual and group counseling today (Lewin, 1942).

Lewin's influence with sensitivity training groups was cut short by his death in 1947. Nonetheless, he is often credited as being the 'spiritual father' of this movement. The significance of the movement was that it advocated sensitivity training for 'normal' people thus greatly expanding the group counseling concept. The initial training seminars were held in Connecticut under the direction of the Research Center for Group Dynamics at MIT. The seminar-orientation was subsequently modified the following year at a special conference held at Bethel, Maine.

Here, distinctions were made between Action Groups (A-Groups) and Sensitivity Training Groups (T-Groups). The laboratory method established boundaries for both types of group encounters (Gestaltan influence) with the A-Groups closely resembling the social/psychological task-oriented groups and the T-Groups emerging as a unique format for interpersonal learning. This method was soon (1950) adopted by the National Education Association (NEA) as a permanent organization know as the National Training Laboratory (NTL).

The T-Group model also provided counseling psychology with much of its terminology and techniques, concepts which clearly reflect the Gestaltan influence and the scientific systemic approach. Notably among these terms and techniques are: 'unfreezing,' 'observant participant,' 'feedback,' 'self-awareness,' 'here-and-now focus,' 'therapeutic environment,' and 'group norms.' Moreover, the focus was on a stepwise process of self-awareness. A related development in sensitivity groups was the wide use of 'structured group exercises,' a phenomenon which may well have expanded from its original function, that as a means toward the larger therapeutic end; now often used as an end-in-itself.

T-Groups soon generated its own off-spring, one which quickly out-distanced its parent organization in popularity during the 1960's and 1970's. This was the Encounter Group movement which gained wide acceptance on the west coast. The Encounter Group counseling orientation is closely associated with Carl Rogers. Rogers already revolutionized individual therapy with his client-oriented technique. Besides, he did much to expan the counseling field beyond the medical profession. Prior to the Second World

War most clinical professionals were medical doctors (psychiarists). Rogers was a psychologist with a PhD and not an MD (Rogers, 1969).

While Rogers is credited with coining the term 'encounter group' this orientation first evolved out of a NTL regional branch established in southern California. Demand for personal growth, self-awareness and sensitivity toward problems with living became paramount considerations within these sessions and soon the new Encounter Group movement was underway. It soon provided a popular vehicle for the new 'humanistic psychology' of the 1960's and 1970's. Encounter reflects the group method whereby members challenge each other during the therapeutic sessions.

A parallel movement within the social science provided evidence which lent support to the counseling psychology movement. The works of Hollingshead and Redlick (1958), H. Warren Dunham (1965), Herbert Hymann (1942) and others did much to challenge the long held myths of mental illness - offering theoretical and empirical information which strongly suggested that mental illness, especailly stress related problems associated with everyday living, are common to all humans. The public response was the development of community mental health centers and the philosophy of preventive and continuing mental health maintenance, programs which best reflect the counseling psychology perspective.

Contravening Cultural-Orientations and Its Impact on Counseling Psychology

Social philosophers have long recognized two basic, albeit contravening, espistemological methodologies. These metaphysical value-orientations direct societies toward either cooperative or competitive ideological foundations. They reflect the artificial and relativistic nature of human society per se. That is, each society, at any given time, interprets life according to its particular social realities (world-view). Consequently, social realitites are actually artificial constructs of reality and that these particular realities then become 'real' to those, and generally only those, who subscribe to a given cultural-orientation (social value system).

Indeed, one of the better discussions of this age-old philosophical phenomenon was put forth by Erich Goode:

> All civilizations set rules concerning what is 'real' and what is not, what is 'true' and what 'false.' All societies select out of the data before them a world, one world, the 'world taken for granted,' and declare that the 'real world.' Each on of these artificially constructed worlds is some degree idiosyncratic, unique. No individual views reality directly, 'in the raw,' so

> to speak. Our preceptions are narrowly channelled through concepts and interpretations... The specific rules governing the perception of the universe which man inhabits are more or less arbitrary, a matter of convention. Every society establishes a kind of epistemological methodology. Meaning, then, does not automatically announce itself. Rather, it is read into every situation, event, entity, object, phenomenon (Goode, 1969:84).

History attests to the intensity of these ideological beliefs and their resulting conflicts. Nevertheless, attempts have been made to analyze the cooperative and competitive world-views within the framework of contemporary Western social philosophies - the post-Enlightenment scientific and technological era. Indeed, the great debates put forth by the British Empiricists (Hobbes, Locke, Rosseau, Hume...) continued into the 20th century with the works of Emile Durkheim, Ferdinand Tonnies, Pitirim Sorokin, among others.

Durkheim (1954) provided an excellent functional analysis of social ideologies suggesting that they provide a shared purpose in life, a purpose articulated through custom, symbols and rituals. Social ideologies (cultural-orientations) provide the group with a shared epistemological methodology, a world view, one which addresses the basic categories of the understanding - the universal properties of culture: time and space, class, number, cause, substance, personality....

Paradoxically, Durkheim (1968) shared the common belief of the time that cooperative societies were anachronisms of a more primitive era. Tonnies (1957) and Sorokin (1928) reinforced this belief in 'progressive social evolution' (circa 1850's to 1920's) and all three scholars' posited theories which viewed cooperative (folk) societies as being inferior to the new technological, competitive social model. Durkheim labelled the cooperative folk society, 'mechanical,' and the new competitive technological societal model, 'organic.' Tonnies used the terms 'gemeinshaft' (folk) and 'gesellscaft' (urban technological) while Skorokin coined traditional folk societies, 'sensate,' and the urban, technological societies as 'ideational' cultures.

This ethnocentric bias was not only reflective in the leading social philosophies of the time, it was also engrained into the basic foundation of Western social/philosophy - the 'Protestant ethic.' Max Weber (1958) did much to articulate the origin, justification and purpose of the Protestant ethic and how this ethos was supportive of the urban, technological, capitalistic society model, that which emerged out of the ruins of the Middle Ages. He noted that the values of certain Protestant groups, Calvinists, Pietists, Methodists and Baptists, lent strong support to the values of capitalism. Certainly, the Protestant ethic was initially based upon the principle of predestination or the 'calling' as well as the concept of asceticism. Within this framework, success and asceticism became reciprocal social and moral indicators of individual superiority within Western societies.

Asceticism eventually became a casualty of secular capitalism while most of the other values associated with the Protestant ethic are still part of the Western value system, including the work ethic, individual achievement and culpability and, of course, individual competition. Accordingly, educational success, occupational status and material wealth are all viewed as important measures of one's social success. The basis for this social world-view is that it is believed that all members of society have equal opportunity to achieve success through the vehicle of individual competition, therefore, the winners of this social 'survival-of-the-fittest' contest should be disproportionately rewarded for their inherent superiority. This world-view, and its corresponding perception of man, is strongly engrained in contemporary counseling psychology (including clinical psychology and psychiatry), with perhaps its strongest influence being the realm of 'humanistic' (existential) psychology where individual self-determination is stressed.

There is little doubt that the competitive, Protestant ethic represents an antithesis to the cooperative folk thesis. American Indians, as diverse a group as they are, universally subscribe to a particualr folk orientation known as the 'harmony ethic' - an aboriginal world-view and resulting value system that directly links man with nature. Not only did the harmony ethic prevail among aboriginal cultures, many of these folk attributes have survived to the present. Here, avoidance and mutual obligations are the main tenet of this ethos. Within this perspective, people try to avoid giving offense to others within their group. Individual autonomy, along with a high valuation placed upon independence, is yet another important ethical value as is its corollary; a resentment of authority and a complementary hesitancy to command others (Kupferer, 1966; Stonequist, 1937).

This ethic also provides projective face-saving techniques for traditional Indians through the use of neutral third persons and/or objects. Moreover, American Indians are enculturated not to display public emotions and to avoid expressive gestures such as direct eye and/or physical contact. Besides, for these avoidance techniques to operate they must be complemented by an equally complex obligatory network.

Those subscribing to this world-view avoid publicly embrassing others while feeling compelled to fulfill the wishes of friends and relatives. Hence, obligatory hositality, public impassivity, the refusal or unwillingness to contradict, a reluctance to assume authority and a strong sense of individual autonomy regarding personal behavior provides a profile of the person socialized within the folk harmony ethic.

This is not to imply that aboriginal Indian cultures were totally passive. Quite the contrary, highly structured avenues of tension release were built into traditional cultures. Wars and rituals played an important tension-management role allowing considerable personal license during these highly emotional activities. Unfortunately, white political, military and religious leaders viewed these activities as manifesting heathen beliefs resulting in most Indian rituals being either outlawed or strongly discouraged. Thus, traditional tribal rituals and festivals were forbidden without being replaced with new avenues for tension release.

Instead a colonial, accommodative model of social control was imposed which attempted to implement policies through secondary institutions making certain to maintain a social and, often, physical distance between them and the group they regulated. This formal separation between the regulators and the regulatees often succeeds in generating an insurmountable communication gap. Indeed, the lack of primary interaction between the two groups actually serves to deny either group adequate opportunity to empathize with the other. Moreover, the flow of communication in these situations is usually one-way being initiated from the dominant regulating agency and directed toward the dependent subordinate group with little or no opportunity for feedback.

Consequently, a small elite of regualators (BIA, ANA...) determine policy according to their beliefs and cultural perspective, here the Protestant ethic, while maintaining rigid physical and social distance between themselves and those being regulated. The reason these programs fail is that once they strip Indians of their cultural identity, denying them access to their traditional ways, the regulating agencies then fail to fill this void with viable substitutes. What usually results is that this process of federal paternalism tends to create adolescent wards who are then torn between the arbitrary expectiations of adult responsibility and those of childhood dependency.

Attempting to make an Indian learn white ways at the expense of his 'Indianism' leads to increased inner turmoil which is often internalized and concealed through alcohol, tension and the like. In rare occurances it errupts in aggressive productivity like that developed by Vine Deloria, Jr., Adolph Dial and other Indian writers and artists. But for most Native Americans the end result is massive self-aggression (alcoholism, mental and physical health problems and suicide) or other-aggression (assault and homicide...). There is little doubt that the most well-adjusted Native Americans are those who are proud of their 'Indianism' and have acceptable avenues of fulfilling that identity.

Ostensibly, any viable Native American therapeutic model must encourage Indian clients to become more responsible, with 'respsonsibility' defined in culturally-relevant terms. Native American behavioral patterns, like those of most groups, seem to be dictated by certain cultural factors. In order to ascertain the nature of an Indian behavioral problem, the therapist must first understand the cultural circumstances surrounding the client's marginality.

Many marginals suffer the dilemma of looking 'Indian' and wanting to be 'Indian' while not knowing the exact nature of their heritage and with little opportunity to find their true identity. For these marginals, Pan-Indianism offers a partial solution. Pan-Indianism attempts to provide a general Indian ethnic image, one that can be readily shared by the some 500 separate Indian groups in the United States and Canada (French, 1978). Nonetheless, access to either the traditional Indian or white middle-class orienations is greatly limited for most marginals. And this factor alone has considerable significance in terms of counseling Indian clients.

Counseling American Indians

While the harmony ethic provides a broad cultural-oreintation and a valuable general perspective toward understanding American Indians, it does not, in itself, answer the more critical questions relevant to counseling psychology. Counselors must first take into account the particular cultural-orientation of the Indian client. For example, the Bureau of Indian Affairs (BIA) has often made the mistake of pairing Indian students, at their boarding schools, who were from diverse cultural backgrounds, and sometimes even traditional enemies. Obviously, a serious error is to mislabel an Indian client.

Ethnocentricism can result in situations whereby counselors exacerbate the same problem(s) the Indian client sought their help for in the first place. The first major consideration in counseling American Indians is to attempt to interpret their situation from their particular tribal--orientation as well as within the larger Pan-Indian, harmony ethos.

Counselors must also remember that time and space, number, substance and the like, are closely linked to nature - Mother Earth and Father Sky - within the traditional Indian culture. Time is recorded by significant events and not be a clock while space is the life cycle or 'hoop.' Life, and consequently space, has closure and this closure is represented by the hoop. The numbers four and seven are also common to American Indians. These numbers reflect the Great Mystery of Life and are incorporated in aboriginal creation myths.

Furthermore, power and personality are related not only to the group, but to nature itself. Clearly, existential and ego psychology has little relevance among traditional Indians. The individual, within the traditional perspective, is always a part of a larger primary network and does not consider himself to be a totally autonomous entity as these psychological orientations seem to suggest. Indian responsibility is to the group and not to oneself. Individual power is also shared. It is viewed as a non-human trait, one that is borrowed from nature and eventually relinquished at death. Vision quests and other rituals are closely associated with the acquisition of power. Besides, within this framework shame, and not guilt, is the most significant control mechanism. Attempting to make an Indian feel guilty is the same as shaming his entire primary network, a mistake that can force a shamed client into the only face-saving option - suicide.

Other considerations revolve around the issue of Indian status and role expectations. Again, considerable differences exist between Indian groups themselves, let alone between Indian and white cultural orientations. For instance, the matrilineal Cherokees had a division of labor which afforded the female considerable power and authority in the area of domestic issues. Females determined who they would marry as well as the size of the family and when and if to abort (infanticide) or divorce. Much of this aboriginal domestic authority has survived to the present.

Another female Indian trait, one widely shared among American Indians in general, is the informal adoption of children - especially those from within their primary clan network. American Indians not only tend to indulge their children, they also freely allow children and kin to gravitate to each other and it is not uncommon, even today, for a family to include both their biological and adopted children - all living in harmony. Western -oriented counselors often interpret these situations as constituting a form of 'family deviance.' Moreover, Indian adult affect, as expressed within the private confines of their home, often involves greater degrees of physical expression than is common to Western societies. And what may be considered spouse abuse within the white-dominant society may well be acceptable behavior according to Indian tradition (French, 1978; 1979).

The counselor has to ask: how do these cultural variations affect basic counseling techniques such as the here-and-now focus, culture building, disclosure, feedback, metacommunication, process illumination and the use of cognitive aids (structured group exercises)? For instance, the here-and-now focus is acceptable if it involves 'significant others' from within the client's primary or tribal network. By the same token, cultural homogeneity is a desired factor within group counseling sessions. This provides a common base not only for culture building but for the processes of disclosure, feedback and process illumination.

Furthermore, metacommunication has significance only when interpreted within the appropriate cultural perspective. Mixed cultural groups tend to increase tension levels often forcing Indian clients out. Moreover, ethnocentric counselors tend to misinterpret Indian eye and body non-verbal communication, often viewing these responses as reflecting guilt when they more likely indicate learned restraint. The same holds true when using structured group exercised. If these techniques are overused, an Indian client may well recognize them as merely game playing. And while this may be an astute and accurate observation, it may also drive the Indian client(s) away..

In summary, it is apparent that many of the common counseling techniques do not apply to Indian clients, especailly as they are currently administered. There is considerable hope for the future, however, providing that counseling psychology adapts to the more viable multicultural perspective.

REFERENCES

Binder, Virginia, et. al. Modern Therapies. Englswood Cliffs, N. J.: Prentice-Hall, 1976.

Cooley, Charles. Human Nature and the Social Order. New York: Charles Scribner's Sons, 1902.

Dunham, H. Warren. Anomie and Deviant Behavior. New York: Free Press, 1965.

Durkheim, Emile. Elementary Forms of the Religious Life (J. Swain, Tran.). Glencoe, Ill.: Free Press, 1954.

- The Rules of Sociological Method (S. A. Solovay & J. H. Mueller, Tran.). Glencoe, Ill.: Free Press, 1968.

Frank, Jerome. Persuasion and Healing. Baltimore: Johns Hopkins Press, 1961.

French, Laurence. "Social Problems among Cherokee Females," American Journal of Psychoanalysis, XXXVI (2), 1976: 163-169.

French, Laurence, and Jim Hornbuckle. "An Analysis of Indian Violence," American Indian Quarterly, 3 (4) (Winter, 1978): 335-356.

-"Indian Stress and Violence," Journal of Alcohol and Drug Education, 25 (1) (Fall, 1979): 36-43.

French, Laurence. "Corrections and the Native American Client," Prison Journal, LIX (1), 1980: 49-60.

-"The Cultural Factor in Defining and Identifying Sex Related Social and Personal Pathologies," British Journal of Sexual Medicine, 5 (July, 1980): 30-33.

Goode, Erich. "Marijuana and the Politics of Reality," Journal of Health and Social Behavior, 10 (June, 1969): 83-94.

Hollingshead, August, and Frederick Redlich. Social Class and Mental Illness. New York: John Wiley, 1958.

Hymann, Herbert. "The Psychology of Status," Archives of Psychology, 269, 1942.

Kupferer, Harriet. "The Principle People," Bureau of Ethnology Bulletin, 196 (78), 1966: 215-325.

Lewin, Kurt. "Field Theory of Learning," National Society for the Study of Education, 41 (Part III), 1942.

Mead, George. Mind, Self and Society (C. Morris, ed.). Chicago: University of Chicago Press, 1934.

Rogers, Carl. Freedom to Learn. Columbus, Ohio: Charles Merrill, 1969.

Shaffer, John, and M. David Galinsky. Models of Group Therapy and Sensitivity Training. Englewood Cliffs, N. J.: Prentice-Hall, 1974.

Sorokin, Pitirim. Contemporary Social Theories. New York: Harper & Row, 1928.

Stonequist, E. The Marginal Man. New York: Russell & Russell, 1937.

Sullivan, Harry Stack. The Interpersonal Theory of Psychiatry. New York: W. W. Norton, 1955.

Thomas, William I. Social Behavior and Personality (E. K. Volkkart, ed.). New York: Social Science Research Council, 1951.

Tonnies, Ferdinand. Community and Society (C. Loomis, Tran.). East Lansing, Mich.: Michigan State University Press, 1957.

Weber, Max. The Protestant Ethic and the Spirit of Capitalism (T. Parsons, Tran.). New York: Charles Scribner's Sons, 1958.

Yalom, Irvin. The Theory and Practice of Group Psychotherapy. New York: Basic Books, 1975.

Postscript

The future for Indian justice is cloudy at best. Paradoxically Native Americans find themselves currently caught between increased autonomy over their land and natural resources while at the same time facing the dire consequences of Reganomics. Unfortunately the most predictable outcome here, predicated upon time-tested public insensitivity toward Indian causes, is that of both increased Indian marginality and cultural genocide.

Clearly American Indians are waging one of the most significant battles in the long continuous war they have been engaged in since the colonial era. Indeed this could be the single most critical battle mainly because this time they are fighting over past injustices. Here Indian attorneys (legal warriors) are counting coup on the majority society winning significant concessions and court settlements for past deceptions. The recent multimillion dollar Penobscot and Passamaquoddy settlement in Maine and pending settlements in Alaska (Alaska Native Claims Settlement Act), Canada, and Martha's Vineyard in Massachusetts, among others, as well as the recent United States Supreme Court ruling favoring Indian-imposed surtaxes on natural resources obtained on tribal lands illustrate these legal successes. In anticipation of the latter energy-rich tribes from ten states established the Council of Energy Resource Tribes (CERT) in 1975. The leader of this group is Peter MacDonald the vocal chairman of the largest United States tribe - the Navajo.

These concessions and settlements, however, may well represent the American Indians' "last hurrah." Some feel that the current legal battles merely represent a convenient vehicle for purging, once and forever, the majority society of past injustices against, and future responsibilities toward, Native Americans. Viewed from this perspective the old status quo becomes readily evident - decreased Indian solidarily through a policy of selective adjudication.

The "divide-and-conquer" methoc fits the adjudication process as well as, perhaps better than, previous government policies (war, genocide, forced removal, reservation internment, federal paternalism...). That is, while the Maine tribes were successful in their land settlement, the Oneida Indians of New York had their (9.2 billion dollars payment for 200 years rent on five million acres in upstate New York) case dismissed by a federal judge. The same argument holds regarding the natural resource surtax. It is clear to most that the northern plains and southwestern tribes stand to profit the most from this decision.

An obvious consequence of this highly publicized dicotomy between American Indians is the creation of a new class of Indians - nouveau'riche Indians. Add the human element of relative deprivation and we have Indians pitched against each other over the distribution of this new found wealth. Not only is intra-group dissension likely to intensify, anti-Indian sentiments are also likely to accelerate among non-Indian neighbors of these nouveau'riche Indians. Moreover, this social double-bind is further exacerbated by minimal transitional resocialization. This component is necessary to facilitate the sudden cultural lag from one of dire poverty to that of instant wealth. If past white/Indian relationships are reliable indicators of future interactions during these transitional periods, then the nouveau' riche Indians need to caution against exploitation, deceit and corruption from both within their own ranks as well as from without. Ostensibly, these judicial "victories" represent a mixed blessing and if the past repeats itself they could prove to be one of the greatest injustices American Indians ever encountered.

Toward an Indian Justice Model:

Given the current political scenario the challenge for the preservation of Native American cultures is indeed considerable. Besides, the causal link between the preservation of Indian culture and Indian justice is a direct one. Intervening cultural variables include, but are not restricted to, religion, education, and tribal autonomy. A viable justice model must be cognizance of these factors.

Native religion and culture are closely intertwined. Aboriginal belief systems adequately prepared American Indians for social lives lived close to nature and its elements. Perhaps it is the continuation of this aboriginal concept which has best prepared Native Americans for survival under seemingly dire social consequences both on and off reservations. Challenges to Indian religion have resulted in bloody confrontations over the years. The Ghost Dance movement initiated nearly a century ago culminated in the Wounded Knee massacre of 1890. This terminated the plains lifestyle. In 1973 the Sioux again felt that their culture and religion were threatened. The result was yet another violent altercation at Wounded Knee. Finally, the American Indian Religious Freedom Act (Public Law 95-341) was passed in 1978. Essentially the act recognized the need to respect the customs, ceremonies and traditions of Native American religions. An assessment of this act was made by the Interior Department through the Federal Agencies Task Force on the American Indian Religious Freedom Act Report (Andrus, 1979):

> Native American tribes, nations and peoples survive as distinct groups within the American society. The policy of the United States is to support their right to cultural and political integrity, while assisting them to adapt to the rapidly changing economic and technological conditions of the modern world. All cultures change with the times and adapt to the conditions of their environment, as a matter of survival. The question is whether the United States government and American society have put unwarranted pressure on these cultures to change.... Federal agencies are now required by law to respect the customs, ceremonies and traditions of Native American religions.... With this new policy, it is now possible to administratively accommodate most of the native religious needs under existing statutory authority...(Andrus, 1979: i,ii).

Judicial ideals aside, the preservation of Indian religion and culture is contingent upon the effective enforcement of Public Law 95-341. Today the Native American Church and tribal medicine men still encounter considerable opposition from the majority society. Indeed, the current era of political conservatism, notably the New Christian Right, could well lead to increased opposition to Indian traditionalism. After all it was the self-righteous ethnocentrism of the policy of "manifest destiny" which rendered Native Americans as heathens worthy of destruction.

Education is another critical cultural variable since it provides the valuable liasion between traditionalism and acceptable social integration into the majority society. Conversely, education is the vehicle through which the larger, majority society becomes exposed to Indian cultures. The greatest challenge facing multicultural education is its ability to provide tribal-specific cultural education to its Indian students while at the same time portraying the essential features of Pan-Indianism and relevant attributes of the majority society. By the same token, majority (non-Indian) students must be exposed to at least a cursory survey of Native American culture - notably the contravening aspects of the Harmony Ethos vis-a-vis that of the Protestant Ethic.

The final cultural element needed for the preservation of Indian culture and justice is that of tribal autonomy. Without tribal-specific Indian input at the local, regional and federal levels Indian policy remains a sham. Yet this remains a considerable challenge as many of the articles within the text attest. None-the-less, Indian autonomy, that based upon each groups unique cultural heritage and molded to the contemporary United States scene, remains the foremost requisite for Indian justice. Indian religion and multicultural education are two significant components of this objective. Reciprocity, however, is the key if cultural pluralism is to prevail. American Indians have to realize that "the days of the buffalo are gone forever" while the majority society must recognize the fact that Indians are here to stay.

REFERENCES

Andrus, Cecil D. American Indian Religious Freedom Act Report, Washington: U. S. Department of Interior, 1979.

About the Authors

Samuel J. Brakel, J.D., is a Research Attorney at the American Bar Foundation and the author of "American Indian Tribal Courts: The Costs of Separate Justice."

John Cross, Ph.D., a Western Seminole (Oklahoma), received his doctorate in Sociology from the University of Missouri and has taught in colleges and universities in Oklahoma, Nebraska, New York, and North Dakota. He has also served as a special consultant and research advisor to a number of local and regional Indian agencies.

Laurence French, Ph.D's, holds the doctorate in Sociology (University of New Hampshire) and in Psychological and Cultural Studies (University of Nebraska). He has taught in universities in North Carolina, Nebraska, and Maine. He has served as a consultant to the Eastern Cherokee, United Southeastern Tribes, Incorporated (USET), Nebraska Indian Commission, and the Lincoln Indian Center. He is currently a psychologist with the New Hampshire Department of Health and Welfare.

Sid Harring, Ph.D., earned his graduate degrees from the University of Wisconsin and is currently affiliated with the John Jay College of Criminal Justice, City University of New York. He has done extensive research on Indian crime, some of it under the direction of Marshall Clinard at the University of Wisconsin. In 1975 - 76, Dr. Harring was a lawyer/jury selection expert at two AIM (American Indian Movement) trials - the Menominee Abbey case in Wisconsin and the Russell Means trial in North Dakota.

Charles "Jim" Hornbuckle, B.A., an enrolled member of the Eastern Band of Cherokee Indians, earned both his A.A. and B.A. degrees at North Carolina schools and is currently working toward his MSW degree. His experiences include that of a BIA Teaching Aid in the reservation schools, Cherokee police officer, Director of the Cherokee Neighborhood Jobs Corps, and cottage patent at the Cherokee Children's Home. Jim is currently the Director of the tribal Alcohol and Mental Health Program - a position he has held since 1974. He sits on, and is a consultant to, a number of local, regional, and national Indian and mental health agencies and organizations.

Richard LaFromboise, J.D., a Turtle Mountain Chippewa (North Dakota), received his law degree from the University of Oklahoma and has served as a consultant to the Nebraska Indian Commission, Lincoln Indian Center, and Omaha, Santee Sioux, and Winnebago Tribes. He currently serves his people in North Dakota.

Theresa LaFromboise, Ph.D., Cherokee, earned her doctorate in Counseling Psychology from the University of Oklahoma and is currently an Assistant Professor of Educational Psychology and Social Foundations at the University of Nebraska. Dr. LaFromboise has served Indian people in the capacity of educator and clinician in Oklahoma, Michigan, Nebraska, North Carolina, North and South Dakota, and Wisconsin.

Elmer R. Rusco, Ph.D., earned his B.A. and M.A. from the University of Kansas and his doctorate from the University of California - all in Political Science. He has held faculty positions at San Diego State College, the University of Idaho, and Parsons College. He currently is a Full Professor at the University of Nevada at Reno. Among his wide academic interests and publications is a strong sentiment toward Native American studies. He is a member of the Indian Rights Committee, American Civil Liberties Union, past-President of the American Civil Liberties Union of Nevada, and former board Chair of the Race Relations Center - Reno, Nevada.

David Wachtel, A.B.D., is completing his Ph.D. in Sociology at the State University of New York at Buffalo. David's experiences include that of a law enforcement officer, college instructor at the Navajo College of Gando (Arizona), Director of Police Training Academy and Criminal Justice at Western New Mexico University and consultant to the Navajo Police Department (Window Rock, Arizona). Currently Mr. Wachtel is an Assistant Professor of Criminal Justice at the University of Alabama at Birmingham. He is also a member of the Minorities and Criminal Justice subcommittee (representing Native American interests) of the Academy of Criminal Justice Sciences (ACJS).

Charles F. Wilkinson, J.D., authored "Basic Doctrines of American Indian Law," the third chapter of the Final Report of the American Indian Policy Review Commission, a report submitted to the

U. S. Congress, May 17, 1977. At that time Professor Wilkinson was affiliated with the School of Law, University of Oregon. Currently he serves as counsel to the Native American Rights Fund (NARF) headquartered in Bolder, Colorado.